PHILIP'S

ROAD ATLAS FRANCE & SPAIN

Contents

II   Driving regulations
III Sights of France, Portugal and Spain
IV   Ski resorts

1   Key to map pages
2   Route planning maps
6   Road maps

63 City plans and approach maps

63   **Alicante** city plan
     Granada city plan

64   **Barcelona** city plan
     Barcelona urban area map
     Bordeaux city plan
     Bordeaux urban area map

65   **Lisboa** city plan
     Lisboa urban area map
     Lyon city plan
     Lyon urban area map

66   **Madrid** city plan
     Madrid urban area map
     Marseille city plan

67   **Paris** urban area map

68   **Paris** city plan
     Sevilla city plan
     Strasbourg city plan

69 Index to road maps

www.philips-maps.co.uk

First published in 2014 by Philip's,
a division of Octopus Publishing Group Ltd
www.octopusbooks.co.uk
Endeavour House, 189 Shaftesbury Avenue,
London WC2H 8JY
An Hachette UK Company · www.hachette.co.uk

First edition 2014, first impression 2014

 **Ordnance Survey®** This product includes mapping data licensed from Ordnance Survey®, with the permission of the Controller of Her Majesty's Stationery Office © Crown copyright 2014. All rights reserved.
Licence number 100011710.

CW00410463

Legend to route

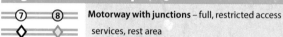

Moto...
tun...
Toll...
Main throug...

European road number, motorway...
National road number

Distances – in kilometres

International boundary, national boundary

LE HAVRE Car ferry and destination

✕ ✈ 1089 ▲ Mountain pass, international airport, height (metres)

Town – population
■ ◙   5 million +
◘ ◙   2–5 million
◘ ◙   1–2 million
◉ ◙   500 000–1 million
◉ ◙   200 000–500 000
◉ ◙   100 000–200 000

○ ◉   50 000–100 000
○ ◉   20 000–50 000
○ ◉   10 000–20 000
○ ◉   5000–10 000
○ ◉   0–5000

The green version of the symbol indicates towns with Low Emission Zones

Scale · pages 2–5

1:3 200 000
1 in = 50.51 miles
1 cm = 32km

| 0 | 10 | 20 | 30 | 40 | 50 | 60 | 70 | 80 | 90 | 100 | 110 miles |
| 0 | 20 | 40 | 60 | 80 | 100 | 120 | 140 | 160 | 180 km |

Legend to road maps pages 6–62

⑦ ⑧ **Motorway with junctions** – full, restricted access
◇ ◇   services, rest area
         tunnel, under construction
Toll Motorway – with toll barrier
Pre-pay motorway – Ⓐ ㏇
'Vignette' must be purchased before travel
Principal trunk highway – single / dual carriageway
         tunnel, under construction
Other main highway – single / dual carriageway
Other important road, other road

E25 A49 European road number, motorway number
135 National road number

▼ Col Bayard 1248 ▲ **Mountain pass**

Scenic route, gradient – arrow points uphill

Distances – in kilometres
⚲ 143 ⚲   major
28   minor

Principal railway with tunnel

Ferry route
Short ferry route

International boundary, national boundary

National park, natural park

✈ Airport
ⴲ Ancient monument
ⵊ Beach
ⴴ Castle or house
⌂ Cave
✦ Other place of interest
❊ Park or garden
† Religious building

ⵊ Ski resort
ⵣ Theme park
◉ World Heritage site
1754▲ Spot height
Sevilla World Heritage town
Poitiers Town of tourist interest
■ ◉ City or town with Low Emission Zone

Scale · pages 6–62

1:753 800
1 inch = 12 miles
1 cm = 7.5km

| 0 | 2 | 4 | 6 | 8 | 10 | 12 | 14 | 16 | 18 | 20 | 22 | 24 | 26 miles |
| 0 | 4 | 8 | 12 | 16 | 20 | 24 | 28 | 32 | 36 | 40km |

Driving regulations

Symbols

🚧 Motorway
⚠ Dual carriageway
⚠ Single carriageway
🏭 Urban area
⊙ Speed limit in kilometres per hour (kph)
🛡 Seat belts
👶 Children
🍷 Blood alcohol level
△ Warning triangle
✚ First aid kit
💡 Spare bulb kit
🔥 Fire extinguisher
⊖ Minimum driving age
📖 Additional documents required
📱 Mobile phones
LEZ Low Emission Zone
★ Other information

Where compulsory, visibility vests should be kept in the passenger compartment and put on before exiting the vehicle in breakdowns or emergencies.

Andorra Principat d'Andorra (AND)

Capital Andorra la Vella
Languages Catalan (official), French, Castilian and Portuguese
Currency Euro = 100 cents
Website http://visitandorra.com

	🚧	⚠	⚠	🏭
⊙	n/a	90	60/90	50

🛡 Compulsory
👶 Under 10 and below 150 cm must travel in an EU-approved restraint system adapted to their size in the rear
🍷 0.05% △ Compulsory
✚ Recommended 💡 Compulsory
🔥 Recommended ⊖ 18
📱 Not permitted whilst driving
★ Dipped headlights compulsory for motorcycles during day and for other vehicles during poor visibility. ★ On-the-spot fines imposed ★ Visibility vests must be carried ★ Winter tyres or snow chains compulsory in poor conditions or when indicated by signs

Belgium Belgique (B)

Capital Brussels/Bruxelles
Languages Dutch, French, German (all official)
Currency Euro = 100 cents
Website www.belgium.be/en

	🚧	⚠	⚠	🏭
⊙	120*	120*	90	50**
If towing trailer				
⊙	90	90	60	50
Over 3.5 tonnes				
⊙	90	90	60	50

*Minimum speed of 70kph may be applied in certain conditions on motorways and some dual carriageways
**Near schools, hospitals and churches the limit may be 30kph

🛡 Compulsory
👶 All under 19s under 135 cm must wear an appropriate child restraint. Airbags must be deactivated if a rear-facing child seat is used in the front
🍷 0.05% △ Compulsory
✚ Recommended 💡 Recommended
🔥 Compulsory ⊖ 18

📱 Only allowed with a hands-free kit
★ Cruise control is not permitted on motorways ★ Dipped headlights mandatory at all times for motorcycles and advised during the day in poor conditions for other vehicles ★ On-the-spot fines imposed ★ Radar detectors prohibited ★ Sticker indicating maximum recommended speed for winter tyres must be displayed on dashboard if using them ★ Visibility vest compulsory

France (F)

Capital Paris
Languages French (official), Breton, Occitan
Currency Euro = 100 cents
Website www.diplomatie.gouv.fr/en/

	🚧	⚠	⚠	🏭
⊙	130	110	90	50
On wet roads or if full driving licence held for less than 2 years				
⊙	110	100	80	50
If towing below / above 3.5 tonnes gross				
⊙	110/90	100/90	90/80	50

50kph on all roads if fog reduces visibility to less than 50m • Licence will be lost and driver fined for exceeding speed limit by over 40kph

🛡 Compulsory in front seats and, if fitted, in rear
👶 In rear, 4 or under must have a child safety seat (rear facing if up to 9 months); if 5–10 must use an appropriate restraint system. Under 10 permitted in the front only if rear seats are fully occupied by other under 10s or there are no rear safety belts. In front, if child is in rear-facing child seat, any airbag must be deactivated.
🍷 0.05%. If towing or with less than 2 years with full driving licence, 0.00% • All drivers/motorcyclists must carry 2 unused breathalysers to French certification standards, showing an NF number.
△ Compulsory
✚ Recommended
💡 Recommended
⊖ 18
📱 Use not permitted whilst driving
LEZ An LEZ operates in the Mont Blanc tunnel
★ Dipped headlights compulsory in poor daytime visibility and at all times for motorcycles ★ GPS must have fixed speed camera function deactivated; radar-detection equipment is prohibited ★ It is compulsory to carry a French-authority-recognised (NF) breathalyser. ★ On-the-spot fines imposed ★ Tolls on motorways. Electronic tag needed if using automatic tolls. ★ Visibility vests must be carried in the passenger compartment; legislation making visibility vests compulsory for motorcyclists and passengers may be reintroduced. ★ Winter tyres recommended. Carrying snow chains recommended in winter as these may have to be fitted if driving on snow-covered roads, in accordance with signage.

Luxembourg (L)

Capital Luxembourg
Currency Euro = 100 cents
Languages, Luxembourgian / Letzeburgish (official), French, German
Website www.visitluxembourg.com

	🚧	⚠	⚠	🏭
⊙	130/110	90	90	50
If towing				
⊙	90	75	75	50

If full driving licence held for less than two years, must not exceed 75 kph • In 20 km/h zones, pedestrians have right of way.

🛡 Compulsory
👶 Children under 3 must use an appropriate restraint system. Airbags must be disabled if a rear-facing child seat is used in the front. Children 3 to 18 and / or under 150 cm must use a restraint system appropriate to their size. If over 36kg a seatbelt may be used in the back only
🍷 0.05%, 0.02% for young drivers, drivers with less than 2 years experience and drivers of taxis and commercial vehicles
△ Compulsory
✚ Compulsory (buses)

💡 Compulsory
⊖ 18
🔥 Compulsory (buses, transport of dangerous goods)
📱 Use permitted only with hands-free kit
★ Dipped headlights compulsory for motorcyclists and in poor visibility for other vehicles ★ On-the-spot fines imposed ★ Visibility vest compulsory ★ Winter tyres compulsory in winter weather

Portugal (P)

Capital Lisbon / Lisboa
Languages Portuguese (official)
Currency Euro = 100 cents
Website www.portugal.gov.pt/en.aspx

	🚧	⚠	⚠	🏭
⊙	120*	90	90	50
If towing				
⊙	100*	90	80	50

*40kph minimum;
90kph maximum if licence held under 1 year

🛡 Compulsory in front seats; compulsory if fitted in rear
👶 Under 12 and below 150cm must travel in the rear in an appropriate child restraint; rear-facing child seats permitted in front only if airbags deactivated
🍷 0.05%
△ Compulsory
✚ Recommended
💡 Recommended
🔥 Recommended
⊖ 18 (motorcycles under 50cc 17)
📖 MOT certificate for vehicles over 3 years old, photographic proof of identity (e.g. driving licence or passport) must be carried at all times.
📱 Only allowed with hands-free kit
LEZ An LEZ prohibits vehicles without catalytic converters from certain parts of Lisbon. There are plans to extend the scheme to the whole of the city
★ Dipped headlights compulsory for motorcycles, compulsory for other vehicles in poor visibility and tunnels ★ On-the-spot fines imposed ★ Radar-detectors prohibited ★ Tolls on motorways; do not use green lanes, these are reserved for auto-payment users. Some motorways require an automatic toll device. ★ Visibility vest compulsory ★ Wearers of spectacles or contact lenses should carry a spare pair

Spain España (E)

Capital Madrid
Languages Castilian Spanish (official), Catalan, Galician, Basque
Currency Euro = 100 cents
Website www.lamoncloa.gob.es/home.htm

	🚧	⚠	⚠	🏭
⊙	110	100	90	50
If towing				
⊙	80	80	70	50

🛡 Compulsory in front seats and if fitted in rear seats
👶 Under 135cm and below 12 must use appropriate child restraint
🍷 0.05%, 0.03% if less than 2 years full licence or if vehicle is over 3.5 tonnes or carries more than 9 passengers
△ Two compulsory (one for in front, one for behind)
✚ Recommended
💡 Compulsory
🔥 Recommended
⊖ 18 (18/21 heavy vehicles;
18 for motorbikes over 125cc;
16 for motorbikes up to 125cc;
14 for mopeds up to 75cc)
📱 Only allowed with hands-free kit
★ Dipped headlights compulsory for motorcycles and in poor daytime visibility for other vehicles. ★ It is recommended that spectacles or contact lens wearers carry a spare pair. ★ Radar-detection equipment is prohibited ★ Snow chains recommended for mountainous areas in winter ★ Spare tyre compulsory ★ Tolls on motorways ★ Visibility vest compulsory

Sights of France, Portugal and Spain

France

http://us.rendezvousenfrance.com/

Albi Old town with rosy brick architecture. The vast Cathédrale Ste-Cécile (begun 13c) holds some good art. The Berbie Palace houses the Toulouse-Lautrec museum. www.albi-tourisme.fr 30 B1

Alps Grenoble, capital of the French Alps, has a good 20c collection in the Museum of Grenoble. The Vanoise Massif has the greatest number of resorts (Val d'Isère, Courchevel). Chamonix has spectacular views on Mont Blanc, France's and Europe's highest peak. www.thealps.com 26 B2

Amiens France's largest Gothic cathedral has beautiful decoration. The Museum of Picardy has unique 16c panel paintings. www.visit-amiens.com 10 B2

Arles Ancient, picturesque town with Roman relics (1c amphitheatre), 11c cathedral, Archaeological Museum (Roman art); Van Gogh centre. www.arlestourisme.com 31 B3

Avignon Medieval papal capital (1309–77) with 14c walls and many ecclesiastical buildings. Vast Palace of the Popes has stunning frescoes. The Little Palace has fine Italian Renaissance painting. The 12–13c Bridge of St Bénézet is famous. www.ot-avignon.fr 31 B3

Bourges The Gothic Cathedral of St Etienne, one of the finest in France, has a superb sculptured choir. Also notable is the House of Jacques Coeur. www.bourgestourisme.com 17 B4

Burgundy *Bourgogne* Rural wine region with a rich Romanesque, Gothic and Renaissance heritage. The 12c cathedral in Autun and 12c basilica in Vézelay have fine Romanesque sculpture. Monasteries include 11c L'Abbaye de Cluny (ruins) and L'Abbaye de Fontenay. Beaune has beautiful Gothic Hôtel-Dieu and 15c Nicolas Rolin hospices. www.burgundy-tourism.com 18 B3

Brittany *Bretagne* Brittany is famous for cliffs, sandy beaches and wild landscape. It is also renowned for megalithic monuments (Carnac) and Celtic culture. Its capital, Rennes, has the Palais de Justice and good collections in the Museum of Brittany (history) and Museum of Fine Arts. Also: Nantes; St-Malo. www.bretagne.com 14–15

Caen City with two beautiful Romanesque buildings: Abbaye aux Hommes; Abbaye aux Dames. The château has two museums (15–20c painting; history). The *Bayeux Tapestry* is displayed in nearby Bayeux. www.tourisme.caen.fr 9 A3

Carcassonne Unusual double-walled fortified town of narrow streets with an inner fortress. The fine Romanesque Church of St Nazaire has superb stained glass. www.tourism-carcassonne.co.uk 30 B1

Chartres The 12–13c cathedral is an exceptionally fine example of Gothic architecture (Royal Doorway, stained glass, choir screen). The Fine Arts Museum has a good collection. www.chartres.com 10 C1

Clermont-Ferrand The old centre contains the cathedral built out of lava and Romanesque basilica. The Puy de Dôme and Puy de Sancy give spectacular views over some 60 extinct volcanic peaks (*puys*). www.clermontferrandtourism.com 24 B3

Colmar Town characterised by Alsatian half-timbered houses. The Unterlinden Museum has excellent German religious art including the famous Isenheim altarpiece. The Dominican church also has a fine altarpiece. Espace André Malraux (contemporary arts). www.ot-colmar.fr 20 A2

Corsica *Corse* Corsica has a beautiful rocky coast and mountainous interior. Napoleon's birthplace of Ajaccio has: Fesch Museum with Imperial Chapel and a large collection of Italian art; Maison Bonaparte; cathedral. Bonifacio, a medieval town, is spectacularly set on a rock over the sea. www.visit-corsica.com 62

Côte d'Azur The French Riviera is best known for its coastline and glamorous resorts. There are many relics of artists who worked here: St-Tropez has Musée de l'Annonciade; Antibes has 12c Château Grimaldi with the Picasso Museum; Cagnes has the Renoir House and Mediterranean Museum of Modern Art; St-Paul-de-Vence has the excellent Maeght Foundation and Matisse's Chapelle du Rosaire. Cannes is famous for its film festival. Also: Marseille, Monaco, Nice. www.frenchriviera-tourism.com 33 B3

Dijon Great 15c cultural centre. The Palais des Ducs et des Etats is the most notable monument and contains the Museum of Fine Arts. Also: the Charterhouse of Champmol. www.visitdijon.com 19 B4

Disneyland Paris Europe's largest theme park follows in the footsteps of its famous predecessors in the United States. www.disneylandparis.com 10 C2

Le Puy-en-Velay Medieval town bizarrely set on the peaks of dead volcanoes. It is dominated by the Romanesque cathedral (cloisters). The Romanesque chapel of St-Michel is dramatically situated on the highest rock. www.ot-lepuyenvelay.fr 25 B3

Loire Valley The Loire Valley has many 15–16c châteaux built amid beautiful scenery by French monarchs and members of their courts. Among the most splendid are Azay-le-Rideau, Chenonceaux and Loches. Also: Abbaye de Fontévraud. www.lvo.com 16 B2

Lyon France's third largest city has an old centre and many museums including the Museum of the History of Textiles and the Museum of Fine Arts (old masters). www.lyon-france.com 25 B4

Marseilles *Marseille* Second lagest city in France. Spectacular views from the 19c Notre-Dame-de-la-Garde. The Old Port has 11-12c Basilique St Victor (crypt, catacombs). Cantini Museum has major collection of 20c French art. Château d'If was the setting of Dumas' *The Count of Monte Cristo*. www.marseille-tourisme.com 31 B4

Mont-St-Michel Gothic pilgrim abbey (11–12c) set dramatically on a steep rock island rising from mud flats and connected to the land by a road covered by the tide. The abbey is made up of a complex of buildings. www.ot-montsaintmichel.com 15 A4

Nancy A centre of Art Nouveau. The 18c Place Stanislas was constructed by dethroned Polish king Stanislas. Museums: School of Nancy Museum (Art Nouveau furniture); Fine Arts Museum. www.ot-nancy.fr 12 C2

Nantes Former capital of Brittany, with the 15c Château des ducs de Bretagne. The cathedral has a striking interior. www.nantes-tourisme.com 15 B4

Nice Capital of the Côte d'Azur, the old town is centred on the old castle on the hill. The seafront includes the famous 19c Promenade des Anglais. The aristocratic quarter of the Cimiez Hill has the Marc Chagall Museum and the Matisse Museum. Also: Museum of Modern and Contemporary Art (especially neo-Realism and Pop Art). www.nicetourism.com 33 B3

Paris Capital of France, one of Europe's most interesting cities. The Île de la Cité area, an island in the River Seine has the 12–13c Gothic Notre Dame (wonderful stained glass) and La Sainte-Chapelle (1240–48), one of the jewels of Gothic art. The Left Bank area: Latin Quarter with the famous Sorbonne university; Museum of Cluny housing medieval art; the Panthéon; Luxembourg Palace and Gardens; Montparnasse, interwar artistic and literary centre; Eiffel Tower; Hôtel des Invalides with Napoleon's tomb. Right Bank: the great boulevards (Avenue des Champs-Élysées joining the Arc de Triomphe and Place de la Concorde); 19c Opéra Quarter; Marais, former aristocratic quarter of elegant mansions (Place des Vosges); Bois de Boulogne, the largest park in Paris; Montmartre, centre of 19c bohemianism, with the Basilique Sacré-Coeur. The Church of St Denis is the first gothic church and the mausoleum of the French monarchy. Paris has three of the world's greatest art collections: The Louvre (to 19c, *Mona Lisa*), Musée d'Orsay (19–20c) and National Modern Art Museum in the Pompidou Centre. Other major museums include: Orangery Museum; Paris Museum of Modern Art; Rodin Museum; Picasso Museum. Notable cemeteries with graves of the famous: Père-Lachaise, Montmartre, Montparnasse. Near Paris are the royal residences of Fontainebleau and Versailles. www.parisinfo.com 10 C2

Pyrenees Beautiful unspoiled mountain range. Towns include: delightful sea resorts of St-Jean-de-Luz and Biarritz; Pau, with access to the Pyrenees National Park; pilgrimage centre Lourdes. 38–39

Reims Together with nearby Epernay, the centre of champagne production. The 13c Gothic cathedral is one of the greatest architectural achievements in France (stained glass by Chagall). Other sights: Palais du Tau with cathedral sculpture, 11c Basilica of St Rémi; cellars on Place St-Niçaise and Place des Droits-des-Hommes. www.reims-tourisme.com 11 B4

Rouen Old centre with many half-timbered houses and 12–13c Gothic cathedral and the Gothic Church of St Maclou with its fascinating remains of a dance macabre on the former cemetery of Aître St-Maclou. The Fine Arts Museum has a good collection. www.rouentourisme.com 9 A5

St-Malo Fortified town (much rebuilt) in a fine coastal setting. There is a magnificent boat trip along the river Rance to Dinan, a splendid well-preserved medieval town. www.saint-malo-tourisme.com 15 A3

Strasbourg Town whose historic centre includes a well-preserved quarter of medieval half-timbered Alsatian houses, many of them set on the canal. The cathedral is one of the best in France. The Palais Rohan contains several museums. www.otstrasbourg.fr 13 C3

Toulouse Medieval university town characterised by flat pink brick (Hôtel Assézat). The Basilique St Sernin, the largest Romanesque church in France, has many art treasures. Marvellous Church of the Jacobins holds the body of St Thomas Aquinas. www.toulouse-tourisme.com 29 C4

Tours Historic town centred on Place Plumereau. Good collections in the Guilds Museum and Fine Arts Museum. www.tours-tourisme.fr 16 B2

Versailles Vast royal palace built for Louis XIV, primarily by Mansart, set in large formal gardens with magnificent fountains. The extensive and much-imitated state apartments include the famous Hall of Mirrors and the exceptional Baroque chapel. www.chateauversailles.fr 10 C2

Vézère Valley Caves A number of prehistoric sites, most notably the cave paintings of Lascaux (some 17,000 years old), now only seen in a duplicate cave, and the cave of Font de Gaume. The National Museum of Prehistory is in Les Eyzies. www.lascaux-dordogne.com/en 29 B4

Portugal

www.visitportugal.com

Alcobaça Monastery of Santa Maria, one of the best examples of a Cistercian abbey, founded in 1147 (exterior 17–18c). The church is Portugal's largest (14c tombs). http://whc.unesco.org/en/list/505 48 A1

Algarve Modern seaside resorts among picturesque sandy beaches and rocky coves (Praia da Rocha). Old towns: Lagos; Faro. www.visitalgarve.pt/visitalgarve/vEN 54 B1

Batalha Abbey is one of the masterpieces of French Gothic and Manueline architecture (tombs, English Perpendicular chapel, unfinished pantheon). http://whc.unesco.org/en/list/264 48 A2

Braga Historic town with cathedral and large Archbishop's Palace. 42 A1

Coimbra Old town with narrow streets set on a hill. The Romanesque cathedral is particularly fine (portal). The university (founded 1290) has a fascinating Baroque library. Also: Museum of Machado de Castro. 42 B1

Évora Centre of the town, surrounded by walls, has narrow streets of Moorish character and medieval and Renaissance architecture. Churches: 12–13c Gothic cathedral; São Francisco with a chapel decorated with bones of some 5000 monks; 15c Convent of Dos Lóis. The Jesuit university was founded in 1559. Museum of Évora holds fine art (particularly Flemish and Portugese). http://whc.unesco.org/en/list/361 48 C3

Guimarães Old town with a castle with seven towers on a vast keep. Churches: Romanesque chapel of São Miguel; São Francisco. Alberto Sampaio Museum and Martins Sarmento Museum are excellent. http://whc.unesco.org/en/list/1031 42 A1

Lisbon *Lisboa* Capital of Portugal. Baixa is the Neoclassical heart of Lisbon with the Praça do Comércio and Rossío squares. São Jorge castle (Visigothic, Moorish, Romanesque) is surrounded by the medieval quarters. Bairro Alto is famous for *fado* (songs). Monastery of Jerónimos is exceptional. Churches: 12c cathedral; São Vicente de Fora; São Roque (tiled chapels); Torre de Belém; Convento da Madre de Deus. Museums: Gulbenkian Museum (ancient, oriental, European), National Museum of Ancient Art; Design Museum; Modern Art Centre; Azulego Museum (decorative tiles). Nearby: palatial monastic complex Mafra; royal resort Sintra. www.visitlisboa.com 48 B1

Porto Historic centre with narrow streets. Views from Clérigos Tower. Churches: São Francisco; cathedral. Soares dos Reis Museum holds fine and decorative arts (18–19c). The suburb of Vila Nova de Gaia is the centre for port wine. www.portoturismo.pt 42 A1

Tomar Attractive town with the Convento de Cristo, founded in 1162 as the headquarters of the Knights Templar (Charola temple, chapter house, Renaissance cloisters). 48 A2

Spain España

www.spain.info

Ávila Medieval town with 2km-long 11c walls. Pilgrimage site to shrines to St Teresa of Avila (Convent of Santa Teresa, Convent of the Incarnation). www.avila.com/avila_tourism 44 B3

Barcelona Showcase of Gothic ('Barri Gòtic': cathedral; Santa María del Mar; mansions on Carrer de Montcada) and *modernista* architecture ('Eixample' area with Manzana de la Discòrdia; Sagrada Familia, Güell Park, La Pedrera). Many

...t boulevards (La Rambla, Passeig de ...ràcia). Museums: Modern Catalan Art, Catalan Archaeology, Picasso Museum, Miró Museum, Tàpies Museum. Nearby: monastery of Montserrat (Madonna); Figueres (Dali Museum). www.barcelonaturisme.com 41 C3

Burgos Medieval town with Gothic cathedral, Moorish-Gothic Royal Monastery and Charterhouse of Miraflores. 37 B3

Cáceres Medieval town surrounded by originally Moorish walls and with several aristocratic palaces with solars. 49 A4

Córdoba Capital of Moorish Spain with a labyrinth of streets and houses with tile-decorated patios. The 8–10c Mezquita is the finest mosque in Spain. A 16c cathedral was added at the centre of the building and a 17c tower replaced the minaret. The old Jewish quarter has 14c synagogue http://english.turismodecordoba.org 50 C3

El Escorial Immense Renaissance complex of palatial and monastic buildings and mausoleum of the Spanish monarchs. www.turismomadrid.es/en/component/guides/monumento/55 45 B3

Granada The Alhambra was hill-top palace-fortress of the rulers of the last Moorish kingdom and is the most splendid example of Moorish art and architecture in Spain. The complex has three principal parts: Alcazaba fortress (11c); Casa Real palace (14c, with later Palace of Carlos V); Generalife gardens. Also: Moorish quarter; gypsy quarter; Royal Chapel with good art in the sacristy. www.turgranada.es 57 A4

León Gothic cathedral has notable stained glass. Royal Pantheon commemorates early kings of Castile and León. 36 B1

Madrid Capital of Spain, a mainly modern city with 17–19c architecture at its centre around Plaza Mayor. Sights: Royal Palace with lavish apartments; Descalzas Reales Convent (tapestries and other works); Royal Armoury museum. Spain's three leading galleries: Prado (15–18c); Queen Sofia Centre (20c Spanish, Picasso's *Guernica*); Thyssen-Bornemisza Museum (medieval to modern). www.turismomadrid.es/en 45 B4

Oviedo Gothic cathedral with 12c sanctuary. Three Visigoth (9c) churches: Santullano, Santa María del Naranco, San Miguel de Lillo. 35 A5

Palma Situated on Mallorca, the largest and most beautiful of the Balearic islands, with an impressive Gothic cathedral. www.palmademallorca.es 60 B2

Picos de Europa Mountain range with river gorges and peaks topped by Visigothic and Romanesque churches. 36 A2

Pyrenees Unspoiled mountain range with beautiful landscape and villages. The Ordesa National Park has many waterfalls and canyons. 38–39

Salamanca Delightful old city with some uniquely Spanish architecture: Renaissance Plateresque is famously seen on 16c portal of the university (founded 1215); Baroque Churrigueresque on 18c Plaza Mayor; both styles at the Convent of San Esteban. Also: Romanesque Old Cathedral; Gothic-Plateresque New Cathedral; House of Shells. www.salamanca.es 44 B2

Santiago di Compostela Medieval city with many churches and religious institutions. The famous pilgrimage to the shrine of St James the Apostle ends here in the magnificent cathedral, originally Romanesque with many later elements (18c Baroque façade). www.santiagodecompostela.org 34 B2

Segovia Old town set on a rock with a 1c Roman aqueduct. Also: 16c Gothic cathedral; Alcázar (14–15c, rebuilt 19c); 12-sided 13c Templar church of Vera Cruz. 45 B3

Seville *Sevilla* City noted for festivals and flamenco. The world's largest Gothic cathedral (15c) retains the Orange Court and minaret of a mosque. The Alcazar is a fine example of Moorish architecture. The massive 18c tobacco factory, now part of the university, was the setting for Bizet's *Carmen*. Barrio de Santa Cruz is the old Jewish quarter with narrow streets and white houses. Also: Casa de Pilatos (15–16c); Museum of Fine Arts. Nearby: Roman Italica with amphitheatre. 56 A2

Tarragona The city and its surroundings have some of the best-preserved Roman heritage in Spain. Also: Gothic cathedral (cloister); Archaeological Museum. www.tarragonaturisme.cat 41 C2

Toledo Historic city with Moorish, Jewish and Christian sights. The small 11c mosque of El Cristo de la Luz is one of the earliest in Spain. Two synagogues have been preserved: Santa María la Blanca; El Tránsito. Churches: San Juan de los Reyes; Gothic cathedral (good artworks). El Greco's *Burial of the Count of Orgaz* is in the Church of Santo Tomé. More of his works are in the El Greco house and, with other art, in Hospital de Santa Cruz. 45 C3

Valencia The old town has houses and palaces with elaborate façades. Also: Gothic cathedral and Lonja de la Seda church. www.turisvalencia.es 53 B3

Zaragoza Town notable for Moorish architecture (11c Aljafería Palace). The Basilica de Nuestra Señora del Pilar, one of two cathedrals, is highly venerated. www.zaragoza.es/turismo 47 A3

Ski resorts

The resorts listed are popular ski centres, therefore road access to most is normally good. However, mountain driving is never predictable and drivers should make sure they take snow chains, emergency provisions and clothing. Listed for each resort are: the atlas page and grid square; the resort/minimum piste altitude (where only one figure is shown, they are at the same height) and maximum altitude of its own lifts; the number of lifts and gondolas (the total for lift-linked resorts); the season start and end dates (snow cover allowing); whether snow is augmented by cannon; the nearest town (with its distance in km) and, where available, the website and/or telephone number of the local tourist information centre or ski centre ('00' prefix required for calls from the UK).

The ❄ symbol indicates resorts with snow cannon

Andorra

Pyrenees

Pas de la Casa / Grau Roig 40 B2 ❄ 2050–2640m • 65 lifts • Dec–Apr • Andorra La Vella (30km) • *Access via Envalira Pass (2407m), highest in Pyrenees, snow chains essential.* www.pasdelacasa-andorra.com

France

Alps

Alpe d'Huez 26 B3 ❄ 1860–3330m • 85 lifts • Dec–Apr • Grenoble (63km) +33 4 76 11 44 44 www.alpedhuez.com • *Snow chains may be required on access road to resort.*

Avoriaz 26 A3 ❄ 1800/1100–2280m • 35 lifts • Dec–May • Morzine (14km) +33 4 50 74 02 11 www.morzine-avoriaz.com • *Chains may be required for access road from Morzine. Car-free resort, park on edge of village. Horse-drawn sleigh service available.*

Chamonix-Mont-Blanc 27 B3 ❄ 49 lifts • 1035–3840m • Dec–Apr • Martigny (38km) +33 4 50 53 00 24 www.chamonix.com

Chamrousse 26 B2 ❄ 1700–2250m • 26 lifts • Dec–Apr • Grenoble (30km) +33 4 76 89 92 65 www.chamrousse.com • *Roads normally cleared, keep chains accessible because of altitude.*

Châtel 27 A3 ❄ 1200/1110–2200m • 41 lifts • Dec–Apr • Thonon-Les-Bains (35km) +33 4 50 73 22 44 http://info.chatel.com/english-version.html

Courchevel 26 B3 ❄ 1750/1300–2470m • 67 lifts • Dec–Apr • Moûtiers (23km) www.courchevel.com • *Roads normally cleared but keep chains accessible. Traffic 'discouraged' within the four resort bases.*

Flaine 26 A3 ❄ 1600–2500m • 26 lifts • Dec–Apr • Cluses (25km) +33 4 50 90 80 01 www.flaine.com • *Keep chains accessible for D6 from Cluses. Car access for depositing luggage and passengers only. 1500-space car park outside resort. Near Sixt-Fer-á-Cheval.*

La Clusaz 26 B3 ❄ 1100–2600m • 55 lifts • Dec–Apr • Annecy (32km) +33 4 50 32 65 00 www.laclusaz.com • *Roads normally clear but keep chains accessible for road from Annecy.*

La Plagne 26 B3 ❄ 2500/1250–3250m • 109 lifts • Dec–Apr Moûtiers (32km) +33 4 79 09 79 79 www.la-plagne.com • *Ten different centres up to 2100m altitude. Road access via Bozel, Landry or Aime normally cleared. Linked to Les Arcs by cablecar*

Les Arcs 27 B3 ❄ 1600/1200–3230m • 77 lifts • Dec–May • Bourg-St-Maurice (15km) +33 4 79 07 12 57 www.lesarcs.com • *Four base areas up to 2000 metres; keep chains accessible. Pay parking at edge of each base resort. Linked to La Plagne by cablecar*

Les Carroz d'Araches 26 A3 ❄ 1140–2500m • 80 lifts • Dec–Apr • Cluses (13km) + 33 4 50 90 00 04 www.lescarroz.com

Les Deux-Alpes 26 C3 ❄ 1650/1300–3600m • 55 lifts • Dec–Apr • Grenoble (75km) +33 4 76 79 22 00 www.les2alpes.com • *Roads normally cleared, however snow chains recommended for D213 up from D1091.*

Les Gets 26 A3 ❄ 1170/1000–2000m • 52 lifts • Dec–Apr • Cluses (18km) +33 4 50 75 80 80 www.lesgets.com

Les Ménuires 26 B3 ❄ 1815/1850–3200m • 40 lifts • Dec–Apr • Moûtiers (27km) +33 4 00 63 77 www.lesmenuires.com • *Keep chains accessible for D117 from Moûtiers.*

Les Sept Laux Prapoutel 26 B3 ❄ 24 lifts • 1350–2400m, • Dec–Apr • Grenoble (38km) +33 4 76 08 17 86 www.les7laux.com • *Roads normally cleared, however keep chains accessible for mountain road up from the A41 motorway. Near St Sorlin d'Arves.*

Megève 26 B3 ❄ 1100/1050–2350m • 79 lifts • Dec–Apr • Sallanches (12km) +33 4 50 21 27 28 www.megeve.com • *Horse-drawn sleigh rides available.*

Méribel 26 B3 ❄ 1400/1100–2950m • 61 lifts • Dec–May • Moûtiers (18km) +33 4 79 08 60 01 www.meribel.net • *Keep chains accessible for 18km to resort on D90 from Moûtiers.*

Morzine 26 A3 ❄ 1000–2460m • 67 lifts, • Dec–Apr • Thonon-Les-Bains (30km) +33 4 50 74 72 72 www.morzine-avoriaz.com

Pra Loup 32 A2 ❄ 1600/1500–2500m • 53 lifts • Dec–Apr • Barcelonnette (10km) +33 4 92 84 10 04 www.praloup.com • *Roads normally cleared but chains accessibility recommended.*

Risoul 26 C3 ❄ 1850/1650–2750m • 51 lifts • Dec–Apr • Briançon (40km) +33 4 92 46 02 60 www.risoul.com • *Keep chains accessible. Near Guillestre. Linked with Vars Les Claux*

St-Gervais Mont-Blanc 26 B3 ❄ 850/1150–2350m • 27 lifts • Dec–Apr • Sallanches (10km) www.st-gervais.com

Serre Chevalier 26 C3 ❄ 1350/1200–2800m • 77 lifts • Dec–Apr • Briançon (10km) + 33 4 92 24 98 98 www.serre-chevalier.com • *Made up of 13 small villages along the valley road, which is normally cleared.*

Tignes 27 B3 ❄ 2100/1550–3450m • 97 lifts • Jan–Dec • Bourg St Maurice (26km) +33 4 79 40 04 40 www.tignes.net • *Keep chains accessible because of altitude.*

Val d'Isère 27 B3 ❄ 1850/1550–3450m • 97 lifts • Dec–Apr • Bourg-St-Maurice (30km) +33 4 79 06 06 60 www.valdisere.com • *Roads normally cleared but keep chains accessible.*

Val Thorens 26 B3 ❄ 2300/1850–3200m • 29 lifts • Dec–Apr • Moûtiers (37km) www.valthorens.com • *Chains essential – highest ski resort in Europe. Obligatory paid parking on edge of resort.*

Valloire 26 B3 ❄ 1430–2600m • 34 lifts • Dec–Apr • Modane (20km) +33 4 79 59 03 96 www.valloire.net • *Road normally clear up to the Col du Galbier, to the south of the resort, which is closed from 1st November to 1st June. Linked to Valmeinier.*

Valmeinier 26 B3 ❄ 1500–2600m • 34 lifts • Dec–Apr • St Michel de Maurienne (47km) +33 4 79 59 53 69 www.valmeinier.com • *Access from north on D1006 / D902. Col du Galbier, to the south of the resort closed from 1st November to 1st June. Linked to Valloire.*

Valmorel 26 B3 ❄ 1400–2550m • 90 lifts • Dec–Apr • Moûtiers (15km) +33 4 79 09 85 55 www.valmorel.com • *Near St Jean-de-Belleville. Linked with ski areas of Doucy-Combelouvière and St François-Longchamp.*

Vars Les Claux 26 C3 ❄ 1850/1650–2750m • 51 lifts • Dec–Apr • Briançon (40km) +33 4 92 46 51 31 www.vars-ski.com • *Four base resorts up to 1850 metres. Keep chains accessible. Linked with Risoul.*

Villard de Lans 26 B2 ❄ 1050/1160–2170m • 28 lifts • Dec–Apr • Grenoble (32km) +33 4 76 95 10 38 www.villarddelans.com

Pyrenees

Font-Romeu 40 B3 ❄ 1800/1600–2200m • 25 lifts • Nov–Apr • Perpignan (87km) +33 4 68 30 68 30 www.font-romeu.fr • *Roads normally clear but keep chains accessible.*

Saint-Lary Soulan 39 B4 ❄ 830/1650/1700–2515m • 31 lifts • Dec–Mar • Tarbes (75km) +33 5 62 39 50 81 www.saintlary.com • *Access roads constantly cleared of snow.*

Vosges

La Bresse-Hohneck 20 A1 ❄ 33 lifts • 500/900–1350m • Dec–Mar • Cornimont (6km) +33 3 29 25 41 29 www.labresse.net

Spain

Pyrenees

Baqueira-Beret/Bonaigua 39 B4 ❄ 1500–2500m • 33 lifts • Dec–Apr • Vielha (15km) +34 902 415 415 www.baqueira.es • *Roads normally clear but keep chains accessible. Near Salardú.*

Sistema Penibetico

Sierra Nevada 57 A4 ❄ 2100–3300m • 24 lifts • Dec–May • Granada (32km) +34 902 70 80 90 http://sierranevada.es • *Access road designed to be avalanche safe and is snow cleared.*

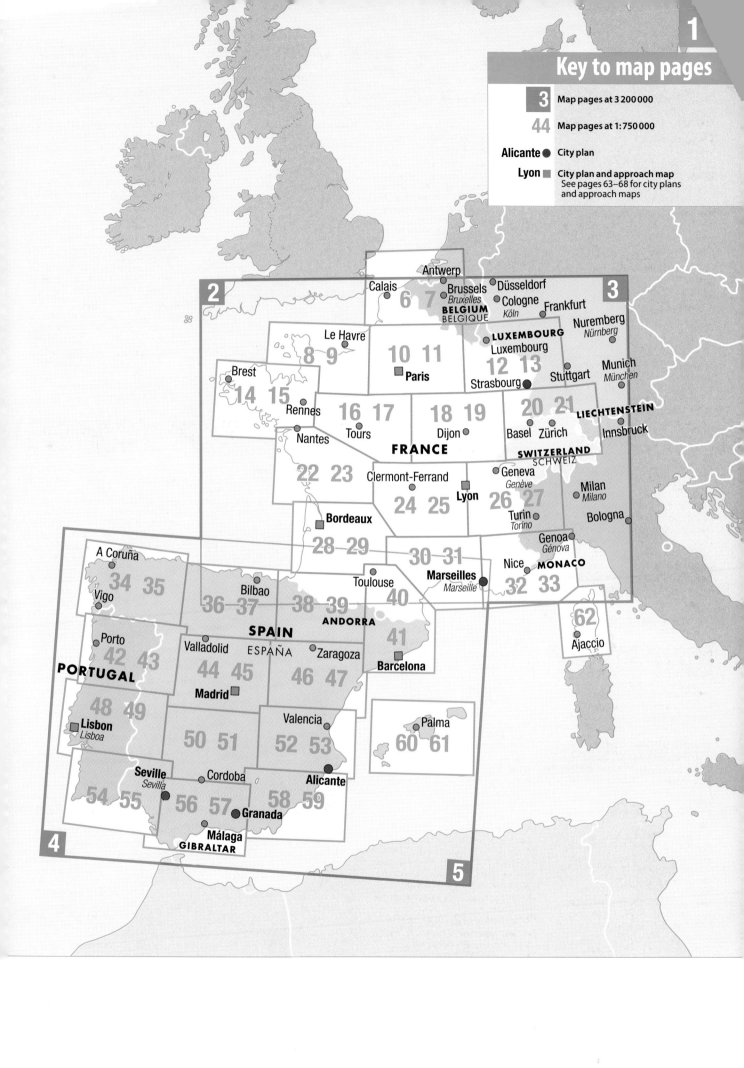

1

Key to map pages

3 Map pages at 3 200 000

44 Map pages at 1:750 000

Alicante ● City plan

Lyon ■ City plan and approach map
See pages 63–68 for city plans
and approach maps

2

3

Antwerp

Calais

6 **7** Brussels
Bruxelles

Düsseldorf

Cologne
Köln

Frankfurt

Nuremberg
Nürnberg

BELGIUM
BELGIQUE

LUXEMBOURG
Luxembourg

Le Havre

8 **9**

10 **11**

12 **13**

Stuttgart

Munich
München

■ **Paris**

Strasbourg ●

Brest

14 **15**

Rennes

16 **17**

18 **19**

20 **21**

LIECHTENSTEIN

Basel Zürich

Innsbruck

Tours

Dijon

Nantes

FRANCE

SWITZERLAND
SCHWEIZ

22 **23**

Clermont-Ferrand

Geneva
Genève

Milan
Milano

24 **25**

■ **Lyon**

26 **27**

Bologna

Bordeaux ■

Turin
Torino

Genoa
Génova

28 **29**

30 **31**

Nice **MONACO**

32 **33**

Toulouse

Marseilles ●
Marseille

A Coruña

34 **35**

Bilbao

38 **39**

40

62

Vigo

36 **37**

ANDORRA

Ajaccio

Porto

42 **43**

SPAIN
ESPAÑA

Valladolid

Zaragoza

41

PORTUGAL

44 **45**

46 **47**

Barcelona ■

■ **Madrid**

48 **49**

Valencia

Palma

■ **Lisbon**
Lisboa

50 **51**

52 **53**

60 **61**

Seville
Sevilla

Cordoba

Alicante ●

54 **55**

56 **57** Granada

58 **59**

Málaga
GIBRALTAR

4

5

COSTA VERDE ST. NAZAIRE POOLE PLYMOUTH PORTSMOUTH PORTSMOUTH

COSTA MONTAÑESA

C. Ortegal C. de Peñas Gijón Xixón

Ortigueira Luarca Avilés Villaviciosa C. de Ajo Santander Santoña Castro Urdiales Getxo Bilbao

Ferrol Vivero Ribadeo Salas Oviedo Pola de Siero Llanes San Vicente de la Barquera Laredo Barakaldo

Pontedeume Mondoñedo Tineo Grado Langreo Torrelavega Reinosa Oña Durango

A Coruña Villalba Cangas de Narcea Mieres Picos de Europa 2648 Potes Briviesca Miranda de

Betanzos Baamonde Fonsagrada Pola de Lena La Pola de Gordon Osorno Santo Domingo de la Calzada

Vimianzo Carballo Lugo Villablino La Robla Saldaña Burgos Salas de los Infantes

Ordes Melide Villafranca del Bierzo León Sahagún Palencia Aranda de Duero Soria

Santiago de Compostela Sarria Ponferrada Astorga La Bañeza Benavente Valladolid Burgo de Osma

Corcubión Chantada Pobra de Trives Valencia de Don Juan Villalón de Campos San Esteban de Gormaz

C. Fisterra O Carballiño Villalpando Medina de Rioseco Picos de Urbión

Noia Lalín A Gudiña Verín Zamora Toro Tordesillas Cuéllar Boceguillas Sigüenza

Muros Padrón Ourense Xinzo de Limia Benavente Medina del Campo Olmedo Medinace

Vilagarcía de Arousa A Estrada Celanova Bragança Fermoselle Arévalo Segovia Medinace

Pontevedra Redondela Ponteareas Chaves Mirandela Miranda do Douro Salamanca Peñaranda de Bracamonte Villacastín El Molar Guadalajara Brihuega

Marin Tui Celorico da Beira Vila Pouca de Aguiar Vila Real Ledesma Vitigudino Alba de Tormes Ávila El Escorial Alcobendas Alcalá de Henares

Vigo Baiono Valença Braga Guimarães Murça Peso da Régua Fuentes de Oñoro Ciudad Rodrigo Béjar San Martín de Valdeiglesias MADRID Leganés Arganda Sace

Caminha Viana do Castelo Amarante Penafiel Lamego Torre de Moncorvo Pinhel Guarda El Barco de Ávila Pico Almanzor 2592 Arenas de San Pedro Navalcarnero Getafe Parla

Póvoa de Varzim Vila do Conde Matosinhos Porto Vila Nova de Gaia São João da Madeira Oliveira de Azeméis Viseu da Beira Manguale Vilar Formoso Fundão Plasencia Coria Talavera de la Reina Illescas Maqueda Aranjuez Tarancón Ocaña

Aveiro Águeda Tondela Mealhada Coimbra Belmonte Covilhã Penamacôr Hoyos Navalmoral de la Mata Toledo Quintanar de la Orden La Alm

Mira Figueira da Foz Miranda do Corvo Pombal Castelo Branco Alcántara Belvís de la Jara Orgaz Pedro Muñoz

Leiria Proença-a-Nova Tomar Abrantes Nisa Trujillo Cáceres Guadalupe Navahermosa Madridejos Alcázar de San Juan Tomelloso Villarrobledo

Caldas da Rainha Torres Novas Gavião Portalegre Valencia de Alcántara Logrosán Malagón Ciudad Real Manzanares

Peniche C. Carvoeiro Santarém Almeirim Ponte de Sor Arronches Monfortinho Zorita Miajadas Villanueva de la Serena Almodóvar del Campo Valdepeñas

Torres Vedras Cartaxo Azambuja Coruche Campo Maior Mérida Don Benito Fuente del Fresno Puertollano Villanueva de los Infantes

Mafra Vila Franca de Xira Estremoz Elvas Badajoz Almendralejo Cástuera Almadén Paso Despeñaperros

Sintra C. da Roca Estoril Oeiras Almada Montijo Barreiro Montemor-o-Novo Évora Reguengos de Monsaraz Olivenza La Albuera Villafranca de los Barros Hinojosa del Duque Pozoblanco La Carolina

LISBOA LISBON Setúbal Alcácer do Sal Viana do Alentejo Jerez de los Caballeros Zafra Los Santos de Maimona Peñarroya-Pueblonuevo Espiel Montoro Andújar Bailén Linares Villacarrillo

C. Espichel B. de Setúbal Grândola Torrão Ferreira do Alentejo Beja Barrancos Moura Llerena Azuaga Fuente Obejuna Córdoba Castro del Río Martos Úbeda Baeza

Santiago do Cacém Aljustrel Mértola Fregenal de la Sierra Aracena Posadas La Carlota Baena Jaén Huelma Cúllar de B

C. de Sines Sines Cercal Odemira Monchique Valverde del Camino Nerva Lora del Río Palma del Río Montilla Cabra Alcalá la Real Priego de Córdoba Guadix Baza

Portimão Lagôa Vila Real de Santo António La Palma del Condado Sanlúcar la Mayor Carmona Écija Lucena Loja Granada

C. de São Vicente Sagres Lagos Albufeira Faro Olhão Tavira Loulé Ayamonte Huelva Almonte Sevilla Seville Dos Hermanas Marchena Osuna Archidona Santa Fe Mulhacén 3478

G. de Cádiz COSTA DE LA LUZ Lebrija Utrera Morón de la Frontera Campillos Antequera Alhama de Granada Orjiva Berja Albuñol Motril

ISLAS CANARIAS Sanlúcar de Barrameda Arcos de la Frontera Ronda Vélez Málaga A44

LAS PALMAS DE GRAN CANARIA SANTA CRUZ DE TENERIFE El Puerto de Santa María Jerez de la Frontera Coín Málaga Torremolinos COSTA DEL SOL Adra Roqu

Cádiz Puerto Real Medina Sidonia Marbella Fuengirola MELILLA AL HOCEIMA

San Fernando Chiclana de la Frontera Vejer de la Frontera Estepona MELILLA

C. Trafalgar Algeciras La Línea de la Concepción Gibraltar (U.K.) SÉTE BARCELONA GENOVA

Str. of Gibraltar Tarifa Ceuta (Esp.) (Spain) Alborán

C. Spartel Tanger Tangier

Tétouan

PORTUGAL ESPAÑA SPAIN

0 40 80 120 160 km

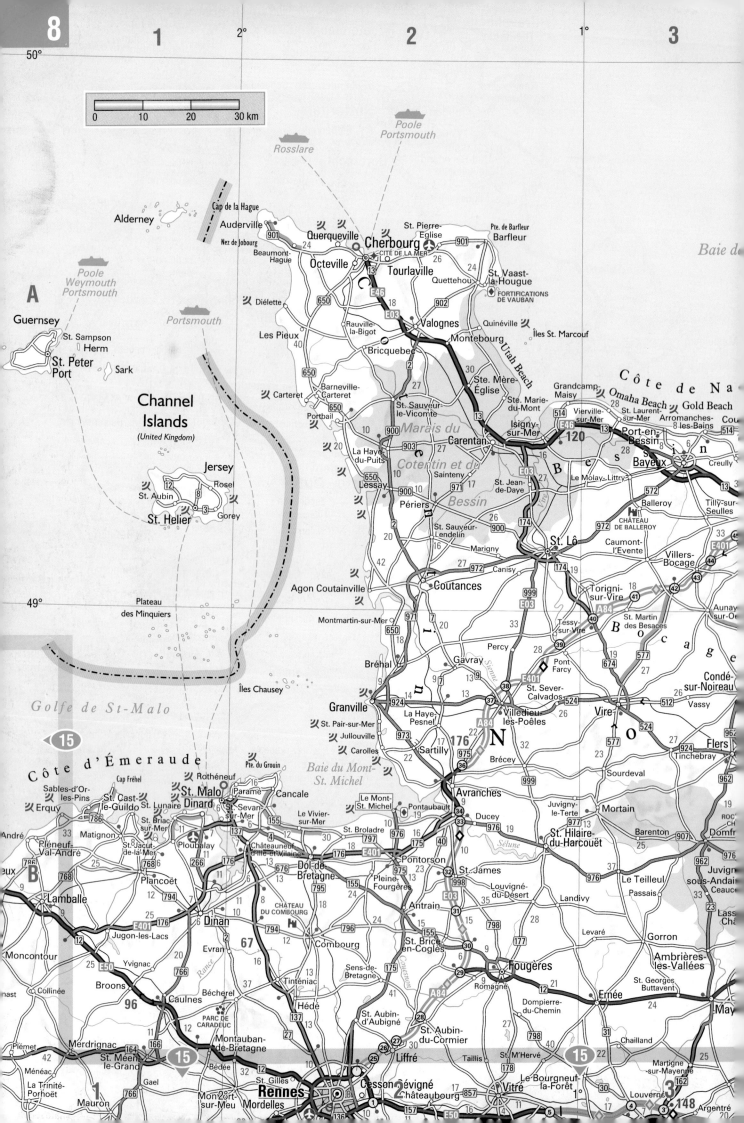

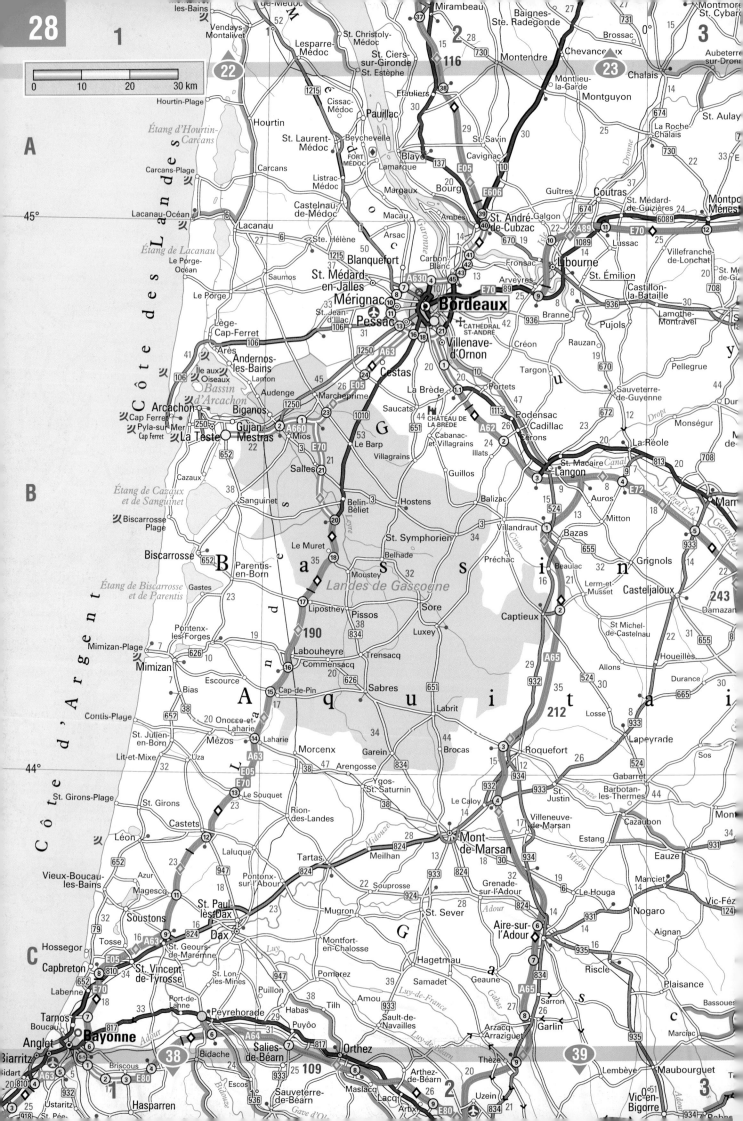

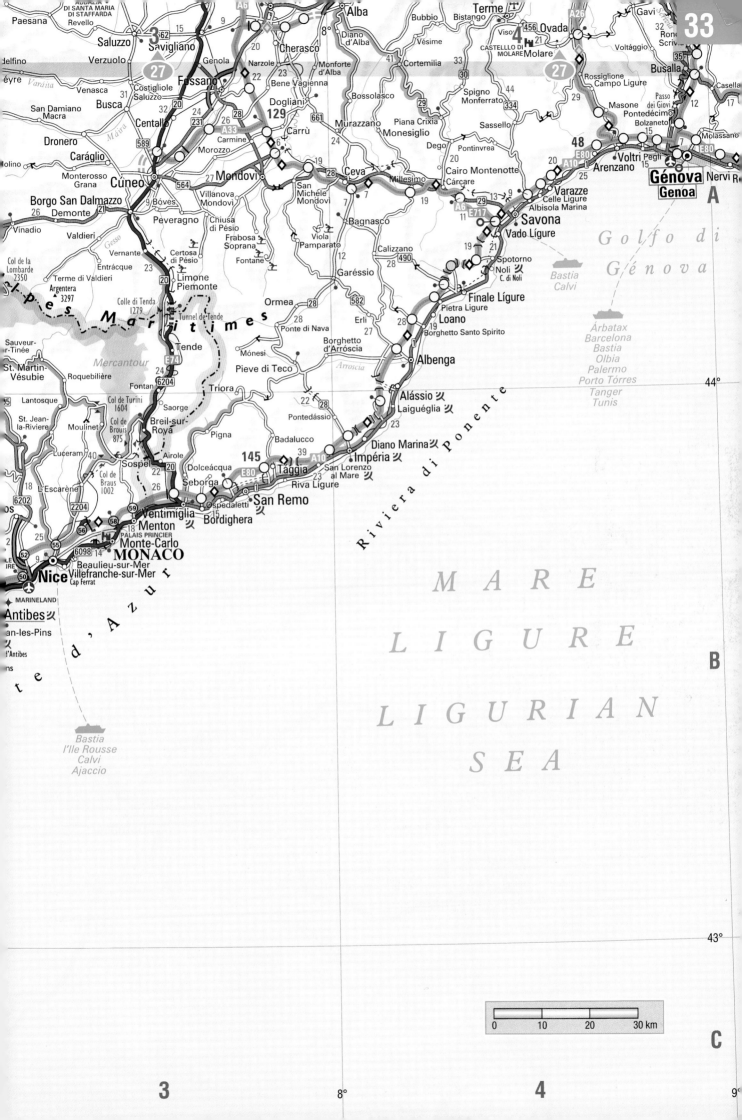

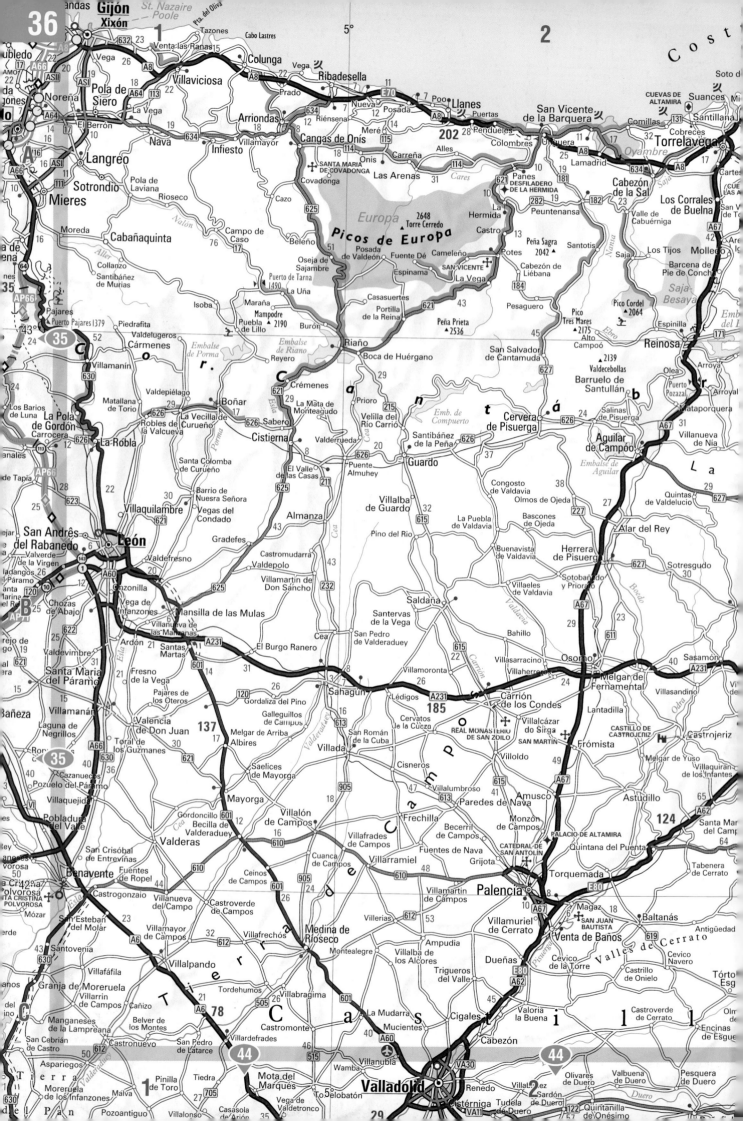

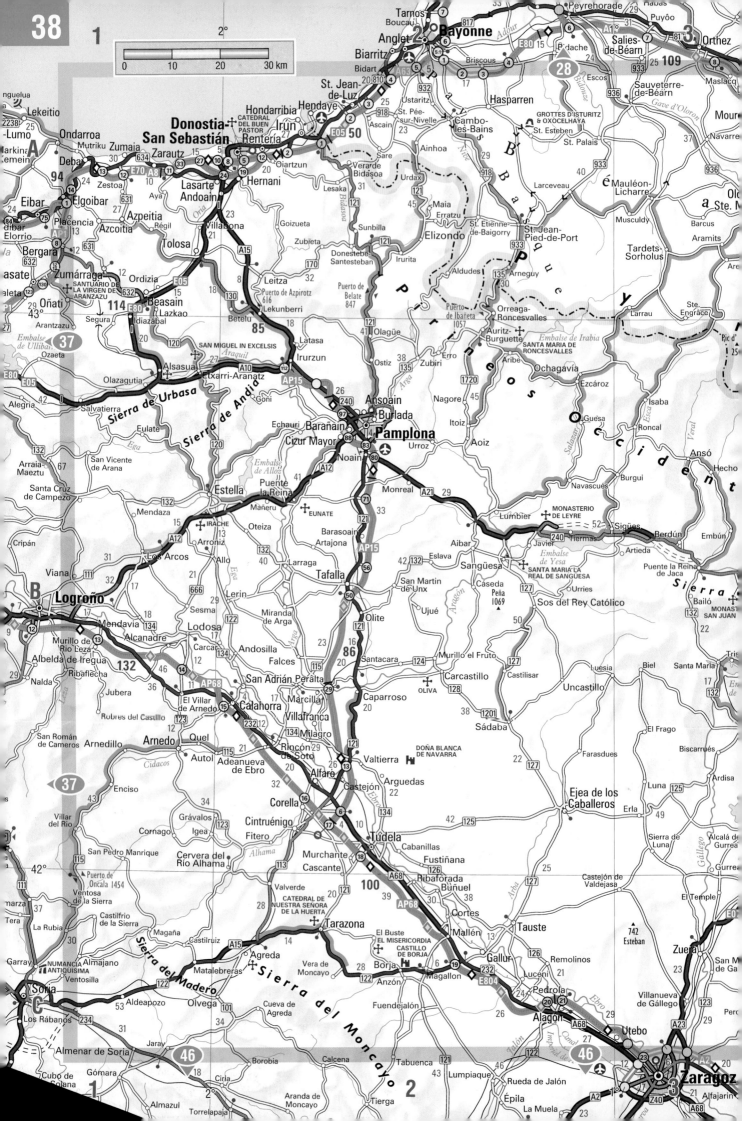

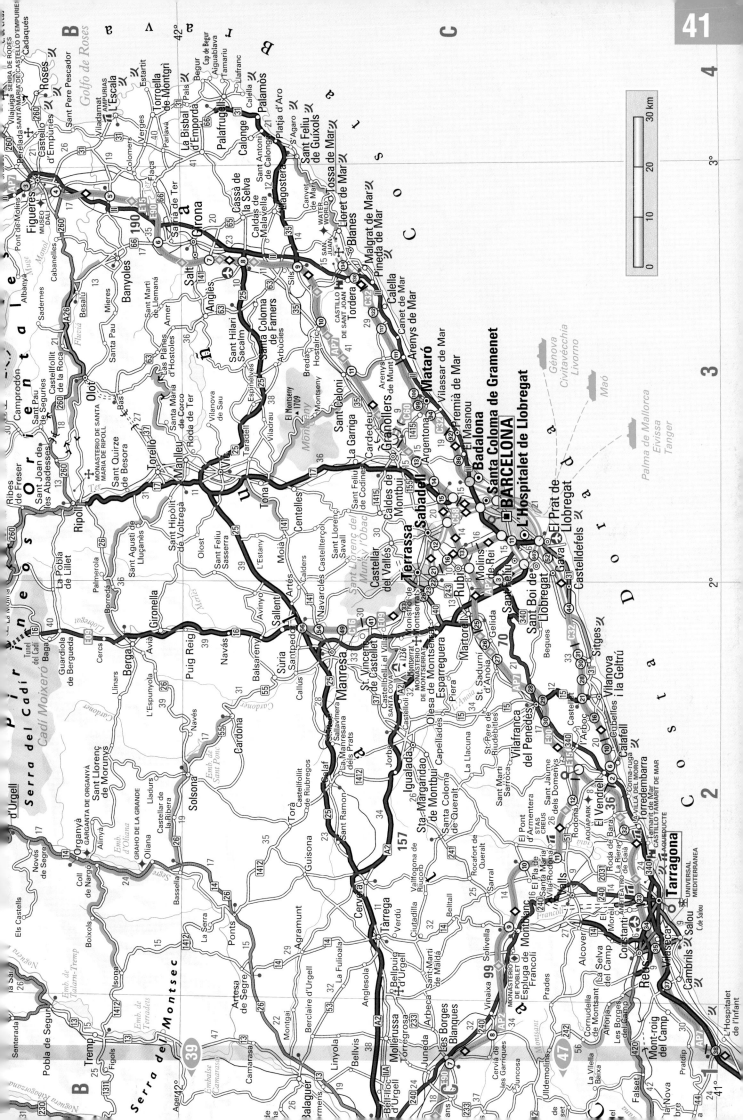

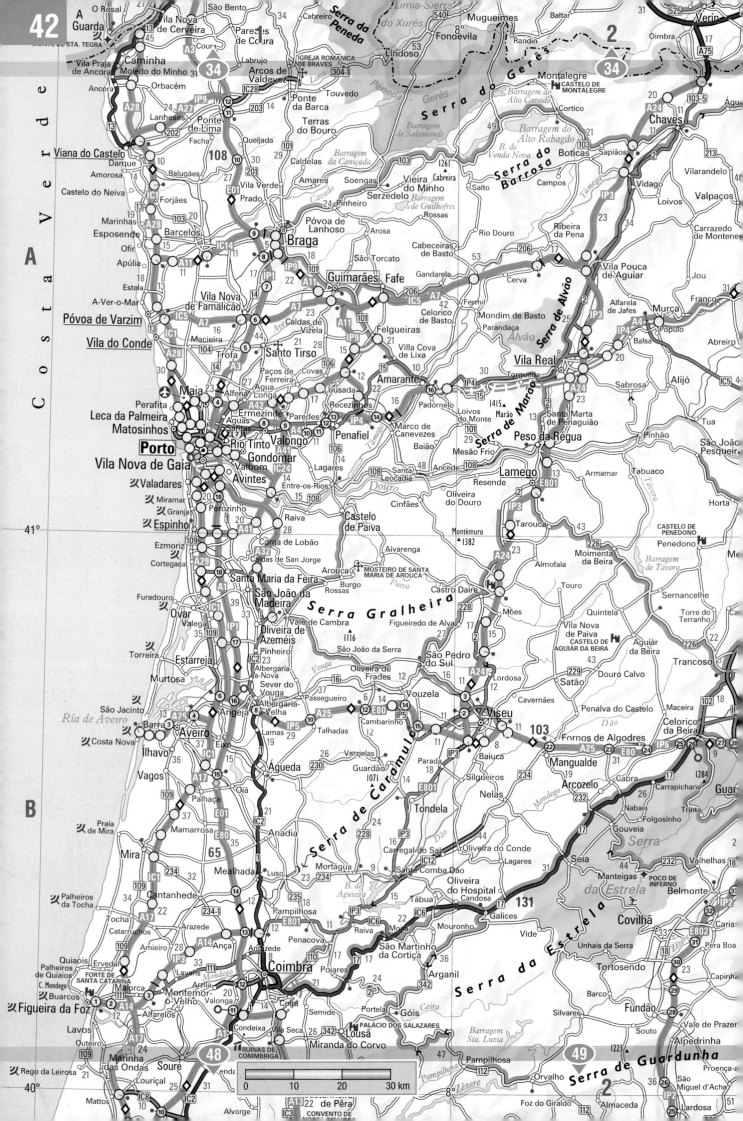

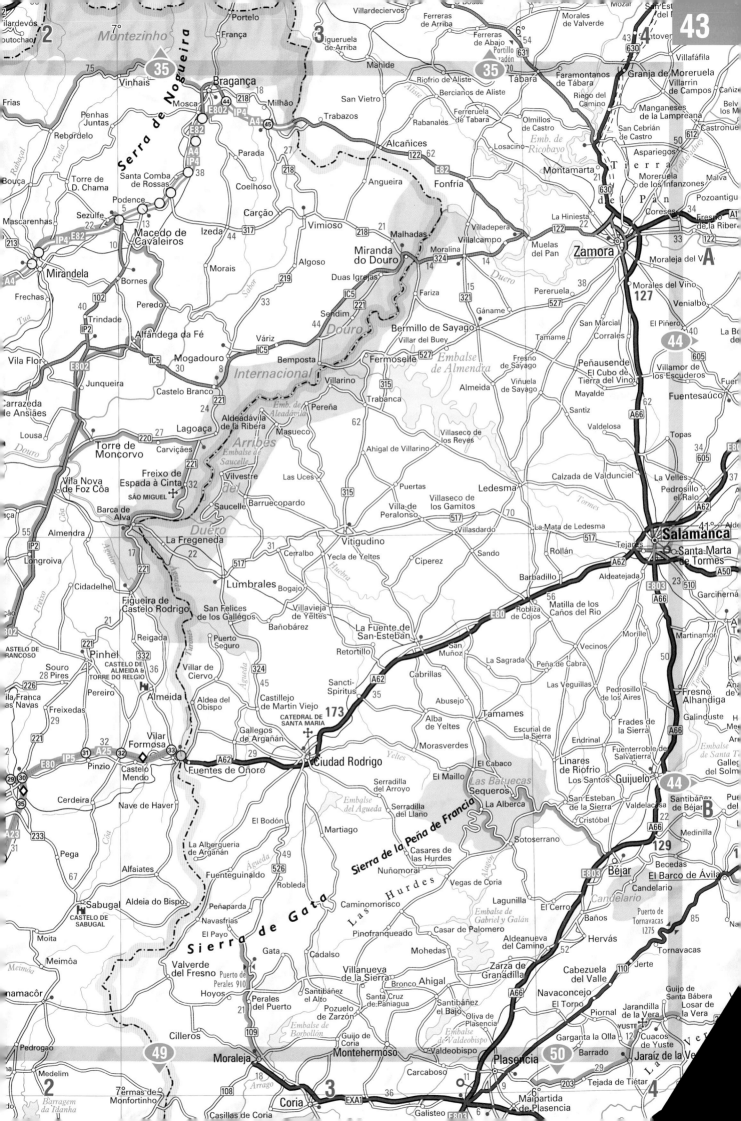

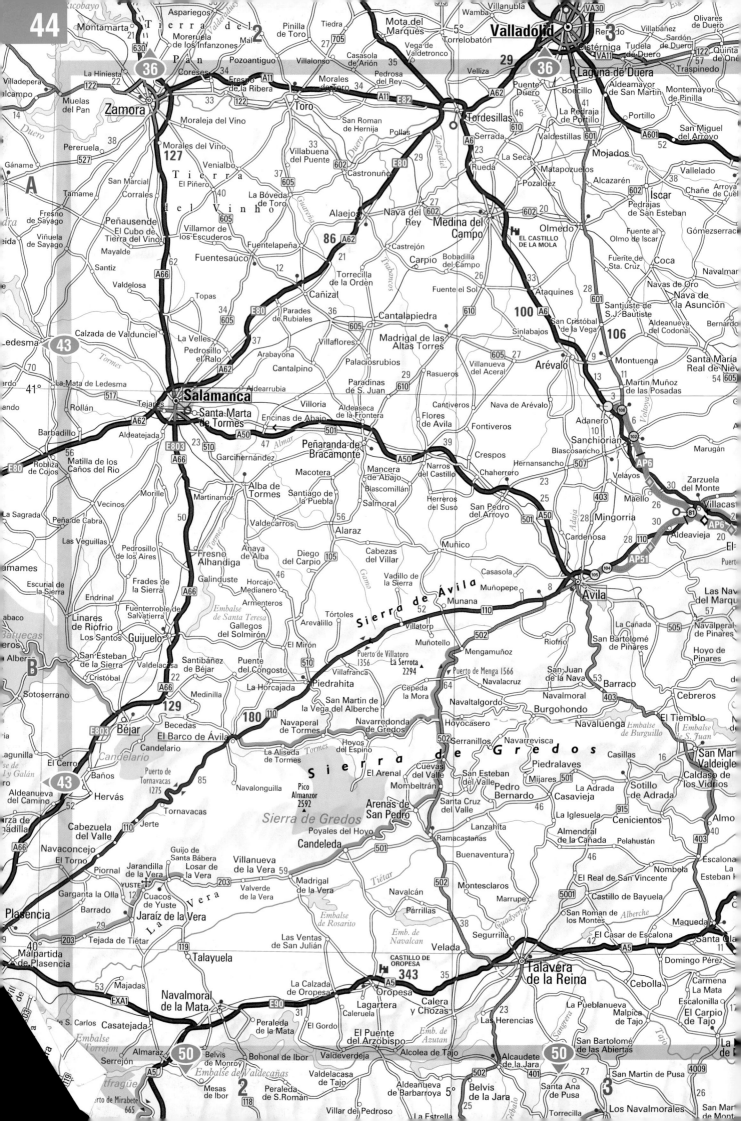

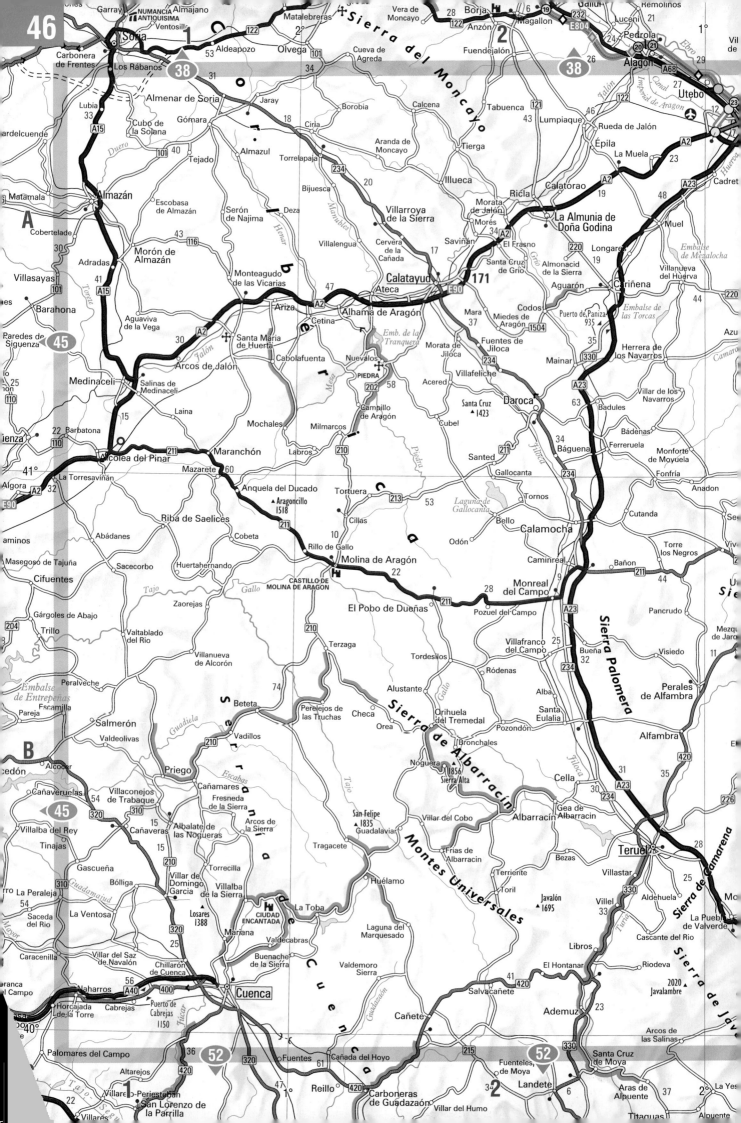

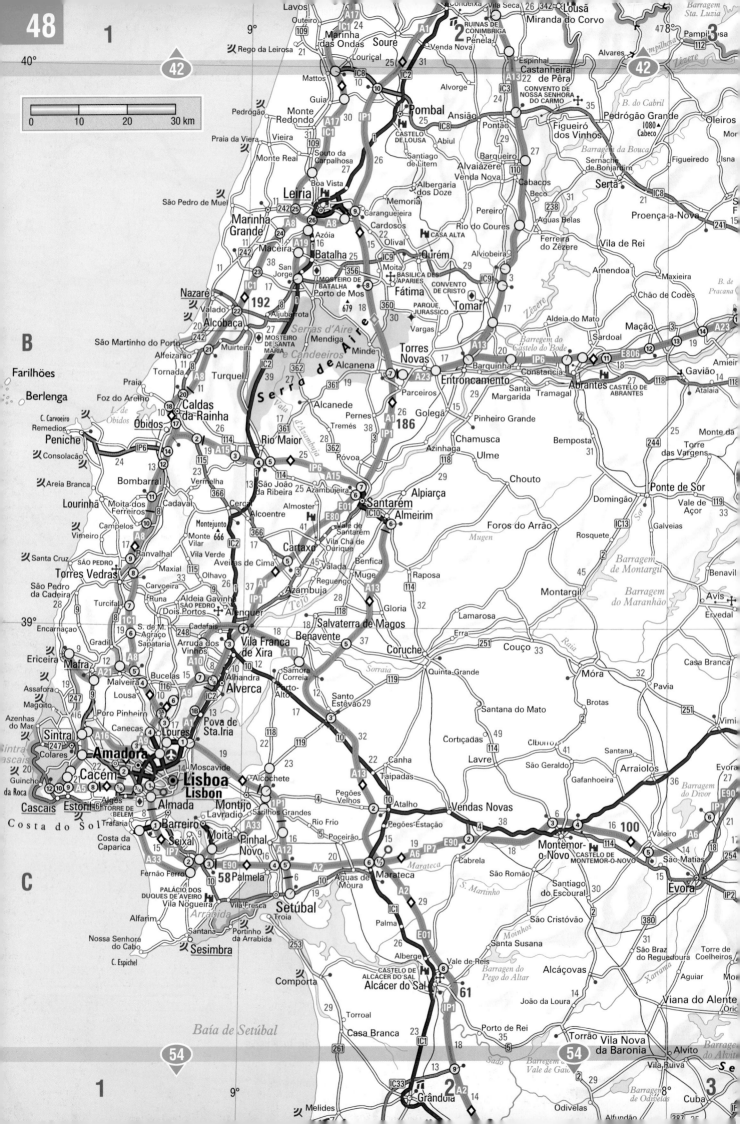

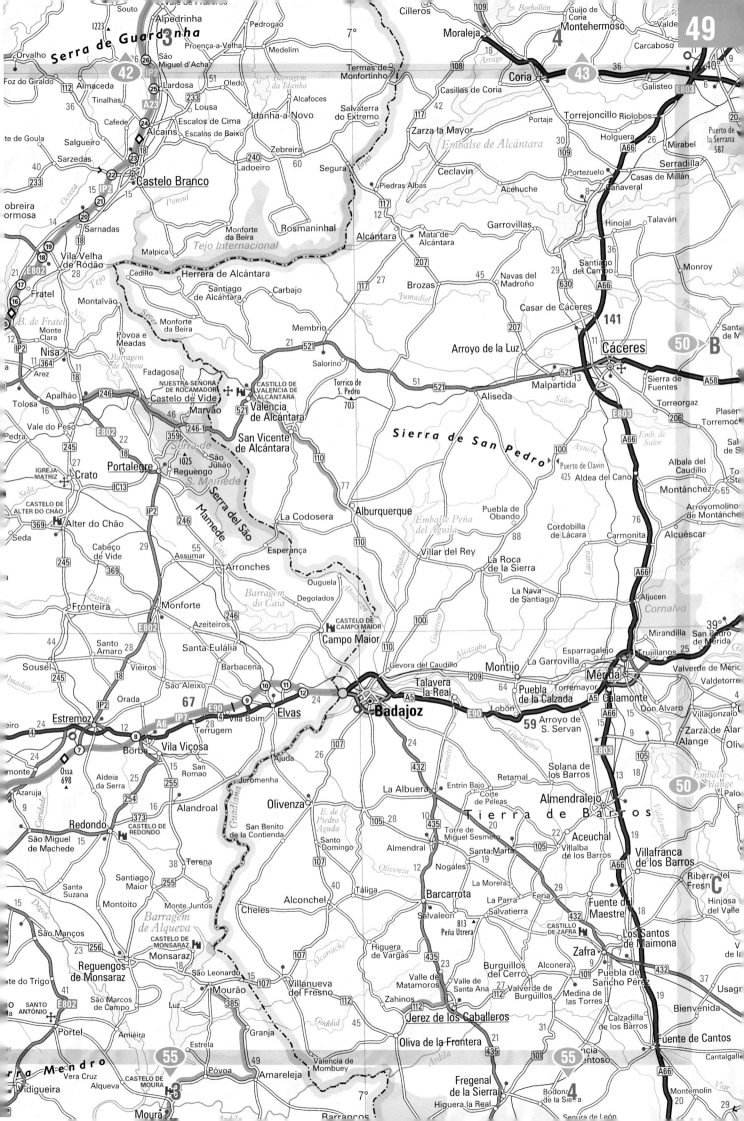

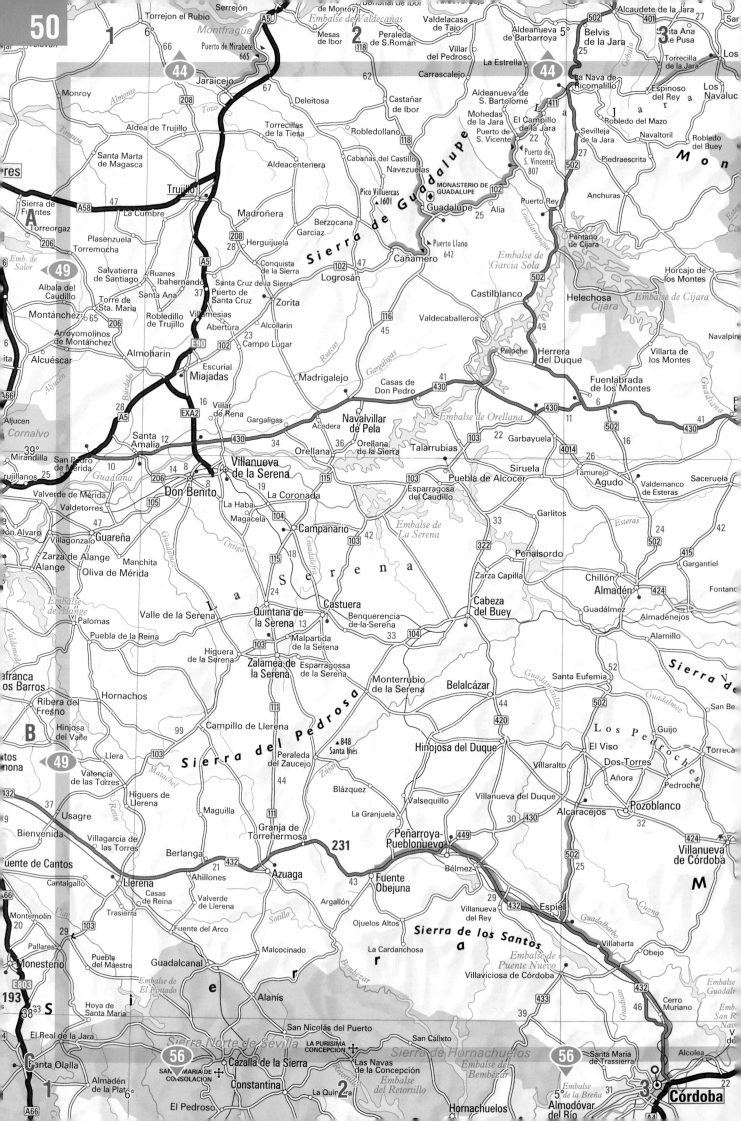

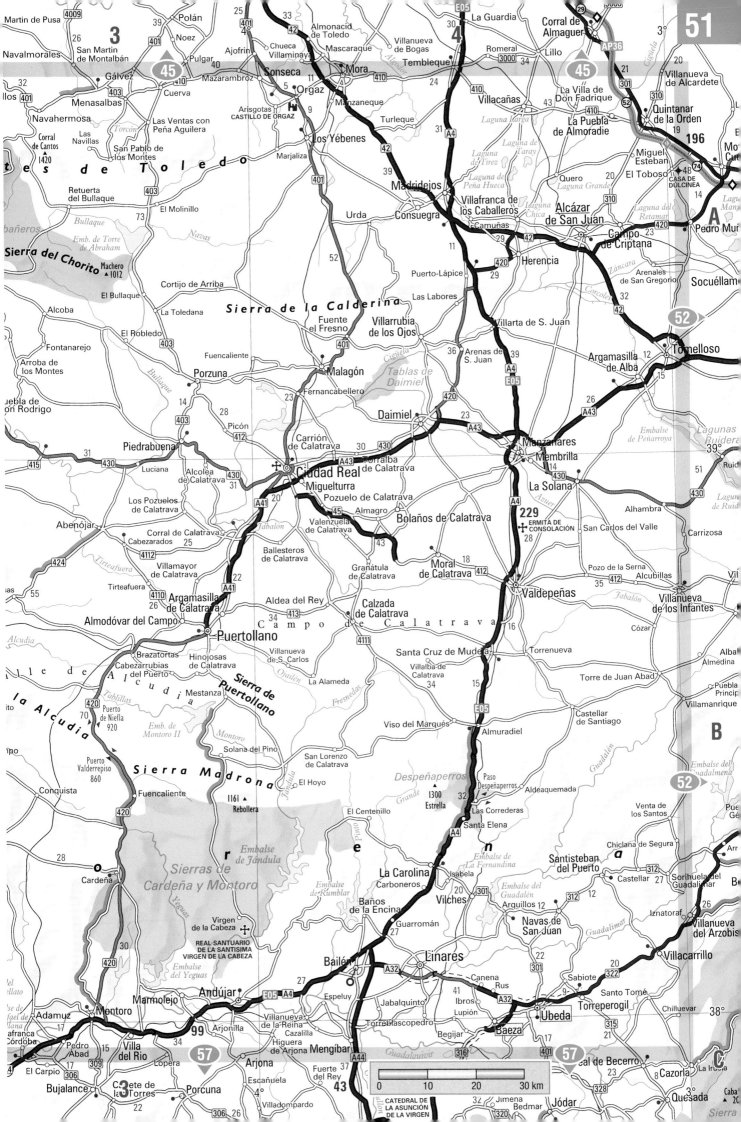

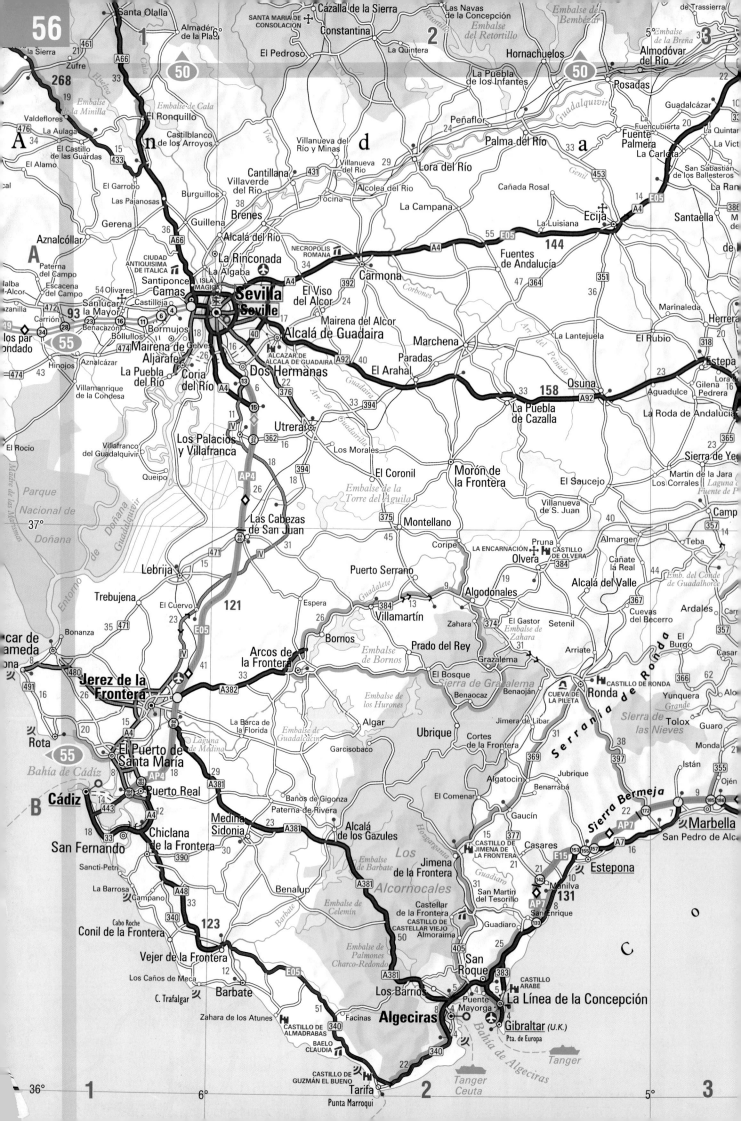

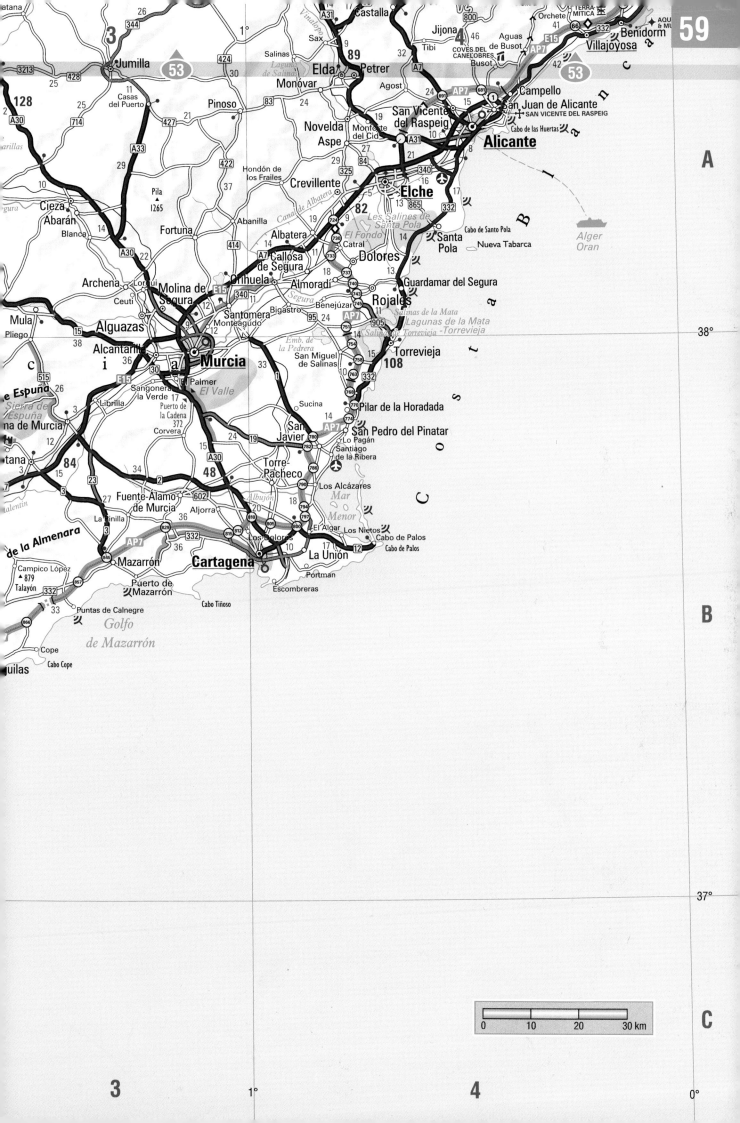

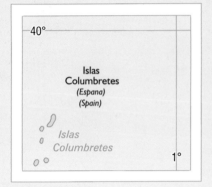

Islas
Columbretes
(España)
(Spain)

*Islas
Columbretes*

ISLAS BALEARES
BALEARIC ISLANDS

Port de Sóller
Fo
Sóller
Deià
Tunel
Sóller Ala
Valldemossa
25
Banyalbufar
Bunyo
Estellencs 39 Esporles 11
Marratx
Puigpunyent
12
10 8
Sa Dragonera **Palma de Mallorca**
Andratx
Calviá 4
Port d'Andratx MA1 Can 6
15 13 12 Pastilla 10
Barcelona Peguera 17 14 Palma
Santa Ponça Nova S'Arenal
Magaluf Cap Enderrocat
Cap de Cala Figuera *Bahía
de Palma*
Maó
Valencia
Mallorca
Eivissa Majorca
Denia

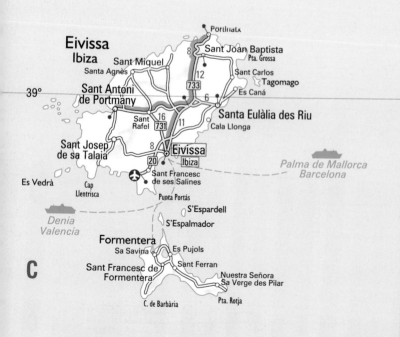

Portinatx
Eivissa
Ibiza Sant Joan Baptista
Sant Miquel Pta. Grossa
Santa Agnès 12 Sant Carlos
Sant Antoni Tagomago
de Portmany 733 Es Caná
6
16 11 **Santa Eulàlia des Riu**
Sant 731 Cala Llonga
Rafel
Sant Josep 8
de sa Talaia Eivissa
20 Ibiza
Es Vedrà Sant Francesc
Cap de ses Salines *Palma de Mallorca
Llentrisca Barcelona*
Punta Portás
S'Espardell
Denia S'Espalmador
Valencia
Formentera
Sa Savina Es Pujols
Sant Francesc de Sant Ferran
Formentera Nuestra Señora
Sa Verge des Pilar
C. de Barbària Pta. Rotja

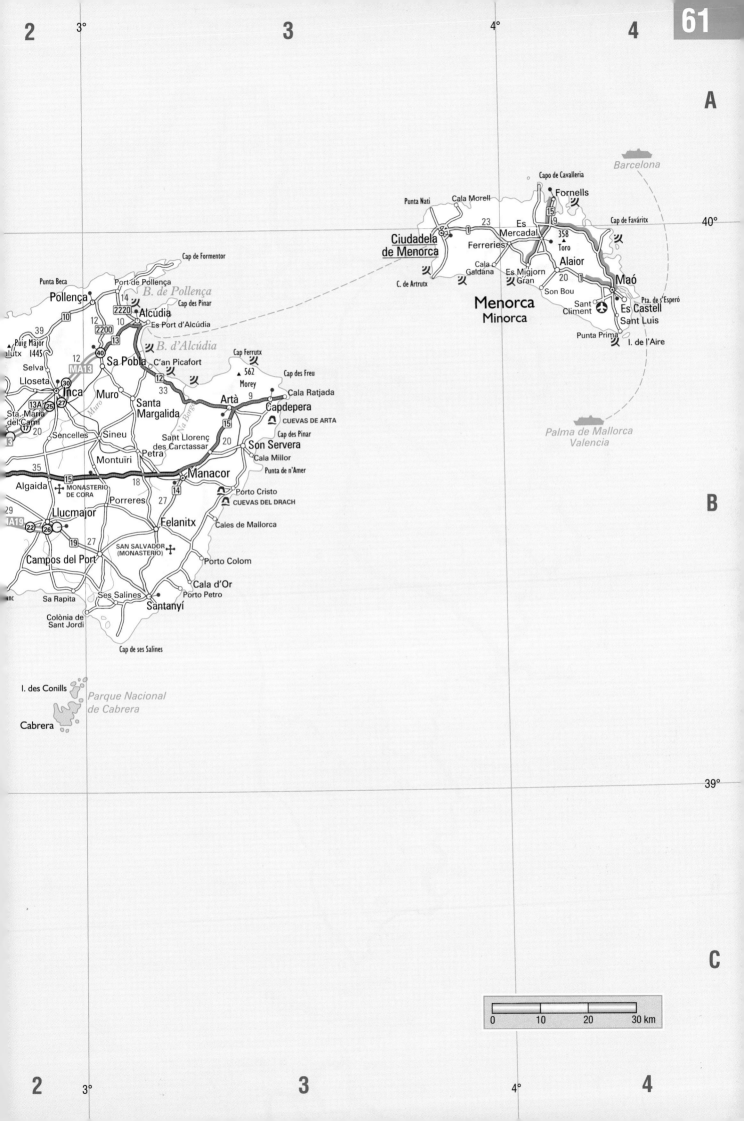

2   3°   3   4°   4

A

40°

Barcelona

Capo de Cavalleria

Punta Nati   Cala Morell   Fornells

Cap de Formentor

15

9

Cap de Faváritx

Cap des Pinar

23   Es Mercadal

Ciudadela de Menorca

Ferreries   358 Toro

Punta Beca   Port de Pollença   B. de Pollença

Pollença

Cala Galdana   Es Migjorn Gran   Alaior

14   2220   Alcúdia

C. de Artrutx   20   1   Maó

10   12   10   Es Port d'Alcúdia

Son Bou   Es Castell

39   2200   B. d'Alcúdia

Menorca   Sant Climent   Sant Luis

Puig Major 1445   13   40   Minorca   Pta. de s'Esperó

alutx   12   MA13   Sa Pobla   C'an Picafort   Cap Ferrutx   Punta Prima

Selva   562 Morey   Cap des Freu   I. de l'Aire

Lloseta   12   33

30   Santa Margalida   Artà   9   Cala Ratjada

27   Inca   Muro   Capdepera

13A   26   15   CUEVAS DE ARTA

Sta. Maria del Camí   Sant Llorenç des Carctassar   Cap des Pinar

17   20   Sencelles   Sineu   Petra   20   Son Servera

3   Cala Millor

Montuïri   Punta de n'Amer

35   15   18   Manacor

Algaida   MONASTERIO DE CORA   14   Porto Cristo

Porreres   27   CUEVAS DEL DRACH

29   Llucmajor   Felanitx

1A19   22   26   Cales de Mallorca

B

19   27   SAN SALVADOR (MONASTERIO)

Campos del Port   Porto Colom

Cala d'Or

nc   Sa Rapita   Ses Salines   Porto Petro

Santanyí

Colònia de Sant Jordi

Cap de ses Salines

I. des Conills

Parque Nacional de Cabrera

Cabrera

39°

C

0   10   20   30 km

Palma de Mallorca Valencia

2   3°   3   4°   4

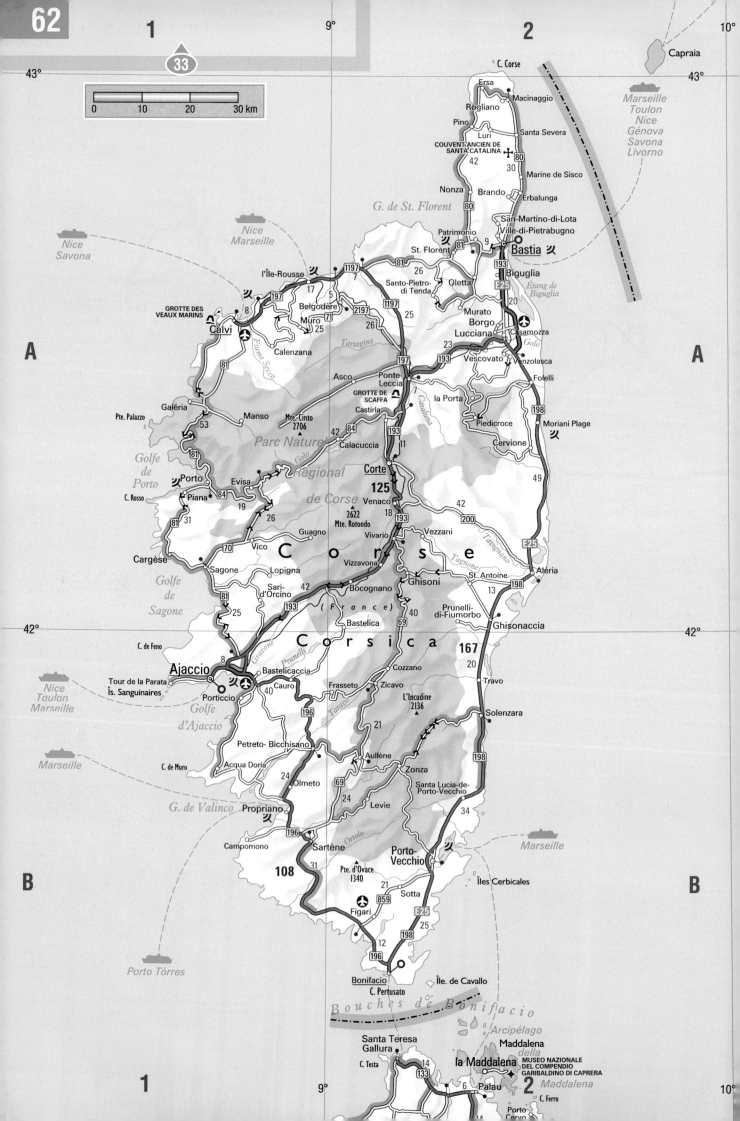

City plans · Plans de villes
Stadtpläne · Piante di città

Approach maps · Agglomérations
Carte régionale · Regionalkarte

Motorway	Autoroute	Autobahn	Autostrada
Major through route	Route principale majeur	Hauptstrecke	Strada di grande communicazione
Through route	Route principale	Schnellstrasse	Strada d'importanza regionale
Secondary road	Route secondaire		
Dual carriageway	Chaussées séparées	Nebenstrasse	Strada d'interesse locale
Other road	Autre route	Zweispurig Schnellstrasse	Strada a carreggiate doppie
Tunnel	Tunnel	Nebenstrecke	Altra strada
Limited access / pedestrian road	Rue réglementée / rue piétonne	Tunnel	Galleria stradale
One-way street	Sens unique	Beschränkter Zugang/ Fussgängerzone	Strada pedonale / a accesso limitato
Parking	Parc de stationnement	Einbahnstrasse	Senso unico
Motorway number	Numéro d'autoroute	Parkplatz	Parcheggio
National road number	Numéro de route nationale	Autobahnnummer	Numero di autostrada
European road number	Numéro de route européenne	Nationalstrassen-nummer	Numero di strada nazionale
Destination	Destination	Europäische Strassennummer	Numero di strada europea
Car ferry	Bac passant les autos	Ziel	Destinazione
Railway	Chemin de fer	Autofähre	Traghetto automobili
Rail / bus station	Gare / gare routière	Eisenbahn	Ferrovia
Underground, metro station	Station de métro	Bahnhof / Busstation	Stazione ferrovia / pullman
Cable car	Téléférique	U-Bahnstation	Metropolitano
Abbey, cathedral	Abbaye, cathédrale	Drahtseilbahn	Funivia
Church of interest	Église intéressante	Abtei, Kloster, Kathedrale	Abbazia, duomo
Synagogue	Synagogue	Interessante Kirche	Chiesa da vedere
Hospital	Hôpital	Synagoge	Sinagoga
Police station	Police	Krankenhaus	Ospedale
Post office	Bureau de poste	Polizeiwache	Polizia
Tourist information	Office de tourisme	Postamt	Ufficio postale
Place of interest	Autre curiosité	Informationsbüro	Ufficio informazioni turistiche
		Sonstige Sehenswürdigkeit	Luogo da vedere

Toll motorway – with motorway number	Autoroute à péage – avec numéro d'autoroute	Gebührenpflichtige Autobahn – mit Autobahnnummer	Autostrada a pedaggio – con numero
Toll-free motorway – with European road number	Autoroute – avec numéro de route européenne	Gebührenfreie Autobahn – Europäische Strassennummer	Autostrada – con numero di strada europea
Pre-pay motorway – vignette required	Autoroute – 'vignette'	Autobahn – 'vignette'	Autostrada – 'vignette'
Motorway services	Aire de service	Autobahnservice	Area di servizio autostradale
Motorway junction full access, restricted access	Échangeur d'autoroute accès libre, accès réglémenté	Autobahnkreuz – voller/begrenzter Zugang	Raccordi autostradali – completo/parziali
Under construction	En construction	Im Bau	In construzione
Tunnel	Tunnel	Tunnel	Galleria stradale
Major route dual carriageway single carriageway	Route principale chausées séparées chausée sans séparation	Hauptstrecke – zweispurige Schnellstrasse	Strada di grande communicazione carreggiata doppia carreggiata unica
Secondary route dual carriageway single carriageway	Route secondaire chausées séparées chausée sans séparation	Nebenstrasse – zweispurige Schnellstrasse	Strada d'interesse locale – carreggiata doppia carreggiata unica
Other road	Autre route	Nebenstrecke	Altra strada
Car ferry	Bac passant les autos	Autofähre	Traghetto automobili
Destination	Destination	Ziel	Destinazione
Railway	Chemin de fer	Eisenbahn	Ferrovia
Railway station	Gare	Hauptbahnhof	Stazione ferrovia
Height – in metres	Altitude – en mètres	Höhe – über dem Meeresspiegel	Altezza in metri
Airport	Aéroport principal	Flughafen	Aeroporto
Airfield	Autre aéroport	Flugplatz	Aerodromo/ campo d'aviazione
City plan coverage area	Région de plan de ville	Vom Stadtplan abgedecktes Gebiet	Area della pianta della città

Alicante

0 km 0.5

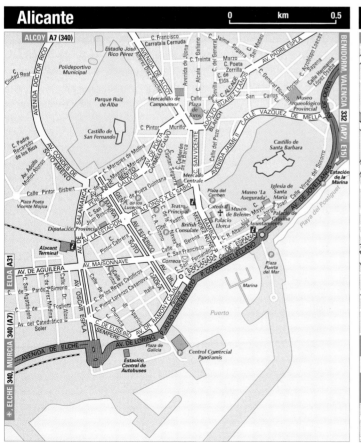

Granada

0 km 0.5

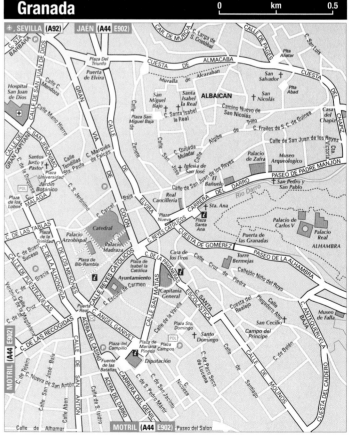

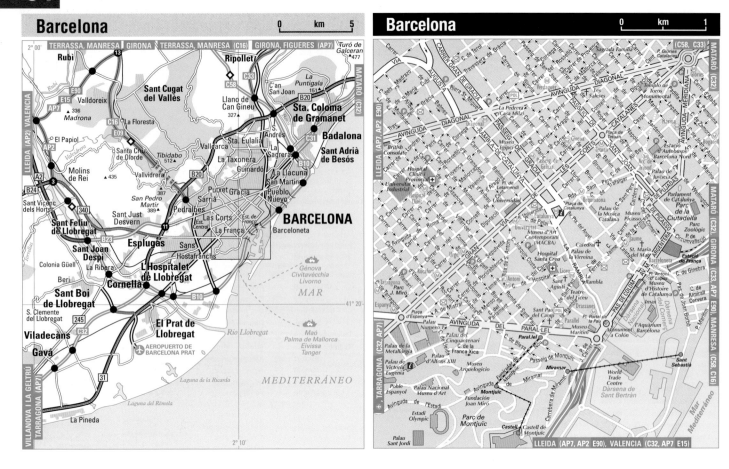

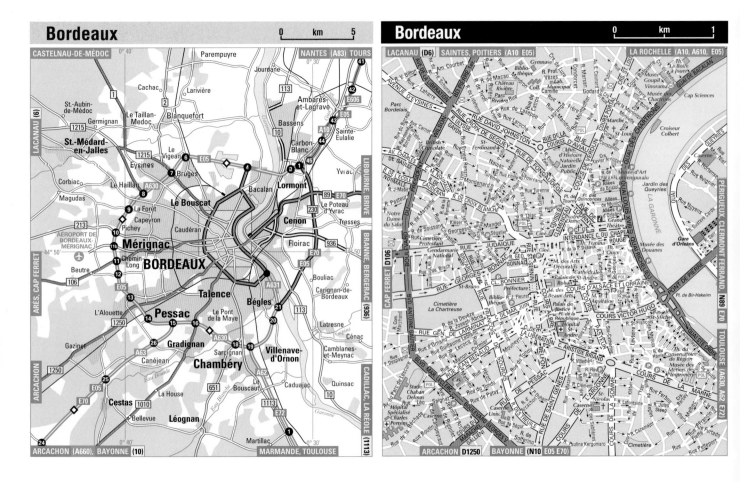

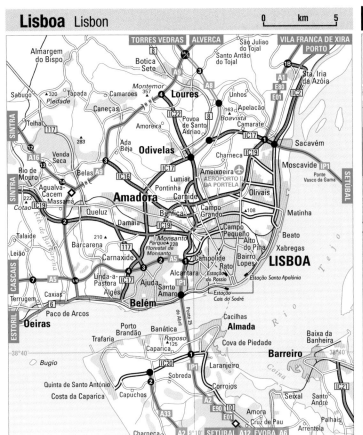

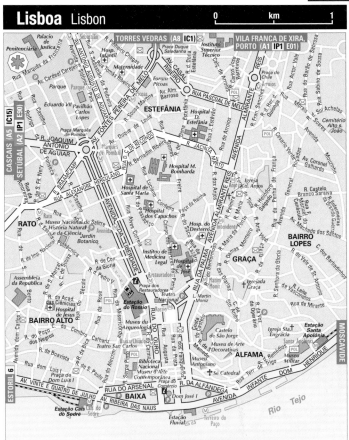

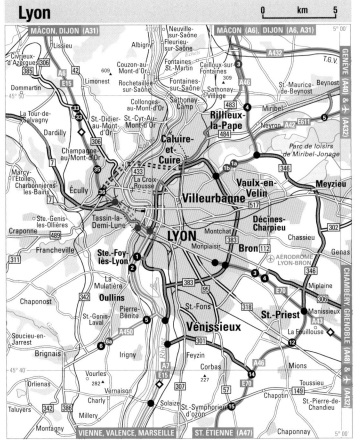

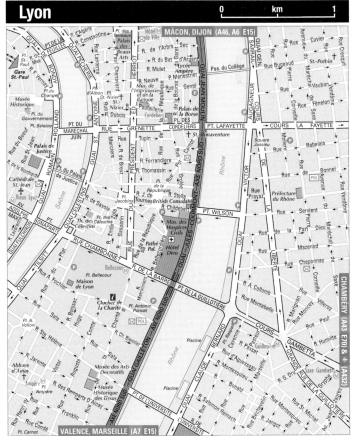

Madrid

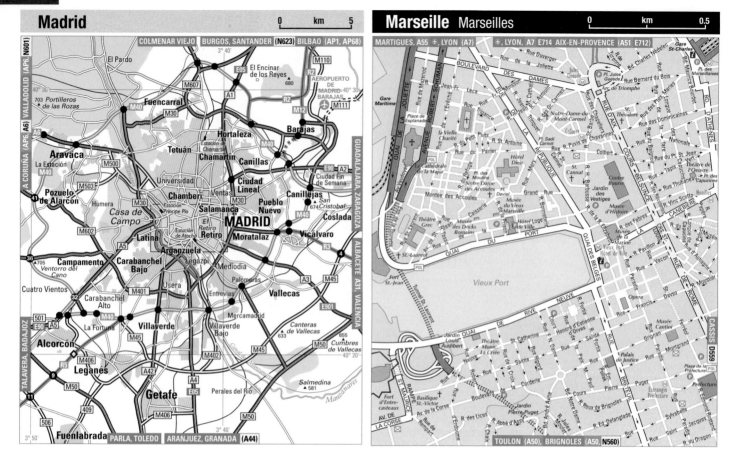

Marseille Marseilles

Madrid

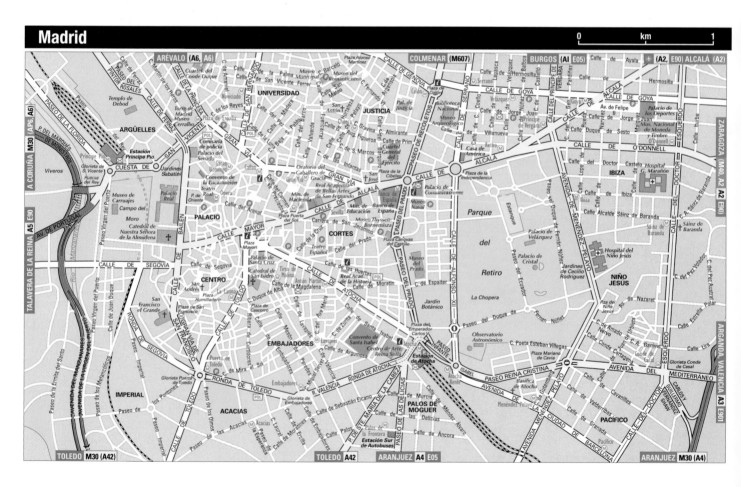

Paris

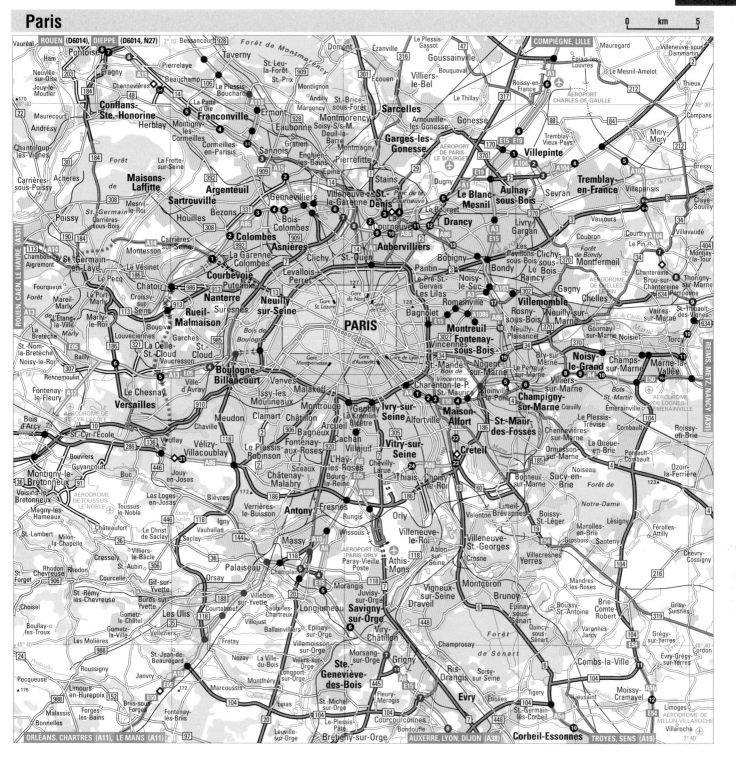

Paris

Sevilla Seville

Strasbourg

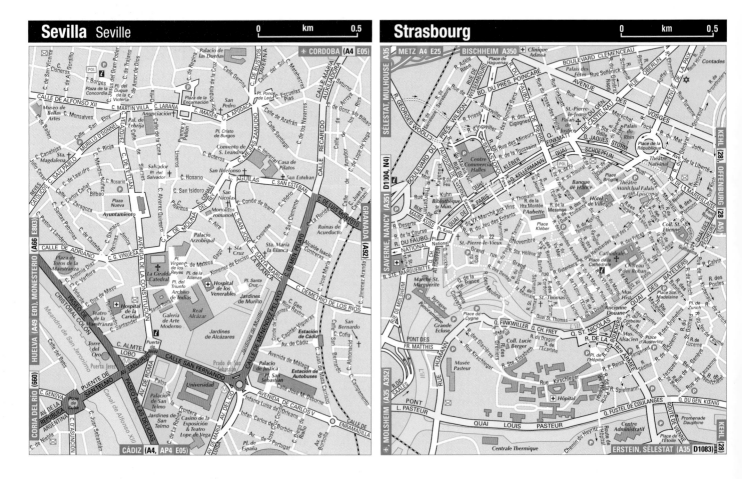

69

Index

A	Austria	Autriche	Österreich	Austria
AND	Andorra	Andorre	Andorra	Andorra
B	Belgium	Belgique	Belgien	Bélgica
CH	Switzerland	Suisse	Schweiz	Suiza
D	Germany	Allemagne	Deutschland	Alemania
E	Spain	Espagne	Spanien	España
F	France	France	Frankreich	Francia
FL	Liechtenstein	Liechtenstein	Liechtenstein	Liechtenstein
GB	United Kingdom	Royaume Uni	Grossbritannien und Nordirland	Reino Unido
GBZ	Gibraltar	Gibraltar	Gibraltar	Gibraltar
I	Italy	Italie	Italien	Italia
L	Luxembourg	Luxembourg	Luxemburg	Luxemburgo
MC	Monaco	Monaco	Monaco	Mónaco
NL	Netherlands	Pays-Bas	Niederlande	Países Bajos
P	Portugal	Portugal	Portugal	Portugal

A

Aach D 21 B4
Aalst B 7 B4
Aalter B 7 A3
Aarau CH 20 B3
Aarberg CH 20 B2
Aarburg CH 20 B2
Aardenburg NL 7 A3
Aarschot B 7 B4
Abádanes E 46 B1
Abades E 45 B3
Abadin E 35 A3
A Baña E 34 B2
Abanilla E 59 A3
Abarán E 59 A3
Abbeville F 10 A1
Abejar E 37 C4
Abela P 54 B1
Abenójar E 51 B3
Abertura E 50 A2
Abiego E 39 B3
Abiul P 48 B2
Abla E 58 B2
Ablis F 10 C1
A Bola E 34 B3
Abondance F 26 A3
Abrantes P 48 B2
Abreiro P 42 A2
Abreschviller F 12 C3
Abrest F 25 A3
Abriès F 27 C3
Abusejo E 43 B3
A Cañiza E 34 B2
A Capela E 34 A2
Accéglio I 32 A2
Accous F 39 A3
Acedera E 50 A2
Acehuche E 49 B4
Acered E 46 A2
Aceuchal E 49 C4
Achene B 7 B5
Achern D 13 C4
Acheux-en-Amienois F 10 A2
A Coruña E 34 A2
Acqua Doria F 62 B1
Acquigny F 9 A5
Ácqui Terme I 27 C5
Acy-en-Multien F 10 B2
Adamuz E 51 B3
Adanero E 44 B3
Adeanueva de Ebro E 38 B2
Adelboden CH 20 C2
Ademuz E 46 B2
Adinkerke B 6 A2
Adliswil CH 21 B3
Adra E 58 C1
Adradas E 46 A1
Adrall E 41 B2
Adzaneta E 47 B3
Aesch CH 20 B2
A Estrada E 34 B2
Affoltern CH 20 B3
A Fonsagrada E 35 A3
Agay F 32 B2
Agde F 30 B2
Agen F 29 B3
Ager E 39 C4
Agnières F 26 C2
Agolada E 34 B2
Agon Coutainville F 8 A2
Agost E 59 A4
Agramón E 52 C2
Agramunt E 41 C2
Agreda E 38 C2
Agrón E 57 A4
Aguadulce
Almería E 58 C2
Sevilla E 56 A3
Agualada E 34 A2
Agua Longa P 42 A1
A Guarda E 34 C2
Aguarón E 46 A2
Aguas E 39 B3
Aguas Belas P 48 B2
Aguas de Busot E 53 C3
Aguas de Moura P 48 C2
Águas Frias P 42 A2
Aguas Santas P 42 A1
Aguaviva E 47 B3
Aguaviva de la Vega E 46 A1
A Gudiña E 35 B3
Agudo E 50 B3
Águeda P 42 B1
Aguessac F 30 A2
Aguiar P 48 C3
Aguiàr da Beira P 42 B2
Aguilafuente E 45 A3
Aguilar de Campóo E 36 B2
Aguilar de la Frontera E 57 A3
Aguilas E 58 B3
Ahigal E 43 B3
Ahigal de Villarino E 43 A3
Ahillones E 50 B2
Ahun F 24 A2
Aibar E 38 B2
Aigle CH 27 A3
Aignan F 28 C3
Aignay-le-Duc F 18 B3
Aigre F 23 C4
Aigrefeuille-d'Aunis F 22 B3
Aigrefeuille-sur-Maine F 15 B4
Aiguablava E 41 C4
Aiguebelle F 26 B3
Aigueperse F 24 A3
Aigues-Mortes F 31 B3
Aigues-Vives F 30 B1
Aiguilles F 27 C3
Aiguillon F 29 B3
Aigurande F 17 C3
Ailefroide F 26 C3
Aillant-sur-Tholon F 18 B2
Ailly-sur-Noye F 10 B2
Ailly-sur-Somme F 10 B2
Aimargues F 31 B3
Aime F 26 B3
Ainhoa F 38 A2
Ainsa E 39 B4
Airaines F 10 B1
Aire-sur-l'Adour F 28 C2
Aire-sur-la-Lys F 6 B2
Airole I 33 B3
Airolo CH 21 C3
Airvault F 16 C1
Aisey-sur-Seine F 18 B3
Aïssey F 19 B5
Aisy-sur-Armançon F 18 B3
Aitona E 47 A4
Aitrach D 21 B5
Aix-en-Othe F 18 A2
Aix-en-Provence F 31 B4
Aixe-sur-Vienne F 23 C5
Aix-les-Bains F 26 B2
Aizenay F 22 B2
Ajac F 40 A3
Ajaccio F 62 B1
Ajain F 24 A1
Ajo E 37 A3
Ajofrín E 51 A4
Ajuda P 49 C3
Ala di Stura I 27 B4
Alaejos E 44 A2
Alagna Valsésia I 27 B4
Alagón E 38 C2
Alaior E 61 B4
Alájar E 55 B3
Alameda E 57 A3
Alameda de la Sagra E 45 B4
Alamedilla E 57 A4
Alamillo E 50 B3
Alaminos E 45 B5
Alandroal P 49 C3
Alange E 50 B1
Alanís E 50 B2
Alaquáso E 53 B3
Alaraz E 44 B2
Alarcón E 52 B1
Alar del Rey E 36 B2
Alaró E 61 B2
Alássio I 33 A4
Alatoz E 52 B2
Alba
E 46 B2
I 27 C5
Albacete E 52 C2
Alba de Tormes E 44 B2
Alba de Yeltes E 43 B3
Albaida E 53 C3
Albaladejo E 52 C1
Albala del Caudillo E 50 A1
Albalat E 53 B3
Albalate de Cinca E 39 C4
Albalate del Arzobispo
E 47 A3
Albalate de las Nogueras
E 46 B1
Albalete de Zorita E 45 B5
Alban F 30 B1
Albánchez E 58 B2
Albanchez de Ubeda E 57 A4
Albanyà E 41 B3
Albares E 45 B4
Albarracín E 46 B2
Albatana E 52 C2
Albatarrec E 47 A4
Albatera E 59 A4
Albbruck D 20 B3
Albedin E 57 A3
Albelda de Iregua E 37 B4
Albenga I 33 A4
Albens F 26 B2
Albergaria-a-Nova P 42 B1
Albergaria-a-Velha P 42 B1
Albergaria dos Doze P 48 B2
Alberge P 48 C2
Alberic E 53 B3
Albernoa P 54 B2
Albert F 10 A2
Albertville F 26 B3
Alberuela de Tubo E 39 C3
Albi F 30 B1
Albires E 36 B1
Albisola Marina I 33 A4
Albocácer E 47 B4
Albolote E 57 A4
Albondón E 58 C1
Alborea E 52 B2
Albox E 58 B2
Albstadt D 21 A4
Albufeira P 54 B1
Albuñol E 58 C1
Albuñuelas E 57 B4
Alburquerque E 49 B3
Alcácer do Sal P 48 C2
Alcáçovas P 48 C2
Alcadozo E 52 C2
Alcafoces P 49 B3
Alcains P 49 B3
Alcaláde Guadaira E 56 A2
Alcaláde Gurrea E 38 B3
Alcaláde Henares E 45 B4
Alcaláde la Selva E 47 B3
Alcaládel Júcar E 52 B2
Alcaláde los Gazules E 56 B2
Alcaládel Rio E 56 A2
Alcaládel Valle E 56 B2
Alcaláde Xivert E 47 B4
Alcalála Real E 57 A4
Alcampell E 39 C4
Alcanadre E 38 B1
Alcanar E 47 B4
Alcanede P 48 B2
Alcanena P 48 B2
Alcañices E 43 A3
Alcántara E 49 B4
Alcantarilha P 54 B1
Alcantarilla E 59 B3
Alcañiz E 47 A3
Alcaracejos E 50 B3
Alcaraz E 52 C1
Alcaria Ruiva P 54 B2
Alcarraz E 47 A4
Alcaudete E 57 A3
Alcaudete de la Jara E 44 C3
Alcázar de San Juan E 51 A4
Alcazarén E 44 A3
Alcoba E 51 A3
Alcobaça P 48 B1
Alcobendas E 45 B4
Alcocer E 45 B5
Alcochete P 48 C2
Alcoentre P 48 B2
Alcolea
Almería E 58 C2
Córdoba E 50 C3
Alcolea de Calatrava E 51 B3
Alcolea de Cinca E 39 C4
Alcolea del Pinar E 46 A1
Alcolea del Rio E 56 A2
Alcolea de Tajo E 44 C2
Alcollarin E 50 A2
Alconchel E 49 C3
Alconera E 49 C4
Alcontar E 58 B2
Alcora E 47 B3
Alcorcón E 45 B4
Alcorisa E 47 B3
Alcossebre E 47 B4
Alcoutim P 54 B2
Alcover E 41 C2
Alcoy E 53 C3
Alcubierre E 39 C3
Alcubilla de Avellaneda
E 37 C3
Alcubilla de Nogales E 35 B5
Alcubillas E 51 B4
Alcublas E 53 B3
Alcúdia E 61 B3
Alcudia de Guadix E 58 B1
Alcuéscar E 49 B4
Aldeacentenera E 50 A2
Aldeadávila de la Ribera
E 43 A3
Aldea del Cano E 49 B4
Aldea del Fresno E 45 B3
Aldea del Obispo E 43 B3
Aldea del Rey E 51 B4
Aldea de Trujillo E 50 A2
Aldealcorvo E 45 A4
Aldealuenga de Santa Maria
E 45 A4
Aldeamayor de San Martin
E 44 A3
Aldeanueva de Barbarroya
E 44 C2
Aldeanueva del Camino
E 43 B4
Aldeanueva del Codonal
E 44 A3
Aldeanueva de San
Bartolomé E 50 A2
Aldeapozo E 38 C1
Aldeaquemada E 51 B4
Aldea Real E 45 A3
Aldearrubia E 44 A2
Aldeaseca de la Frontera
E 44 B2
Aldeasoña E 45 A3
Aldeatejada E 44 B2
Aldeavieja E 44 B3
Aldehuela E 46 B2
Aldehuela de Calatañazor
E 37 C4
Aldeia da Serra P 49 C3
Aldeia do Bispo P 43 B3
Aldeia do Mato P 48 B2
Aldeia Gavinha P 48 B1
Aldeire E 58 B1
Aldudes F 38 A2
Aledo E 59 B3
Alegria E 37 B4
Alençon F 9 B4
Alenquer P 48 B1
Alenya F 40 B3
Aléria F 62 A2
Alès F 31 A3
Alet-les-Bains F 40 B3
Aleyrac F 31 A3
Alfacar E 57 A4
Alfaiates P 43 B3
Alfajarin E 47 A3
Alfambra
E 46 B2
P 54 B1
Alfândega da Fé P 43 A3
Alfarela de Jafes P 42 A2
Alfarelos P 42 B1
Alfarim P 48 C1
Alfarnate E 57 B3
Alfaro E 38 B2
Alfarràs E 39 C4
Alfaz del Pi E 53 C3
Alfeizarão P 48 B1
Alfena P 42 A1
Alferce P 54 B1
Alforja E 41 C1
Alfoz E 35 A3
Alfundão P 54 A1
Algaida E 61 B2
Algar E 56 B2
Algarinejo E 57 A3
Algarrobo E 57 B3
Algatocin E 56 B2
Algeciras E 56 B2
Algemesí E 53 B3
Algés P 48 C1
Algete E 45 B4
Alginet E 53 B3
Algodonales E 56 B2
Algodor
E 45 C4
P 54 B2
Algora E 45 B5
Algoso P 43 A3
Algoz P 54 B1
Alguaire E 39 C4
Alguazas E 59 A3
Alhama de Almería E 58 C2
Alhama de Aragón E 46 A2
Alhama de Granada E 57 B4
Alhama de Murcia E 59 B3
Alhambra E 51 B4
Alhandra P 48 C1
Alhaurin de la Torre E 57 B3
Alhaurín el Grande E 57 B3
Alhendin E 57 A4
Alhóndiga E 45 B5
Alia E 50 A2
Aliaga E 47 B3
Alicante E 59 A4
Alicún de Ortega E 58 B1
Alija del Infantado E 35 B5
Alijó P 42 A2
Alinyà E 41 B2
Aliseda E 49 B4
Alixan F 25 C5
Aljaraque E 55 B2
Aljezur P 54 B1
Aljorra E 59 B3
Aljubarrota P 48 B2
Aljucen E 49 B4
Aljustrel P 54 B1
Alken B 7 B5
Allaines F 17 A3
Allaire F 15 B3
Allanche F 24 B2
Allariz E 34 B3
Allassac F 29 A4
Allauch F 31 B4
Allègre F 25 B3
Allemont F 26 B3
Allepuz E 47 B3
Alles E 36 A2
Allevard F 26 B3
Allmannsdorf D 21 B4
Allo E 38 B1
Allogny F 17 B4
Allones
Eure et Loire F 10 C1
Maine-et-Loire F 16 B2
Allonnes F 16 B2
Allons F 28 B2
Allos F 32 A2
Almaceda P 49 B3
Almacelles E 39 C4
Almachar E 57 B3
Almada P 48 C1
Almadén E 50 B3
Almadén de la Plata E 55 B3
Almadenejos E 50 B3
Almadrones E 45 B5
Almagro E 51 B4
Almajano E 38 C1
Almansa E 53 C2
Almansil P 54 B1
Almanza E 36 B1
Almaraz E 44 C2
Almargen E 56 B2
Almarza E 37 C4
Almassora E 53 B3
Almazán E 46 A1
Almazul E 46 A1
Almedina E 52 C1
Almedinilla E 57 A3
Almeida
E 43 A3
P 43 B3
Almeirim P 48 B2
Almenar E 39 C4
Almenara E 53 B3
Almenar de Soria E 46 A1
Almendra P 43 B2
Almendral E 49 C4
Almendral de la Cañada
E 44 B3
Almendralejo E 49 C4
Almería E 58 C2
Almerimar E 58 C2
Almese I 27 B4
Almexial P 54 B2
Almodôvar P 54 B1
Almodóvar del Campo
E 51 B3
Almodóvar del Pinar E 52 B2
Almodóvar del Rio E 56 A2
Almofala P 42 B2
Almogia E 57 B3
Almoharín E 50 A1
Almonacid de la Sierra
E 46 A2
Almonacid de Toledo E 51 A4
Almonaster la Real E 55 B3
Almonte E 55 B3
Almoradí E 59 A4
Almoraima E 56 B2
Almorox E 44 B3
Almoster P 48 B2
Almudena E 58 A3
Almudévar E 39 B3
Almuñécar E 57 B4
Almuradiel E 51 B4
Almussafes E 53 B3
Álora E 57 B3
Alos d'Ensil E 40 B2
Alosno E 55 B2
Alozaina E 56 B3
Alpedrete de la Sierra E 45 B4
Alpedrinha P 42 B2
Alpera E 53 C2
Alpiarça P 48 B2
Alpignano I 27 B4
Alpirsbach D 13 C4
Alpuente E 53 B2
Alqueva P 54 A2
Alquézar E 39 B4
Alsasua E 38 B1
Altarejos E 52 B1
Altdorf CH 21 C3
Alte P 54 B1
Altea E 53 C3
Altenheim D 13 C3
Altensteig D 13 C4
Alter do Chão P 49 B3
Altkirch F 20 B2
Alto Campoó E 36 A2
Altshausen D 21 B4
Altstätten CH 21 B4
Altura E 53 B3
Altusried D 21 B5
Alustante E 46 B2
Alvaiázere P 48 B2
Alvalade P 54 B1
Alvarenga P 42 B1
Alvares P 48 A2
Alverca P 48 C1
Alvignac F 29 B4
Alvimare F 9 A4
Alviobeira P 48 B2
Alvito P 54 A2
Alvor P 54 B1
Alvorge P 48 B2
Alzénau D 13 A5
Alzey D 13 B4
Alzira E 53 B3
Alzonne F 40 A3
Amadora P 48 C1
Amance F 19 B5
Amancey F 19 B5
Amarante P 42 A1
Amareleja P 55 A2
Amares P 42 A1
Amay B 7 B5
Ambazac F 23 C5
Ambérieu-en-Bugey F 26 B2
Ambérieux-en-Dombes
F 25 A4
Ambert F 25 B3
Ambès F 28 A2
Ambleteuse F 6 B1

Aac–Aos

Amboise F 16 B2
Ambrières-les-Vallées F 8 B3
Amden CH 21 B4
Amélie-les-Bains-Palalda
F 40 B3
Amendoa P 48 B2
Amendoeira P 54 B2
Amer E 41 B3
A Merca E 34 B3
Amièira P 49 C3
Amieira P 48 B3
Amieiro P 42 B1
Amiens F 10 B2
Amorebieta E 37 A4
Amorosa P 42 A1
Amou F 28 C2
Amplepuis F 25 B4
Amposta E 47 B4
Ampudia E 36 C2
Ampuero E 37 A3
Amriswil CH 21 B4
Amtzell D 21 B4
Amurrio E 37 A4
Amusco E 36 B2
Anadia P 42 B1
Anadon E 46 B2
Anaya de Alba E 44 B2
Ança P 42 B1
Ancede P 42 A1
Ancenis F 15 B4
Ancerville F 11 C5
Anchuras E 50 A3
Ancora P 42 A1
Ancy-le-Franc F 18 B3
Andance F 25 B4
Andeer CH 21 C4
Andelfingen CH 21 B3
Andelot-Blanchville F 19 A4
Andelot-en-Montagne F 19 C4
Andenne B 7 B5
Anderlues B 7 B4
Andermatt CH 21 C3
Andernos-les-Bains F 28 B1
Andoain E 38 A1
Andolsheim F 20 A2
Andorra E 47 B3
Andorra La Vella AND 40 B2
Andosilla E 38 B2
Andratx E 60 B2
Andrest F 39 A4
Andrezieux-Bouthéon F 25 B4
Andújar E 51 B3
Anduze F 31 A2
Añes E 37 A3
Anet F 10 C1
Angaïs F 39 A3
Angeja P 42 B1
Angers F 16 B1
Angerville F 10 C2
Anglès E 41 C3
Anglés F 30 B1
Angles F 22 B2
Anglesola E 41 C2
Angles sur l'Anglin F 23 B4
Anglet F 28 C1
Anglure F 11 C3
Angoulême F 23 C4
Angoulins F 22 B2
Angueira P 43 A3
Angües E 39 B3
Anguiano E 37 B4
Anhée B 7 B4
Aniane F 30 B2
Aniche F 6 B3
Anizy-le-Château F 11 B3
Anlezy F 18 C2
Annecy F 26 B3
Annemasse F 26 A3
Annevoie-Rouillon B 7 B4
Annonay F 25 B4
Annot F 32 B2
Annweiler D 13 B3
Añora E 50 B3
Anould F 20 A1
Anquela del Ducado E 46 B1
Anse F 25 B4
Anseroeul B 7 B3
Ansião P 48 B2
Ansó E 38 B3
Ansoain E 38 B2
Antas E 58 B3
Antequera E 57 A3
Antibes F 32 B3
Antigüedad E 36 C2
Antoing B 7 B3
Antrain F 8 B2
Antronapiana I 27 A5
Antuzede P 42 B1
Antwerp = Antwerpen B 7 A4
Antwerpen = Antwerp B 7 A4
Anvin F 6 B2
Anzat-le-Luguet F 24 B3
Anzón E 38 C2
Aoiz E 38 B2
Aosta I 27 B4

Apalhão P 49 B3
A Peroxa E 34 B3
A Pontenova E 35 A3
Appenzell CH 21 B4
Appoigny F 18 B2
Apremont-la-Forêt F 12 C1
Apt F 31 B4
Apúlia P 42 A1
Arabayona E 44 A2
Aracena E 55 B3
Aragnouet F 39 B4
Aramits F 38 A3
Aramon F 31 B3
Aranda de Duero E 37 C3
Aranda de Moncayo E 46 A2
Aranjuez E 45 B4
Arantzazu E 37 B4
Aranzueque E 45 B4
Aras de Alpuente E 53 B2
Arauzo de Miel E 37 C3
Arazede P 42 B1
Arbas F 39 B4
Arbeca E 41 C1
Arbois F 19 C4
Arbon CH 21 B4
Arbório I 27 B5
Arbúcies E 41 C3
Arbuniel E 57 A4
Arcachon F 28 B1
Arc-en-Barrois F 19 B3
Arces-Dilo F 18 A2
Arc-et-Senans F 19 B4
Arcey F 20 B1
Archena E 59 A3
Archez E 57 B4
Archiac F 23 C3
Archidona E 57 A3
Archivel E 58 A3
Arcis-sur-Aube F 11 C4
Arc-lès-Gray F 19 B4
Arcones E 45 A4
Arcos E 37 B3
Arcos de Jalón E 46 A1
Arcos de la Frontera E 56 B2
Arcos de la Sierra E 46 B1
Arcos de las Salinas E 53 B2
Arcos de Valdevez P 42 A1
Arcozelo P 42 B2
Arc-sur-Tille F 19 B4
Arcusa E 39 B4
Arcy-sur-Cure F 18 B2
Ardales E 56 B3
Ardentes F 17 C3
Ardes F 24 B3
Ardez CH 21 C5
Ardisa E 38 B3
Ardón E 36 B1
Ardooie B 6 B3
Ardres F 6 B1
Areia Branca P 48 B1
Arenales de San Gregorio
  E 51 A4
Arenas E 57 B3
Arenas de Iguña E 36 A2
Arenas del Rey E 57 B4
Arenas de San Juan E 51 A4
Arenas de San Pedro E 44 B2
Arendonk B 7 A5
Arengosse F 28 B2
Arenys de Mar E 41 C3
Arenys de Munt E 41 C3
Arenzano I 33 A4
Areo E 40 B2
Ares E 34 A2
Arès F 28 B1
Ares del Maestrat E 47 B3
Arette F 38 A3
Aretxabaleta E 37 A4
Arevalillo E 44 B2
Arévalo E 44 A3
Arez P 49 B3
Arfeuilles F 25 A3
Argallón E 50 B2
Argamasilla de Alba E 51 A4
Argamasilla de Calatrava
  E 51 B1
Arganda E 45 B4
Arganil P 42 B1
Argelès-Gazost F 39 A3
Argelès-sur-Mer F 40 B4
Argentan F 9 B3
Argentat F 24 B2
Argentera I 32 A2
Argenteuil F 10 C2
Argenthal D 13 B3
Argentona E 41 C3
Argenton-Château F 16 C1
Argenton-sur-Creuse F 17 C3
Argentré F 16 A1
Argentré-du-Plessis F 15 A4
Argent-sur-Sauldre F 17 B4
Argote E 37 B4
Arguedas E 38 B2
Arguis F 10 B1
Aribe E 38 B2
Ariño E 47 A3
Arinthod F 26 A2
Arisgotas E 51 A4
Ariza E 46 A1
Arjona E 51 C3
Arjonilla E 51 C3
Arlanc F 25 B3
Arlanzón E 37 B3
Arlebosc F 25 B4
Arles F 31 B3
Arles-sur-Tech F 40 B3
Arlon B 12 B1
Armação de Pera P 54 B1
Armamar P 42 A2
Armeno I 27 B5
Armenteros E 44 B2
Armentières F 6 B2
Armilla E 57 A4
Armiñón E 37 B4
Armuña de Tajuña E 45 B4
Arnac-Pompadour F 23 C5
Arnage F 16 B2
Arnas F 25 A4
Arnay-le-Duc F 18 B3
Arnedillo E 38 B1
Arnedo E 38 B1
Arneguy F 38 A2
Arnés E 47 B4

Aroche E 55 B3
Arolla CH 27 A4
Arona I 27 B5
Arosa
  CH 21 C4
  P 42 A1
Arouca P 42 B1
Arpajon F 10 C2
Arpajon-sur-Cère F 24 C2
Arques F 6 B2
Arques-la-Bataille F 9 A5
Arquillos E 51 B4
Arraia-Maeztu E 37 B4
Arraiolos P 48 C2
Arrancourt F 12 C2
Arras F 6 B2
Arrasate E 37 A4
Arreau F 39 B4
Arredondo E 37 A3
Arrens-Marsous F 39 B3
Arriate E 56 B2
Arrifana P 54 B1
Arrigorriaga E 37 A4
Arriondas E 36 A1
Arroba de los Montes E 51 A3
Arromanches-les-Bains
  F 8 A3
Arronches P 49 B3
Arroniz E 38 B1
Arrou F 17 A3
Arroya E 36 B2
Arroya de Cuéllar E 44 A3
Arroyal E 36 B2
Arroyo de la Luz E 49 B4
Arroyo del Ojanco E 58 A2
Arroyo de San Servan
  E 49 C4
Arroyomolinos de León
  E 55 A3
Arroyomolinos de
  Montánchez E 50 A1
Arruda dos Vinhos P 48 C1
Arsac F 28 B2
Ars-en-Ré F 22 B2
Ars-sur-Moselle F 12 B2
Artà E 61 B3
Artajona E 38 B2
Arteixo E 34 A2
Artemare F 26 B2
Artenay F 17 A3
Artés E 41 C2
Artesa de Segre E 41 C2
Arth CH 21 B3
Arthez-de-Béarn F 39 A3
Arthon-en-Retz F 15 B4
Artieda E 38 B3
Artix F 39 A3
Artziniega E 37 A3
A Rúa E 35 B3
Arudy F 39 A3
Arveyres F 28 B2
Arvieux F 26 C3
Arzacq-Arraziguet F 28 C2
Arzano F 14 B2
Arzila P 42 B1
Arzúa E 34 B2
Asasp F 39 A3
Aschaffenburg D 13 B5
Ascó E 47 A4
Asco F 62 A2
Ascoux F 17 A4
Asfeld F 11 B4
As Neves E 34 B2
As Nogais E 35 B3
Aspariegos E 43 A4
Aspe E 59 A4
Aspet F 39 A4
As Pontes de Garcia
  Rodríguez E 34 A3
Aspres-sur-Buëch F 32 A1
Asse B 7 B4
Asselborn L 12 A1
Assemini I 7 A3
Assesse B 7 B5
Asson F 39 A3
Assumar P 49 B3
Astaffort F 29 B3
Asti I 27 C5
Astorga E 35 B4
Astudillo E 36 B2
Atalaia P 48 B3
Atalho P 48 C2
Atanzón E 45 B4
Ataquines E 44 A3
Atarfe E 57 A4
Ateca E 46 A2
A Teixeira E 35 B3
Ath B 7 B3
Athies F 10 B2
Athies-sous-Laon F 11 B3
Attichy F 10 B3
Attigny F 11 B4
Au A 21 B4
Aubagne F 32 B1
Aubange B 12 B1
Aubenas F 25 C4
Aubenton F 11 B4
Auberive F 19 B4
Aubeterre-sur-Dronne F 28 A3
Aubiet F 29 C3
Aubigné F 23 B3
Aubigny F 22 B2
Aubigny-au-Bac F 6 B3
Aubigny-en-Artois F 6 B2
Aubigny-sur-Nère F 17 B4
Aubin F 30 A1
Aubonne CH 19 C5
Aubrac F 24 C2
Aubusson F 24 B2
Auch F 29 C3
Auchy-au-Bois F 6 B2
Audenge F 28 B1
Auderville F 8 A2
Audincourt F 20 B1
Audruicq F 6 B2
Audun-le-Roman F 12 B1
Audun-le-Tiche F 12 B1
Augignac F 23 C4
Aulendorf D 21 B4
Aullène F 62 B2
Aulnay F 23 B3
Aulnoye-Aymeries F 7 B3

Ault F 10 A1
Aulus-les-Bains F 40 B2
Aumale F 10 B1
Aumetz F 12 B1
Aumont-Aubrac F 24 C3
Aunay-en-Bazois F 18 B2
Aunay-sur-Odon F 8 A3
Auneau F 10 C1
Auneuil F 10 B1
Aups F 32 B2
Auray F 14 B3
Aurignac F 39 A4
Aurillac F 24 C2
Auriol F 32 B1
Auritz-Burguete E 38 B2
Auros F 28 B2
Auroux F 25 C3
Auterive F 40 A2
Autheuil-Authouillet F 9 A5
Authon F 32 A2
Authon-du-Perche F 16 A2
Autol E 38 B2
Autreville F 12 C1
Autrey-lès-Gray F 19 B4
Autun F 18 C3
Auty-le-Châtel F 17 B4
Auvelais B 7 B4
Auvillar F 29 B3
Auxerre F 18 B2
Auxi-le-Château F 6 B2
Auxon F 18 A2
Auxonne F 19 B4
Auxy F 18 C3
Auzances F 24 A2
Auzon F 25 B3
Availles-Limouzine F 23 B4
Avallon F 18 B2
A Veiga E 35 B3
Aveiras de Cima P 48 B2
Aveiro P 42 B1
Avelgem B 7 B3
A-Ver-o-Mar P 42 A1
Avenches CH 20 C2
Avesnes-le-Comte F 6 B2
Avesnes-sur-Helpe F 11 A3
Avià E 41 B2
Avigliana I 27 B4
Avignon F 31 B3
Ávila E 44 B3
Avilés E 35 A5
Avilley F 19 B5
Avintes P 42 A1
Avinyo E 41 C2
Avioth F 12 B1
Avis P 48 B3
Avize F 11 C4
Avon F 10 C2
Avord F 17 B4
Avranches F 8 B2
Avril F 12 B1
Avrillé F 16 B1
Awans B 7 B5
Axat F 40 B3
Axel NL 7 A3
Ax-les-Thermes F 40 B2
Ay F 11 B4
Aya E 38 A1
Ayamonte E 55 B2
Ayelo de Malferit E 53 C3
Ayer CH 27 A4
Ayerbe E 38 B3
Ayette F 6 B2
Ayllón E 45 A4
Ayna E 52 C1
Ayódar E 53 B3
Ayora E 53 B2
Ayron F 23 B4
Azaila E 47 A3
Azambuja P 48 B2
Azambujeira P 48 B2
Azannes-et-Soumazannes
  F 12 B1
Azanúy-Alins E 39 C4
Azaruja P 49 C3
Azay-le-Ferron F 23 B5
Azay-le-Rideau F 16 B2
Azcoitia E 37 A4
Azé F 25 A4
Azeiteiros P 49 B3
Azenhas do Mar P 48 C1
Azinhaga P 48 B2
Azinhal P 54 B2
Azinheira dos Bairros P 54 A1
Aznalcázar E 55 B3
Aznalcóllar E 55 B3
Azóia P 48 B1
Azpeitia E 38 A1
Azuaga E 50 B2
Azuara E 47 A3
Azuqueca de Henares E 45 B4
Azur F 28 C1

B

Baad A 21 B5
Baamonde E 34 A3
Baar CH 21 B3
Baarle-Nassau B 7 A4
Babenhausen
  Bayern D 21 A5
  Hessen D 13 B4
Bacares E 58 B2
Baccarat F 12 C2
Bacharach D 13 A3
Bacqueville-en-Caux F 9 A5
Badajoz E 49 C4
Badalona E 41 C3
Badalucco I 33 B3
Bad Bergzabern D 13 B3
Bad Buchau D 21 A4
Bad Dürkheim D 13 B4
Bad Dürrheim D 21 A3
Baden CH 20 B3
Baden-Baden D 13 C4
Badenweiler D 20 B2
Bad Friedrichshall D 13 B5
Bad Herrenalb D 13 C4
Bad Innerlaterns A 21 B4
Bad Kemmeriboden CH 20 C2
Bad König D 13 B5
Bad Kreuznach D 13 B3
Bad Krozingen D 20 B2
Bad Liebenzell D 13 C4
Badolatosa E 57 A3

Badonviller F 12 C2
Bad Peterstal D 13 C4
Bad Ragaz CH 21 C4
Bad Rappenau D 13 B5
Bad Säckingen D 20 B2
Bad Schönborn D 13 B4
Bad Schussenried D 21 A4
Badules E 46 A2
Bad Waldsee D 21 B4
Bad Wurzach D 21 B4
Baells E 39 C4
Baena E 57 A3
Baeza E 51 C4
Baga E 41 B2
Bagnasco I 33 A4
Bagnères-de-Bigorre F 39 A4
Bagnères-de-Luchon F 39 B4
Bagnoles-de-l'Orne F 9 B3
Bagnols-en-Forêt F 32 B2
Bagnols-sur-Cèze F 31 A3
Báguena E 46 A2
Bahabón de Esgueva E 37 C3
Bahillo E 36 B2
Baião P 42 A1
Baiersbronn D 13 C4
Baignes-Ste Radegonde
  F 23 C3
Baigneux-les-Juifs F 18 B3
Bailén E 51 B4
Baileux B 11 A4
Bailleul F 6 B2
Baillonville B 7 B5
Bailó E 38 B3
Bain-de-Bretagne F 15 B4
Bains F 25 B3
Bains-les-Bains F 19 A5
Baio E 34 A2
Baiona E 34 B2
Bais F 9 B3
Baiuca P 42 B2
Bakio E 37 A4
Balaguer E 39 C4
Balazote E 52 C1
Balbigny F 25 B4
Balboa E 35 B4
Baleira E 35 A3
Baleizao P 54 A2
Balen B 7 A5
Balerma E 58 C2
Balingen D 21 A3
Balizac F 28 B2
Ballancourt-sur-Essonne
  F 10 C2
Ballerias E 39 C3
Balleroy F 8 A3
Ballesteros de Calatrava
  E 51 B4
Ballobar E 47 A4
Ballon F 16 A2
Balmaseda E 37 A3
Balme I 27 B4
Balmuccia I 27 B5
Balneario de Panticosa E 39 B3
Balsa P 42 A2
Balsareny E 41 C2
Balsthal CH 20 B2
Baltanás E 36 C2
Baltar E 34 C3
Balugães P 42 A1
Bande
  B 7 B5
  E 34 B3
Bandol F 32 B1
Bañeres E 53 C3
Bangor F 14 B2
Bannalec F 14 B2
Bannes F 11 C3
Bañobárez E 43 B3
Bañon E 46 B2
Banon F 32 A1
Baños F 43 B4
Baños de Gigonza E 56 B2
Baños de la Encina E 51 B4
Baños de Molgas E 34 B3
Baños de Rio Tobia E 37 B4
Baños de Valdearados
  E 37 C3
Bantheville F 11 B5
Bantzenheim F 20 B2
Banyalbufar E 60 B2
Banyoles E 41 B3
Banyuls-sur-Mer F 40 B4
Bapaume F 10 A2
Barahona E 45 A5
Barajas de Melo E 45 B4
Barakaldo E 37 A4
Baralla E 35 B3
Barañain E 38 B2
Baraqueville F 30 A1
Barasoain E 38 B2
Barbacena P 49 C3
Barbadás E 34 B3
Barbadillo E 43 B4
Barbadillo de Herreros
  E 37 B3
Barbadillo del Mercado
  E 37 B3
Barbadillo del Pez E 37 B3
Barbastro E 39 B4
Barbate E 56 B2
Barbatona E 46 A1
Barbâtre F 22 B1
Barbazan F 39 A4
Barbeitos E 35 A3
Barbentane F 31 B3
Barbezieux-St Hilaire F 23 C3
Barbonne-Fayel F 11 C3
Bárcabo E 39 B4
Barca de Alva P 43 A3
Barcarrota E 49 C4
Barcelona E 41 C3
Barcelonette F 32 A2
Barcelos P 42 A1
Bárcena del Monasterio
  E 35 A4
Barcena de Pie de Concha
  E 36 A2
Barco P 42 B2
Barcones E 45 A5
Barcus F 38 A3
Bardonécchia I 26 B3
Barèges F 39 B4
Barentin F 9 A4

Barenton F 8 B3
Barfleur F 8 A2
Bargas E 45 C3
Barge I 27 C4
Bargemon F 32 B2
Barjac F 31 A3
Barjols F 32 B1
Barjon F 19 B3
Bar-le-Duc F 11 C5
Barles F 32 A2
Barneville-Carteret F 8 A2
Baron F 10 B2
Barqueiro P 48 B2
Barquinha P 48 B2
Barr F 13 C3
Barra P 42 B1
Barracas E 53 A3
Barraco E 44 B3
Barrado E 44 B2
Barranco do Velho P 54 B2
Barrancos P 55 A3
Barrax E 52 B1
Barre-des-Cévennes F 30 A2
Barreiro P 48 C1
Barreiros E 35 A3
Barrême F 32 B2
Barret-le-Bas F 32 A1
Barrio de Nuesra Señora
  E 36 B1
Barruecoparado E 43 A3
Barruelo de Santullán
  E 36 B2
Barruera E 39 B4
Bar-sur-Aube F 18 A3
Bar-sur-Seine F 18 A3
Barzana E 35 A4
Bas E 41 B3
Basauri E 37 A4
Basconcillos del Tozo
  E 37 B3
Bascones de Ojeda E 36 B2
Basécles B 7 B3
Basel CH 20 B2
Bassecourt CH 20 B2
Bassella E 41 B2
Bassou F 18 B2
Bassoues F 28 C3
Bastelica F 62 A2
Bastelicaccia F 62 B1
Bastia F 62 A2
Bastogne B 12 A1
Batalha P 48 B2
Batea E 47 A4
Bätterkinden CH 20 B2
Baud F 14 B2
Baudour B 7 B3
Baugé F 16 B1
Baugy F 17 B4
Bauma CH 21 B3
Baume-les-Dames F 19 B5
Baumholder D 13 B3
Bavay F 7 B3
Bavilliers F 20 B1
Bayel F 19 A3
Bayeux F 8 A3
Bayon F 12 C2
Bayonne F 28 C1
Bayons F 32 A2
Baza E 58 B2
Bazas F 28 B2
Baziege F 40 A2
Bazoches-les-Gallerandes
  F 17 A4
Bazoches-sur-Hoëne F 9 B4
Beade E 34 B2
Beas E 55 B3
Beasain E 38 A1
Beas de Segura E 58 A1
Beaubery F 25 A4
Beaucaire F 31 B3
Beaufort F 26 B3
Beaufort-en-Vallée F 16 B1
Beaugency F 17 B3
Beaujeu
  Alpes-de-Haute-Provence
  F 32 A2
  Rhône F 25 A4
Beaulac F 28 B2
Beaulieu F 17 B4
Beaulieu-sous-la-Roche
  F 22 B2
Beaulieu-sur-Dordogne
  F 29 B4
Beaulieu-sur-Mer F 33 B3
Beaulon F 18 C2
Beaumesnil F 9 A4
Beaumetz-lès-Loges F 6 B2
Beaumont
  B 7 B4
  F 29 B3
Beaumont-de-Lomagne
  F 29 C3
Beaumont-du-Gâtinais
  F 17 A4
Beaumont-en-Argonne
  F 11 B5
Beaumont-la-Ronce F 16 B2
Beaumont-le-Roger F 9 A4
Beaumont-sur-Oise F 10 B2
Beaumont-sur-Sarthe F 16 A2
Beaune F 19 B3
Beaune-la-Rolande F 17 A4
Beaupréau F 15 B5
Beauraing B 11 A4
Beaurepaire F 25 B5
Beaurepaire-en-Bresse
  F 19 C4
Beaurières F 32 A1
Beauvais F 10 B2
Beauval F 10 A2
Beauville F 29 B3
Beauvoir-sur-Mer F 22 B1
Beauvoir-sur-Niort F 23 B3
Becedas E 44 B2
Beceite E 47 B4
Becerreá E 35 B3
Becerril de Campos E 36 B2
Bécherel F 15 A4
Becilla de Valderaduey
  E 36 C1

Bédarrides F 31 A3
Bédée F 15 A4
Bedmar E 57 A4
Bédoin F 31 A4
Bedretto CH 21 C3
Beerfelden D 13 B4
Beernem B 6 A3
Beflelay CH 20 B2
Bégard F 14 A2
Begijar E 51 C4
Begijnendijk B 7 A4
Begues E 41 C2
Begur E 41 C4
Beine-Nauroy F 11 B4
Beinwil CH 20 B3
Beja P 54 A2
Béjar E 43 B4
Bélabre F 23 B5
Belalcázar E 50 B2
Belcaire F 40 B2
Belchite E 47 A3
Beleño E 36 A1
Bélesta F 40 B2
Belfort F 20 B1
Belgentier F 32 B1
Belgodère F 62 A2
Belhade F 28 B2
Belin-Béliet F 28 B2
Belinchón E 45 B4
Bellac F 23 B5
Belleau F 10 B3
Bellegarde
  Gard F 31 B3
  Loiret F 17 B4
Bellegarde-en-Diois F 32 A1
Bellegarde-en-Marche F 24 B2
Bellegarde-sur-Valserine
  F 26 A2
Belle-Isle-en-Terre F 14 A2
Bellême F 9 B4
Bellenaves F 24 A3
Bellentre F 26 B3
Bellevaux F 26 A3
Bellevesvre F 19 C4
Belleville F 25 A4
Belleville-sur-Vie F 22 B2
Bellevue-la-Montagne F 25 B3
Belley F 26 B2
Bellheim D 13 B4
Bell-lloc d'Urgell E 47 A4
Bello E 46 B2
Bellpuig d'Urgell E 41 C2
Bellreguart E 53 C3
Belltall E 41 C2
Bellver de Cerdanya E 40 B2
Bellvis E 41 C1
Bélmez E 50 B2
Belmez de la Moraleda
  E 57 A4
Belmont-de-la-Loire F 25 A4
Belmonte
  Asturias E 35 A4
  Cuenca E 52 B1
  P 42 B2
Belmonte de San José
  E 47 B3
Belmonte de Tajo E 45 B4
Belmont-sur-Rance F 30 B1
Beloeil B 7 B3
Belorado E 37 B3
Belp CH 20 C2
Belpech F 40 A2
Belvédère
  Campomoro F 62 B1
Belver de Cinca E 47 A4
Belver de los Montes E 36 C1
Belvès F 29 B3
Belvezet F 30 A2
Belvis de la Jara E 44 C2
Belvis de Monroy E 44 C2
Belz F 14 B2
Bembibre E 35 B4
Bemposta
  Bragança P 43 A3
  Santarém P 48 B2
Benabarre E 39 B4
Benacazón E 55 B3
Benaguacil E 53 B3
Benahadux E 58 C2
Benalmádena E 57 B3
Benalúa de Guadix E 58 B1
Benalúa de las Villas E 57 A4
Benalup E 56 B2
Benamargosa E 57 B3
Benamaurel E 58 B2
Benameji E 57 A3
Benamocarra E 57 B3
Benaocaz E 56 B2
Benaoján E 56 B2
Benarrabá E 56 B2
Benasque E 39 B4
Benavente
  E 36 B1
  P 48 C2
Benavides de Órbigo E 35 B5
Benavila P 48 B3
Benejama E 53 C3
Benejúzar E 59 A4
Bénestroff F 12 C2
Benet F 22 B3
Bene Vagienna I 33 A3
Bénévent-l'Abbaye F 24 A1
Benfeld F 13 C3
Benfica P 48 B2
Benicarló E 47 B4
Benicàssim E 47 B4
Benidorm E 53 C3
Benifaió E 53 B3
Beniganim E 53 C3
Benisa E 53 C3
Bénodet F 14 B1
Benquerencia de la Serena
  E 50 B2
Bensafrim P 54 B1
Bensheim D 13 B4
Beranga E 37 A3
Bérat F 40 A2
Berbegal E 39 C3
Berberana E 37 B3
Bercedo E 37 A3
Bercenay-le-Hayer F 11 C3
Berchem B 7 B3
Bérchules E 57 B4
Bercianos de Aliste E 43 A3
Berck F 6 B1
Berclaire d'Urgell E 41 C1
Berdoias E 34 A1
Berducedo E 35 A4

Berdún E 38 B3
Berga E 41 B2
Bergara E 37 A4
Bergen op Zoom NL 7 A4
Bergerac F 29 B3
Bergères-lés-Vertus F 11 C4
Bergeyk NL 7 A5
Berghausen D 13 C4
Bergues F 6 B2
Bergün Bravuogn CH 21 C4
Beringel P 54 A2
Beringen B 7 A5
Berja E 58 C2
Berkheim D 21 A5
Berlanga E 50 B2
Berlanga de Duero E 45 A5
Bermeo E 37 A4
Bermillo de Sayago E 43 A4
Bern CH 20 C2
Bernardos E 44 A3
Bernau D 20 B3
Bernaville F 10 A2
Bernay F 9 A4
Bernkastel-Kues D 12 B3
Bernués E 39 B3
Beromünster CH 20 B3
Berre-l'Etang F 31 B4
Berrocal E 55 B3
Bertamiráns E 34 B2
Berthelming F 12 C2
Bertincourt F 10 A2
Bertogne B 12 A1
Bertrix B 11 B5
Berville-sur-Mer F 9 A4
Berzocana E 50 A2
Besalú E 41 B3
Besançon F 19 B5
Besenfeld D 13 C4
Besigheim D 13 C5
Besle F 15 B4
Bessais-le-Fromental F 17 C4
Bessan F 30 B2
Besse-en-Chandesse F 24 B2
Bessèges F 31 A3
Bessé-sur-Braye F 16 B2
Bessines-sur-Gartempe
F 23 B5
Best NL 7 A5
Betanzos E 34 A2
Betelu E 38 A2
Bétera E 53 B3
Beteta E 46 B1
Béthenville F 11 B4
Béthune F 6 B2
Beton-Bazoches F 10 C3
Bettembourg L 12 B2
Betterdorf L 12 B2
Betxi E 53 B3
Betz F 10 B2
Beuil F 32 A2
Beuzeville F 9 A4
Beveren B 7 A4
Bex CH 27 A4
Beychevelle F 28 A2
Beynat F 29 A4
Bezas E 46 B2
Bezau A 21 B4
Bèze F 19 B4
Bezenet F 24 A2
Béziers F 30 B2
Biandrate I 27 B5
Biar E 53 C3
Biarritz F 38 A2
Bias F 28 B1
Biberach
Baden-Württemberg
D 13 C4
Baden-Württemberg D 21 A4
Biblis D 13 B4
Bicorp E 53 B3
Bicos P 54 B1
Bidache F 28 C1
Bidart F 38 A2
Biel
CH 20 B2
E 38 B3
Biella I 27 B5
Bielsa E 39 B4
Bienservida E 52 C1
Bienvenida E 50 B1
Bierné F 16 B1
Bierwart B 7 B5
Biescas E 39 B3
Bietigheim-Bissingen D 13 C5
Bièvre B 11 B5
Biganos F 28 B2
Bigas P 42 B2
Bigastro E 59 A4
Bignasco CH 27 A5
Biguglia F 62 A2
Bijuesca E 46 A2
Bilbao E 37 A4
Billom F 24 B3
Binaced E 39 C4
Binche B 7 B4
Binefar E 39 C4
Bingen D 13 B3
Binic F 14 A3
Bionaz I 27 B4
Birkenfeld
Baden-Württemberg
D 13 C4
Rheinland-Pfalz D 12 B3
Bisbal de Falset E 47 A4
Biscarosse F 28 B1
Biscarosse Plage F 28 B1
Biscarrués E 38 B3
Bischheim F 13 C3
Bischofszell CH 21 B4
Bischwiller F 13 C3
Bisingen D 13 C4
Bissen L 12 B2
Bistango I 27 C5
Bitburg D 12 B2
Bitche F 13 B3
Bitschwiller F 20 B2
Biville-sur-Mer F 9 A5
Biwer L 12 B2
Blacy F 11 C4
Blagnac F 29 C4
Blaichach D 21 B5
Blain F 15 B4
Blainville-sur-l'Eau F 12 C2
Blajan F 39 A4
Blâmont F 12 C2
Blanca E 59 A3
Blancos E 34 C3
Blanes E 41 C3
Blangy-sur-Bresle F 10 B1
Blankenberge B 6 A3
Blanquefort F 28 B2
Blanzac F 23 C4
Blanzy F 18 C3
Blascomillán E 44 B2
Blascosancho E 44 B3
Blatten CH 27 A4
Blaye F 28 A2
Blaye-les-Mines F 30 A1
Blázquez E 50 B2
Blecua E 39 B3
Bléneau F 18 B1
Blérancourt F 10 B3
Bléré F 16 B2
Blesle F 24 B3
Blet F 17 C4
Bletterans F 19 C4
Blieskastel D 12 B3
Bligny-sur-Ouche F 18 B3
Blois F 17 B3
Blonville-sur-Mer F 9 A4
Bludenz A 21 B4
Blumberg D 21 B3
Boal E 35 A4
Boa Vista P 48 B2
Bobadilla
Logroño E 37 B4
Málaga E 57 A3
Bobadilla del Campo E 44 A2
Bobadilla del Monte E 45 B4
Bóbbio Pellice I 27 C4
Bobigny F 10 C2
Böblingen D 13 C5
Boboras E 34 B2
Boca de Huérgano E 36 B2
Bocairent E 53 C3
Boceguillas E 45 A4
Bocognano F 62 A2
Bodonal de la Sierra E 55 A3
Boecillo E 44 A3
Boëge F 26 A3
Boën F 25 B3
Bogajo E 43 B3
Bogarra E 52 C1
Bogarre E 57 A4
Bognanco Fonti I 27 A5
Bohain-en-Vermandois
F 11 B3
Bohonal de Ibor E 44 C2
Boiro E 34 B2
Bois-d'Amont F 19 C5
Boisseron F 31 B3
Boixols E 41 B2
Bolaños de Calatrava E 51 B4
Bolbec F 9 A4
Bolea E 39 B3
Boliqueime P 54 B1
Bollène F 31 A3
Bólliga E 46 B1
Bollullos E 55 B3
Bollullos par del Condado
E 55 B3
Bologne F 19 A4
Boltaña E 39 B4
Boltigen CH 20 C2
Bolzaneto I 33 A4
Bombarral P 48 B1
Bona F 18 B2
Bonaduz CH 21 C4
Bonanza E 55 C3
Boñar E 36 B1
Bonares E 55 B3
Bondorf D 13 C4
Bon-Encontre F 29 B3
Bonete E 52 C2
Bonifacio F 62 B2
Bonigen CH 20 C2
Bonnat F 24 A1
Bonndorf D 20 B3
Bonnétable F 16 A2
Bonnétage F 20 B1
Bonneuil-les-Eaux F 10 B2
Bonneuil-Matours F 23 B4
Bonneval F 17 A3
Bonneval-sur-Arc F 27 B4
Bonneville F 26 A3
Bonnières-sur-Seine F 10 B1
Bonnieux F 31 B4
Bönnigheim D 13 B5
Bonny-sur-Loire F 17 B4
Bono E 39 B4
Boom B 7 A4
Boos F 9 A5
Boqueixón E 34 B2
Boran-sur-Oise F 10 B2
Borba P 49 C3
Bordeaux F 28 B2
Bordeira P 54 B1
Bordighera I 33 B3
Bordón E 47 B3
Borghetto d'Arróscia I 33 A3
Borghetto Santo Spirito
I 33 A4
Borgloon B 7 B5
Borgo F 62 A2
Borgofranco d'Ivrea I 27 B4
Borgomanero I 27 B5
Borgomasino I 27 B4
Borgo San Dalmazzo I 33 A3
Borgosésia I 27 B5
Borgo Vercelli I 27 B5
Borja E 38 C2
Bormes-les-Mimosas F 32 B2
Bórmio I 21 C5
Bormujos E 55 B3
Bornes P 43 A2
Bornos E 56 B2
Borobia E 46 A2
Borox E 45 B4
Borredá E 41 B2
Borrenes E 35 B4
Borriol E 53 A3
Bort-les-Orgues F 24 B2
Bossast E 39 B4
Bossolasco I 33 A4
Bot E 47 A4
Boticas P 42 A2
Bötzingen D 20 A2
Bouaye F 15 B4
Bouça P 43 A2
Boucau F 28 C1
Bouchain F 6 B3
Bouchoir F 10 B2
Boudreville F 19 B3
Boudry CH 20 C1
Bouesse F 17 C3
Bouguenais F 15 B4
Bouhy F 18 B2
Bouillargues F 31 B3
Bouillon B 11 B5
Bouilly F 18 A2
Bouin F 22 B2
Boulay-Moselle F 12 B2
Boulazac F 29 A3
Boule-d'Amont F 40 B3
Bouligny F 12 B1
Boulogne-sur-Gesse F 39 A4
Boulogne-sur-Mer F 6 B1
Bouloire F 16 B2
Bouquemaison F 6 B2
Bourbon-Lancy F 18 C2
Bourbon-l'Archambault
F 18 C2
Bourbonne-les-Bains F 19 B4
Bourbourg F 6 B2
Bourbriac F 14 A2
Bourcefranc-le-Chapus
F 22 C2
Bourdeaux F 31 A4
Bouresse F 23 B4
Bourg F 28 A2
Bourg-Achard F 9 A4
Bourganeuf F 24 B1
Bourg-Argental F 25 B4
Bourg-de-Péage F 25 B5
Bourg-de-Thizy F 25 A4
Bourg-de-Visa F 29 B3
Bourg-en-Bresse F 26 A2
Bourges F 17 B4
Bourg-et-Comin F 11 B3
Bourg-Lastic F 24 B2
Bourg-Madame F 40 B2
Bourgneuf-en-Retz F 22 A2
Bourgogne F 11 B4
Bourgoin-Jallieu F 26 B2
Bourg-St Andéol F 31 A3
Bourg-St Maurice F 27 B3
Bourgtheroulde F 9 A4
Bourgueil F 16 B2
Bourmont F 19 A4
Bourneville F 9 A4
Bournezeau F 22 B2
Bourran F 29 B3
Bourret F 29 C4
Bourron-Marlotte F 10 C2
Boussac F 24 A2
Boussens F 39 A4
Boutersem B 7 B4
Bouttencourt F 10 B1
Bouvières F 31 A4
Bouvron F 15 B4
Bouxwiller F 13 C3
Bouzas E 34 B2
Bouzonville F 12 B2
Bóveda E 35 B3
Boves F 10 B2
Bóves I 33 A3
Boxtel NL 7 A5
Bozouls F 30 A1
Bra I 27 C4
Bracieux F 17 B3
Brackenheim D 13 B5
Braga P 42 A1
Bragança P 43 A3
Braine F 11 B3
Braine-le-Comte B 7 B4
Braives B 7 B5
Brakel B 7 B3
Bram F 40 A3
Bramafan F 32 B2
Brand A 21 B4
Brando F 62 A2
Brandomil E 34 A2
Branne F 28 B2
Brantôme F 23 C4
Bras d'Asse F 32 B2
Brasparts F 14 A2
Brassac F 30 B1
Brassac-les-Mines F 24 B3
Brasschaat B 7 A4
Bray Dunes F 6 A2
Bray-sur-Seine F 10 C3
Bray-sur-Somme F 10 B2
Brazatortas E 51 B3
Brazey-en-Plaine F 19 B4
Brea de Tajo E 45 B4
Brécey F 8 B2
Brecht B 7 A4
Brécy F 17 B4
Breda
E 41 C3
NL 7 A4
Bregenz A 21 B4
Bréhal F 8 B2
Breidenbach F 13 B3
Breil-sur-Roya F 33 B3
Breisach D 20 A2
Breitenbach CH 20 B2
Bremgarten CH 20 B3
Brem-sur-Mer F 22 B2
Brenes E 56 A2
Brénod F 26 A2
Brensbach D 13 B4
Breskens NL 7 A3
Bresles F 10 B2
Bressuire F 16 C1
Brest F 14 A1
Bretenoux F 29 B4
Breteuil
Eure F 9 B4
Oise F 10 B2
Brétigny-sur-Orge F 10 C2
Bretten D 13 B4
Bretteville-sur-Laize F 9 A3
Breuil-Cervinia I 27 B4
Bréziers F 32 A2
Brezolles F 9 B5
Briançon F 26 C3
Brianconnet F 32 B2
Briare F 17 B4
Briatexte F 29 C4
Briaucourt F 19 A4
Bricquebec F 8 A2
Briec F 14 A1
Brie-Comte-Robert F 10 C2
Brienne-le-Château F 11 C4
Brienon-sur-Armançon
F 18 B2
Brienz CH 20 C3
Brieva de Cameros E 37 B4
Briey F 12 B1
Brig CH 27 A5
Brignogan-Plage F 14 A1
Brignoles F 32 B2
Brihuega E 45 B5
Brillon-en-Barrois F 11 C5
Brinches P 54 A2
Brinon-sur-Beuvron F 18 B2
Brinon-sur-Sauldre F 17 B4
Brión E 34 B2
Briones E 37 B4
Brionne F 9 A4
Brioude F 25 B3
Brioux-sur-Boutonne F 23 B3
Briouze F 9 B3
Briscous F 38 A2
Brissac-Quincé F 16 B1
Brive-la-Gaillarde F 29 A4
Briviesca E 37 B3
Brocas F 28 B2
Broglie F 9 B4
Bromont-Lamothe F 24 B2
Bronchales E 46 B2
Bronco E 43 B3
Broons F 15 A3
Broquies F 30 A1
Brossac F 23 C3
Brotas P 48 C2
Broto E 39 B3
Brou F 17 A3
Brouage F 22 C2
Broût-Vernet F 24 A3
Brouvelieures F 20 A1
Brouwershaven NL 7 A3
Brozas E 49 B4
Bruay-la-Buissière F 6 B2
Bruchsal D 13 B4
Brue-Auriac F 32 B1
Bruen CH 21 C3
Bruère-Allichamps F 17 C4
Brugg CH 20 B3
Brugge B 6 A3
Bruinisse NL 7 A4
Brûlon F 16 B1
Brumath F 13 C3
Brunehamel F 11 B4
Brunete E 45 B3
Brunnen CH 21 C3
Brusasco I 27 B5
Brusque F 30 B1
Brussels = Bruxelles B 7 B4
Brusson I 27 B4
Bruxelles = Brussels B 7 B4
Bruyères F 20 A1
Bruz F 15 A4
Buarcos P 42 B1
Bubbio I 27 C5
Bubry F 14 B2
Bucelas P 48 C1
Buchboden A 21 B4
Buchenberg D 21 B5
Buchères F 18 A3
Buchs CH 21 B4
Buchy F 9 A5
Bucy-lés-Pierreport F 11 B3
Budens P 54 B1
Budia E 45 B5
Bueña E 46 B2
Buenache de Alarcón E 52 B1
Buenache de la Sierra E 46 B2
Buenaventura E 44 B3
Buenavista de Valdavia
E 36 B2
Buendia E 45 B5
Bueu E 34 B2
Buezo E 37 B3
Bugarra E 53 B3
Bugeat F 24 B1
Bühl
Baden-Württemberg
D 13 C4
Bayern D 21 B5
Bühlertal D 13 C4
Buis-les-Baronnies F 31 A4
Buitrago del Lozoya E 45 B4
Bujalance E 51 C3
Bujaraloz E 47 A3
Bujedo E 37 B3
Bülach CH 21 B3
Bulgnéville F 19 A4
Bullas E 58 A3
Bulle CH 20 C2
Buño E 34 A2
Buñol E 53 B3
Bunsbeek B 7 B4
Buñuel E 38 C2
Bunyola E 60 B2
Burdons-sur-Rognon F 19 A4
Burela E 35 A3
Büren an der Aare CH 20 B2
Burgau P 54 B1
Burgdorf CH 20 B2
Burgo P 42 B1
Burgohondo E 44 B3
Burgos E 37 B3
Burgui E 38 B3
Burguillos E 56 A2
Burguillos del Cerro E 49 C4
Burguillos de Toledo E 45 C4
Burie F 22 C3
Burjassot E 53 B3
Burlada E 38 B2
Burladingen D 21 A4
Burón E 36 A1
Buronzo I 27 B5
Burret F 40 B2
Burriana E 53 B3
Bürs A 21 B4
Bürstadt D 13 B4
Burujón E 45 C3
Busano I 27 B4
Busca I 33 A3
Busot E 53 C3
Busquistar E 57 B4
Bussang F 20 B1
Bussière-Badil F 23 C4
Bussière-Poitevine F 23 B4
Bussoleno I 27 B4
Bütschwil CH 21 B4
Buxières-les-Mines F 18 C1
Buxy F 18 C3
Buzançais F 17 C3
Buzancy F 11 B4
Buzy F 39 A3

C

Cabacos P 48 B2
Cabana E 34 A2
Cabanac-et-Villagrains
F 28 B2
Cabañaquinta E 36 A1
Cabanas P 54 B2
Cabañas del Castillo E 50 A2
Cabañas de Yepes E 45 C4
Cabanelles E 41 B3
Cabanes E 47 B4
Cabanillas E 38 B2
Cabasse F 32 B2
Cabdella E 40 B2
Cabeceiras de Basto P 42 A1
Cabeço de Vide P 49 B3
Cabeza del Buey E 50 B2
Cabeza la Vaca E 55 A3
Cabezamesada E 45 C4
Cabezarados E 51 B3
Cabezarrubias del Puerto
E 51 B3
Cabezas del Villar E 44 B2
Cabezas Rubias E 55 B2
Cabezón E 36 C2
Cabezón de la Sal E 36 A2
Cabezón de Liébana E 36 A2
Cabezuela E 45 A4
Cabezuela del Valle E 43 B4
Cabo de Gata E 58 C2
Cabo de Palos E 59 B4
Cabolafuenta E 46 A1
Cabourg F 9 A3
Cabra
E 57 A3
P 42 B2
Cabra del Santo Cristo
E 57 A4
Cabreiro P 34 C2
Cabreiros E 34 A3
Cabrejas E 46 B1
Cabrela P 48 C2
Cabrillas E 43 B3
Cacabelos E 35 B4
Cacela P 54 B2
Cacém P 48 C1
Cáceres E 49 B4
Cachafeiro E 34 B2
Cachopo P 54 B2
Cacin E 57 A4
Cadafais P 48 C1
Cadalen F 29 C5
Cadalso E 43 B3
Cadaqués E 41 B4
Cadaval P 48 B1
Cadavedo E 35 A4
Cadéac F 39 B4
Cadenet F 31 B4
Cadeuil F 22 C3
Cádiar E 58 C1
Cadillac F 28 B2
Cádiz E 56 B1
Cadouin F 29 B3
Cadours F 29 C4
Cadrete E 46 A3
Caen F 9 A3
Cafede P 49 B3
Cagnes-sur-Mer F 32 B3
Cahors F 29 B4
Caion E 34 A2
Cairo Montenotte I 33 A4
Cajarc F 29 B4
Cala E 55 B3
Calaceite E 47 B4
Calacuccia F 62 A2
Cala d'Or E 61 B3
Calaf E 41 C2
Calafell E 41 C2
Cala Galdana E 61 B3
Calahonda
Granada E 57 B4
Málaga E 57 B3
Calahorra E 38 B2
Calais F 6 B1
Cala Llonga E 60 C1
Cala Millor E 61 B3
Calamocha E 46 B2
Calamonte E 49 C4
Cala Morell E 61 A3
Calañas E 55 B3
Calanda E 47 B3
Cala Ratjada E 61 B3
Calasparra E 58 A3
Calatayud E 46 A2
Calatorao E 46 A2
Calcena E 46 A2
Caldas da Rainha P 48 B1
Caldas de Boi E 39 B4
Caldas de Malavella E 41 C3
Caldas de Reis E 34 B2
Caldas de San Jorge P 42 B1
Caldas de Vizela P 42 A1
Caldaso de los Vidrios
E 44 B3
Caldearenas E 39 B3
Caldelas P 42 A1
Calders E 41 C2
Caldes de Montbui E 41 C3
Calella
Barcelona E 41 C3
Girona E 41 C4
Calenzana F 62 A1
Calera de León E 55 A3
Calera y Chozas E 44 C3
Caleruega E 37 C3
Caleruela E 44 C2
Cales de Mallorca E 61 B3
Calizzano I 33 A4
Callac F 14 A2
Callas F 32 B2
Calliano I 27 B5
Callosa de Ensarriá E 53 C3
Callosa de Segura E 59 A4
Callús E 41 C2
Calmbach D 13 C4
Calonge E 41 C4
Calpe E 53 C4
Caltojar E 45 A5
Caluire-et-Cuire F 25 B4
Caluso I 27 B4
Calvi F 62 A1
Calviá E 60 B2
Calvinet F 24 C2
Calvisson F 31 B3
Calw D 13 C4
Calzada de Calatrava E 51 B4
Calzada de Valdunciel
E 44 A2
Calzadilla de los Barros
E 49 C4
Camarasa E 39 C4
Camarena E 45 B3
Camarès F 30 B1
Camaret-sur-Aigues F 31 A3
Camaret-sur-Mer F 14 A1
Camarillas E 47 B3
Camariñas E 34 A1
Camarma E 45 B4
Camarzana de Tera E 35 B4
Camas E 56 A1
Cambados E 34 B2
Cambarinho P 42 B1
Cambil E 57 A4
Cambligeu F 6 B2
Cambo-les-Bains F 38 A2
Cambrai F 6 B3
Cambre E 34 A2
Cambrils E 41 C2
Cameleño E 36 A2
Camelle E 34 A1
Caminha P 42 A1
Caminomorisco E 43 B3
Camineral E 46 B2
Camors F 14 B3
Campan F 39 A4
Campanario E 50 B2
Campanillas E 57 B3
Campano E 56 B1
Campaspero E 45 A3
Campello E 59 A4
Campelos P 48 B1
Campico López E 59 B3
Campillo de Altobuey E 52 B2
Campillo de Aragón E 46 A2
Campillo de Arenas E 57 A4
Campillo de Llerena E 50 B2
Campillos E 56 A3
Campo E 39 B4
Campo da Feira E 34 A3
Campo de Bacerros E 35 B3
Campo de Caso E 36 A1
Campo de Criptana E 51 A4
Campofrio E 55 B3
Campo Ligure I 33 A4
Campo Lugar E 50 A2
Campo Maior P 49 B3
Campomanes E 35 A5
Campo Molino I 33 A3
Campomono F 62 B1
Campo Real E 45 B4
Camporrells E 39 C4
Camporrobles E 52 B2
Campos P 42 A2
Camposa P 42 A1
Campos del Port E 61 B3
Camposines E 47 A4
Campotéjar E 57 A4
Camprodón E 41 B3
Campsegret F 29 B3
Camuñas E 51 A4
Cañada del Hoyo E 52 B2
Cañadajuncosa E 52 B1
Cañada Rosal E 56 A2
Canale I 27 C4
Canales
Asturias E 35 B5
Castellón de la Plana
E 53 B3
Canals E 53 C3
Cañamares E 46 B1
Cañamero E 50 A2
Cañar E 57 B4
Cañate la Real E 56 B2
Cañaveral E 49 B4
Cañaveral de León E 55 A3
Cañaveras E 46 B1
Cañaveruelas E 45 B5
Cancale F 8 B2
Cancon F 29 B3
Canda E 35 B4
Candamil E 34 A3
Candanchu E 39 B3
Candas E 35 A5
Candasnos E 47 A4
Candé F 15 B4
Candelario E 44 B2
Candeleda E 44 B2
Candin E 35 B4
Candosa P 42 B2
Canecas P 48 C1
Canelli I 27 C5
Canena E 51 B4
Canencia E 45 B4
Canero E 35 A4
Canet F 30 B2
Canet de Mar E 41 C3
Canet d'en Berenguer E 53 B3
Cañete E 52 A2
Cañete de las Torres E 57 A3
Canet-Plage F 40 B4
Canfranc E 39 B3
Cangas
Lugo E 35 A3
Pontevedra E 34 B2
Cangas de Narcea E 35 A4
Cangas de Onís E 36 A1
Canha P 48 C2
Canhestros P 54 A1
Canicosa de la Sierra E 37 C3
Caniles E 58 B2
Canillas de Aceituno E 57 B3
Canisy F 8 A2
Cañizal E 44 A2
Cañizo E 36 C1
Canjáyar E 58 C2
Cannes F 32 B3
Can Pastilla E 60 B2
C'an Picafort E 61 B3
Cantalapiedra E 44 A2
Cantalejo E 45 A4
Cantalgallo E 55 A3
Cantalpino E 44 A2
Cantanhede P 42 B1
Cantavieja E 47 B3
Cantillana E 56 A2
Cantiveros E 44 B3
Cantoria E 58 B2

Cany-Barville F 9 A4
Canyet de Mar E 41 C3
Caparroso E 38 B2
Capbreton F 28 C1
Capdenac-Gare F 24 C2
Capdepera E 61 B3
Cap-de-Pin F 28 B2
Capellades E 41 C2
Capendu F 40 A3
Capestang F 30 B2
Cap Ferret F 28 B1
Capileira E 57 B4
Capinha P 42 B2
Captieux F 28 B2
Capvern F 39 A4
Carabaña E 45 B4
Carabias E 45 A4
Caracenilla E 46 B1
Caráglio I 33 A3
Caraman F 40 A2
Caranga E 35 A4
Caranguejeira P 48 B2
Carantec F 14 A2
Caravaca de la Cruz E . . .58 A3
Carbajal E 57 B3
Carbajo E 49 B3
Carballeda E 34 B3
Carballeda de Avia E 34 A2
Carballo E 34 A2
Carbon-Blanc F 28 B2
Carbonera de Frentes E 37 C4
Carboneras E 58 C3
Carboneras de Guadazaón
  E 52 B2
Carbonero el Mayor E . . .45 A3
Carboneros E 51 B4
Carbonne F 40 A2
Carcaboso E 43 B3
Carcabuey E 57 A3
Carcaixent E 53 B3
Carcans F 28 A1
Carcans-Plage F 28 A1
Carção P 43 A3
Carcar E 38 B2
Cárcare I 33 A4
Carcassonne F 40 A3
Carcastillo E 38 B2
Carcedo de Burgos E 37 B3
Carcelén E 53 B2
Carcès F 32 B2
Carchelejo E 57 A4
Cardedeu E 41 C3
Cardeña E 51 B3
Cardenete E 52 B2
Cardeñosa E 44 B3
Cardona E 41 C2
Cardosos P 48 B2
Carentan F 8 A2
Carentoir F 15 B3
Cargèse F 62 A1
Carhaix-Plouguer F 14 A2
Caria P 42 B2
Carignan F 11 B5
Carignano I 27 C4
Cariñena E 46 A2
Cariño E 34 A3
Carlepont F 10 B3
Carlet E 53 B3
Carmagnola I 27 C4
Carmaux F 30 A1
Carmena E 44 C3
Cármenes E 36 B1
Carmine I 33 A3
Carmona E 56 A2
Carmonita E 49 B4
Carnac F 14 B2
Carnon Plage F 31 B2
Carnota E 34 B1
Carolles F 8 B2
Carpentras F 31 A4
Carpignano Sésia I 27 B5
Carpio E 44 A2
Carquefou F 15 B4
Carqueiranne F 32 B2
Carral E 34 A2
Carranque E 45 B4
Carrapichana P 42 B2
Carrascalejo E 50 A2
Carrascosa del Campo
  E 45 B5
Carratraca E 56 B3
Carrazeda de Ansiães
  P 42 A2
Carrazedo de Montenegro
  P 42 A2
Carregal do Sal P 42 B1
Carreña E 36 A2
Carrión E 55 B3
Carrión de Calatrava E . . .51 A4
Carrión de los Condes
  E 36 B2
Carrizo de la Ribera E . . .35 B5
Carrizosa E 51 B5
Carro F 31 B4
Carrocera E 36 B1
Carros F 33 B3
Carrouge CH 20 C1
Carrouges F 9 B3
Carrù I 33 A3
Carry-le-Rouet F 31 B4
Cartagena E 59 B4
Cártama E 57 B3
Cartaxo P 48 B2
Cartaya E 55 B2
Carteret F 8 A2
Cartes E 36 A2
Carviças P 43 A3
Carvin F 6 B2
Carvoeiro P 48 B1
Carvoeiro P 54 B1
Casabermeja E 57 B3
Casa Branca
  Portalegre P 48 C3
  Setúbal P 48 C2
Casaio E 35 B4
Casalarreina E 37 B4
Casalborgone I 27 B4
Casale Monferrato I 27 B5
Casamozza F 62 A2
Casarabonela E 56 B3
Casar de Cáceres E 49 B4
Casar de Palomero E 43 B3
Casarejos E 37 C3

Casares E 56 B2
Casares de las Hurdes
  E 43 B3
Casariche E 57 A3
Casarrubios del Monte
  E 45 B3
Casas de Don Pedro E . . .50 A2
Casas de Fernando Alonso
  E 52 B1
Casas de Haro E 52 B1
Casas de Juan Gil E 53 B2
Casas del Juan Núñez
  E 52 B2
Casas del Puerto E 53 C2
Casas del Rio E 53 B2
Casas de Millán E 49 B4
Casas de Reina E 50 B2
Casas de Ves E 53 B2
Casas-Ibáñez E 52 B2
Casasimarro E 52 B1
Casas Nuevas E 58 B3
Casasola E 44 B3
Casasola de Arión E 44 A2
Casasuertes E 36 A2
Casatejada E 44 C2
Casavieja E 44 B3
Cascais P 48 C1
Cascante E 38 C2
Cascante del Rio E 46 B2
Cáseda E 38 B2
Caselle Torinese I 27 B4
Caseres E 47 A4
Casével P 54 B1
Casillas E 44 B3
Casillas de Coria E 49 B4
Casinos E 53 B3
Caspe E 47 A4
Cassàde la Selva E 41 C3
Cassagnas F 30 A2
Cassagnes-Bégonhès
  F 30 A1
Cassel F 6 B2
Cassine I 27 C5
Cassis F 32 B1
Cassuéjouls F 24 C2
Castalla E 53 B3
Castañar de Ibor E 50 A2
Castanheira de Pêra P . . .48 A2
Casteição P 42 B2
Castejón E 38 B2
Castejón de Monegros
  E 47 A3
Castejón de Sos E 39 B4
Castejón de Valdejasa
  E 38 C3
Castel del Cabra E 47 B3
Casteldelfino I 32 A3
Casteljaloux F 28 B3
Castellamonte I 27 B4
Castellane F 32 B2
Castellar de la Frontera
  E 56 B2
Castellar de la Ribera E . .41 B2
Castellar del Vallès E 41 C3
Castellar de Santiago E . .51 B4
Castellbell i Villar E 41 C2
Castelldans E 47 A4
Castell de Cabres E 47 B4
Castell de Castells E 53 C3
Castelldefels E 41 C2
Castell de Ferro E 57 B4
Castellet E 41 C2
Castellfollit de la Roca
  E 41 B3
Castellfollit de Riubregos
  E 41 C2
Castellfort E 47 B3
Castellóde Farfaña E 39 C4
Castellóde la Plana E 53 B3
Castello d'Empúries E . . .41 B4
Castelloli E 41 C2
Castelló de Rugat E 53 C3
Castellote E 47 B3
Castellterçol E 41 C3
Castelmoron-sur-Lot F . . .29 B3
Castelnaudary F 40 A2
Castelnau-de-Médoc E . . .28 A2
Castelnau-de-Montmirail
  F 29 C4
Castelnau-Magnoac F 39 A4
Castelnau-Montratier F . . .29 B4
Castelnou E 47 A3
Castelnuovo Don Bosco
  I 27 B4
Castelo Branco
  Bragança P 43 A3
  Castelo Branco P 49 B3
Castelo de Paiva P 42 A1
Castelo de Vide P 49 B3
Castelo do Neiva P 42 A1
Castelo Mendo P 43 B3
Castelsarrasin F 29 B4
Castelserás E 47 B3
Castets E 28 C1
Castilblanco E 50 A2
Castilblanco de los Arroyos
  E 55 B4
Castil de Peones E 37 B3
Castilfrio de la Sierra E . .38 C1
Castilgaleu E 39 B4
Castilisar E 38 B2
Castilleja E 55 B3
Castillejar E 58 B2
Castillejo de Martin Viejo
  E 43 B3
Castillejo de Mesleón E . .45 A4
Castillejo de Robledo E . .45 A4
Castillo de Bayuela E 44 B3
Castillo de Locubín E 57 A4
Castillonès F 29 B3
Castillon-la-Bataille F 28 B2
Castillon-Len-Couserans
  F 40 B2
Castillonroy E 39 C4
Castilruiz E 38 C1
Castirla F 62 A2
Castrejón E 44 A2
Castrelo del Valle E 35 B3
Castries F 31 B2
Castril E 58 B2
Castrillo de Duero E 45 A4
Castrillo de la Vega E 37 C3
Castrillo de Onielo E 36 C2

Castro E 36 A2
Castrocabón E 35 B5
Castro-Caldelas E 35 B3
Castrocontrigo E 35 B4
Castro Daire P 42 B2
Castro del Rio E 57 A3
Castro de Rey E 35 A3
Castrogonzaio E 36 B1
Castrojeriz E 36 B2
Castro Laboreiro P 34 B2
Castro Marim P 54 B2
Castromonte E 36 C1
Castromudarra E 36 B1
Castronuevo E 36 C1
Castronuño E 44 A2
Castropol E 35 A3
Castroserracin E 45 A4
Castro-Urdiales E 37 A3
Castroverde E 35 A3
Castro Verde P 54 B1
Castroverde de Campos
  E 36 C1
Castroverde de Cerrato
  E 36 C2
Castuera E 50 B2
Catadau E 53 B3
Catarroja E 53 B3
Catarruchos P 42 B1
Cati E 47 B4
Catillon F 11 A3
Catoira E 34 B2
Catral E 59 A4
Caudebec-en-Caux F 9 A4
Caudete E 53 C3
Caudete de las Fuentes
  E 53 B2
Caudiel E 53 B3
Caudiès-de-Fenouillèdes
  F 40 B3
Caudry F 11 A3
Caulnes F 15 A3
Caumont-l'Evente F 8 A3
Caunes-Minervois F 40 A3
Cauro F 62 B1
Caussade F 29 B4
Causse-de-la-Selle F 30 B2
Cauterets F 39 B3
Cavaglia I 27 B5
Cavaillon F 31 B4
Cavalaire-sur-Mer F 32 B2
Cavaleiro P 54 B1
Cavallermaggiore I 27 C4
Cavernães P 42 B2
Cavignac F 28 A2
Cavour I 27 C4
Cayeux-sur-Mer F 6 B1
Caylus F 29 B4
Cayres F 25 C3
Cazalilla E 51 C4
Cazalla de la Sierra E 50 C2
Cazals F 29 B4
Cazanuecos E 36 B1
Cazaubon F 28 C2
Cazaux F 28 B1
Cazavet F 40 A2
Cazères F 40 A2
Cazis CH 21 C4
Cazo E 36 A1
Cazorla E 58 B2
Cazouls-lès-Béziers F 30 B2
Cea
  León E 36 B1
  Orense E 34 B3
Ceánuri E 37 A4
Ceauce F 8 B3
Cebolla E 44 C3
Cebreros E 44 B3
Ceclavin E 49 B4
Cedeira E 34 A2
Cedillo E 49 B3
Cedillo del Condado E . . .45 B4
Cedrillas E 47 B3
Cée E 34 B1
Cehegin E 58 A3
Ceilhes-et-Rocozels F . . .30 B2
Ceinos de Campos E 36 B1
Ceira P 42 B1
Celanova E 34 B3
Cella E 46 B2
Celle Ligure I 33 A4
Celles F 7 B4
Celles-sur-Belle F 23 B3
Celorico da Beira P 42 B2
Celorico de Basto P 42 A1
Cenicientos E 44 B3
Cenicero E 37 B4
Cenicientos E 44 B3
Censeau F 19 C5
Centallo I 33 A3
Centelles E 41 C3
Cepeda la Mora E 44 B2
Cépet F 29 C4
Cérans Foulletourte F 16 B2
Cerbère F 41 B4
Cercadillo E 45 A5
Cercal
  Lisboa P 48 B1
  Setúbal P 54 B1
Cerceda E 45 B4
Cercedilla E 45 B4
Cercs E 41 B2
Cercy-la-Tour F 18 C2
Cerdedo E 34 B2
Cerdeira P 43 B2
Cerdon F 17 B4
Ceres I 27 B4
Ceresole-Reale I 27 B4
Cereste F 32 B1
Céret F 40 B3
Cerezo de Abajo E 45 A4
Cerezo de Riotirón E 37 B3
Cerfontaine B 7 B4
Cergy F 10 B2
Cérilly F 17 C4
Cerisiers F 18 A2
Cerizay F 22 B3
Cernay F 20 B2
Cernégula E 37 B3
Cérons F 28 B2
Cerralbo E 43 B3
Cerro Muriano E 50 B3
Certosa di Pésio I 33 A3
Cerva P 42 A2
Cervatos de la Cueza E . .36 B2
Cervera E 41 C2
Cervera de la Cañada E . .46 A2
Cervera del Llano E 52 B1

Cervera del Rio Alhama
  E 38 B2
Cervera de Pisuerga E . . .36 B2
Cerviáde les Garrigues
  E 41 C1
Cervione F 62 A2
Cervo E 35 A3
Cervon F 18 B2
Cesana Torinese I 27 C3
Cessenon F 30 B2
Cesson-Sévigné F 15 A4
Cestas F 28 B2
Cesuras E 34 A2
Cetina E 46 A2
Ceuti E 59 A3
Ceva I 33 A4
Cevico de la Torre E 36 C2
Cevico Navero E 36 C2
Cevins F 26 B3
Cévio CH 27 A5
Ceyrat F 24 B3
Ceyzériat F 26 A2
Chaam NL 7 A4
Chabanais F 23 C4
Chabeuil F 25 C5
Chablis F 18 B2
Châbons F 26 B2
Chabreloche F 25 B3
Chabris F 17 B3
Chagny F 19 C3
Chaherrero E 44 B3
Chailland F 8 B3
Chaillé-les-Marais F 22 B2
Chailles F 17 B3
Chailley F 18 A2
Chalabre F 40 B3
Chalais F 28 A3
Chalamont F 26 B2
Châlette-sur-Loing F 17 A4
Chalindrey F 19 B4
Challans F 22 B2
Challes-les-Eaux F 26 B2
Chalmazel F 25 B3
Chalmoux F 18 C2
Chalonnes-sur-Loire F . . .16 B1
Châlons-en-Champagne
  F 11 C4
Chalon-sur-Saône F 19 C3
Chálus F 23 C4
Cham CH 20 B3
Chamberet F 24 B1
Chambéry F 26 B2
Chambilly F 25 A4
Chambley F 12 B1
Chambly F 10 B2
Chambois F 9 B4
Chambon-sur-Lac F 24 B2
Chambon-sur-Voueize
  F 24 A2
Chambord F 17 B3
Chamborigaud F 31 A2
Chamboulive F 24 B1
Chamonix-Mont Blanc
  F 26 B3
Champagnac-le-Vieux F . .25 B3
Champagney F 20 B1
Champagnole F 19 C4
Champagny-Mouton F 23 B4
Champaubert F 11 C3
Champdeniers-St Denis
  F 22 B3
Champdieu F 25 B4
Champdôtre F 19 B4
Champeix F 24 B3
Champéry CH 27 A3
Champigne F 16 B1
Champignelles F 18 B2
Champigny-sur-Veude
  F 16 B2
Champlitte-et-le-Prelot
  F 19 B4
Champoluc I 27 B4
Champoly F 25 B3
Champorcher F 27 B4
Champrond-en-Gâtine F . .9 B5
Champs-sur-Tarentaine
  F 24 B2
Champs-sur-Yonne F 18 B2
Champtoceaux F 15 B4
Champtoceaux F 15 B4
Chamrousse F 26 B2
Chamusca P 48 B2
Chanac F 30 A2
Chanaleilles F 25 C2
Checa E 46 B2
Chef-Boutonne F 23 B3
Cheles E 49 C3
Chella E 53 B3
Chelles F 10 C2
Chelva E 53 B2
Chémery F 17 B3
Chemery-sur-Bar F 11 B4
Chemillé F 16 B1
Chemin F 19 C4
Chénerailles F 24 A2
Cheniménil F 20 A1
Chenonceaux F 17 B3
Chenôve F 19 B3
Chera E 53 B3
Cherasco I 27 C4
Cherbonnières F 23 C3
Cherbourg F 8 A2
Chéroy F 18 A1
Chessy-lès-Pres F 18 A2
Cheste E 53 B3
Chevagnes F 18 C2
Chevanceaux F 23 C3
Chevillon F 11 C5
Chevilly F 17 A3
Chézery-Forens F 26 A2
Chialamberto I 27 B4
Chianale I 27 C4
Chiché F 16 C1
Chiclana de la Frontera
  E 56 B1
Chiclana de Segura E 58 A1
Chillarón de Cuenca E . . .46 B1
Chillarón del Rey E 45 B5
Chilleurs-aux-Bois F 17 A4
Chillón E 50 B3
Chilluevar E 58 B1
Chiloeches E 45 B4
Chimay B 11 A4
Chimeneas E 57 A4
Chinchilla de Monte Aragón
  E 52 C2

Château-d'Olonne F . . .22 B2
Château-du-Loir F 16 B2
Châteaudun F 17 A3
Châteaugiron F 15 A4
Château-Gontier F 16 B1
Château-Landon F 17 A4
Château-la-Vallière F 16 B2
Château-l'Evêque F 29 A3
Châteaulin F 14 A1
Châteaumeillant F 17 C4
Châteauneuf
  Nièvre F 18 B2
  Saône-et-Loire F 25 A4
Châteauneuf-de-Randon
  F 25 C3
Châteauneuf-d'Ille-et-
  Vilaine F 8 B2
Châteauneuf-du-Faou F . .14 A2
Châteauneuf-du-Pape F . 31 A3
Châteauneuf-en-Thymerais
  F 9 B5
Châteauneuf la-Forêt F . .24 B1
Châteauneuf-le-Rouge
  F 32 B1
Châteauneuf-sur-Charente
  F 23 C3
Châteauneuf-sur-Cher
  F 17 C4
Châteauneuf-sur-Loire
  F 17 B4
Châteauneuf-sur-Sarthe
  F 16 B1
Châteauponsac F 23 B5
Château-Porcien F 11 B4
Châteauredon F 32 A2
Châteaurenard
  Bouches du Rhône F . . 31 B3
  Loiret F 18 B1
Château-Renault F 16 B2
Châteauroux F 17 C3
Châteauroux-les-Alpes
  F 26 C3
Château-Salins F 12 C2
Château-Thierry F 11 B3
Châteauvillain F 19 A3
Châtel F 27 A3
Châtelaillon-Plage F 22 B2
Châtelaudren F 14 A3
Châtel-Censoir F 18 B2
Châtel-de-Neuvre F 24 A3
Châtelet B 7 B4
Châtelguyon F 24 B3
Châtellerault F 23 B4
Châtel-Montagne F 25 A3
Châtel-St Denis CH 20 C1
Châtel-sur-Moselle F 12 C2
Châtelus-Malvaleix F 24 A2
Châtenois F 19 A4
Châtenois-les-Forges F . .20 B1
Châtillon F 27 B4
Châtillon-Coligny F 17 B4
Châtillon-en-Bazois F 18 B2
Châtillon-en-Diois F 26 C2
Châtillon-sur Chalaronne
  F 25 A4
Châtillon-sur-Indre F 17 C3
Châtillon-sur-Loire F 17 B4
Châtillon-sur-Marne F 11 B3
Châtillon-sur-Seine F 18 B3
Châtres F 11 C3
Chauchina E 57 A4
Chaudes-Aigues F 24 C3
Chaudrey F 11 C4
Chauffailles F 25 A4
Chaulnes F 10 B2
Chaument Gistoux B 7 B4
Chaumergy F 19 C4
Chaumont F 19 A4
Chaumont-en-Vexin F 10 B1
Chaumont-Porcien F 11 B4
Chaumont-sur-Aire F 11 C5
Chaumont-sur-Loire F 17 B3
Chaunay F 23 B4
Chauny F 10 B3
Chaussin F 19 C4
Chauvigny F 23 B4
Chavagnes-en-Paillers
  F 22 B2
Chavanges F 11 C4
Chaves P 42 A2
Chavignon F 11 B3
Chazelles-sur-Lyon F 25 B4
Chazey-Bons F 26 B2
Checa E 46 B2
Chef-Boutonne F 23 B3
Cheles E 49 C3
Chella E 53 B3
Chelles F 10 C2
Chelva E 53 B2
Chémery F 17 B3
Chemery-sur-Bar F 11 B4
Chemillé F 16 B1
Chemin F 19 C4
Chénerailles F 24 A2
Cheniménil F 20 A1
Chenonceaux F 17 B3
Chenôve F 19 B3
Chera E 53 B3
Cherasco I 27 C4
Cherbonnières F 23 C3
Cherbourg F 8 A2
Chéroy F 18 A1
Chessy-lès-Pres F 18 A2
Cheste E 53 B3
Chevagnes F 18 C2
Chevanceaux F 23 C3
Chevillon F 11 C5
Chevilly F 17 A3
Chézery-Forens F 26 A2
Chialamberto I 27 B4
Chianale I 27 C4
Chiché F 16 C1
Chiclana de la Frontera
  E 56 B1
Chiclana de Segura E 58 A1
Chillarón de Cuenca E . . .46 B1
Chillarón del Rey E 45 B5
Chilleurs-aux-Bois F 17 A4
Chillón E 50 B3
Chilluevar E 58 B1
Chiloeches E 45 B4
Chimay B 11 A4
Chimeneas E 57 A4
Chinchilla de Monte Aragón
  E 52 C2

Chinchón E 45 B4
Chinon F 16 B2
Chiomonte I 27 B3
Chipiona E 55 C3
Chirac F 30 A2
Chirens F 26 B2
Chirivel E 58 B2
Chissey-en-Morvan F 18 B3
Chiusa di Pésio I 33 A3
Chiva E 53 B3
Chivasso I 27 B4
Cholet F 22 A3
Chomérac F 25 C4
Chorges F 32 A2
Chouilly F 11 B4
Chouto P 48 B2
Chouzy-sur-Cisse F 17 B3
Chozas de Abajo E 36 B1
Chueca E 51 A4
Chur CH 21 C4
Churriana E 57 B3
Churwalden CH 21 C4
Ciadoncha E 37 B3
Ciborro P 48 C2
Cidadelhe P 43 B2
Cidones E 37 C4
Ciempozuelos E 45 B4
Cierp-Gaud F 39 B4
Ciervana E 37 A3
Cieutat F 39 A4
Cieza E 59 A3
Cifuentes E 45 B5
Cigales E 36 C2
Cigliano I 27 B5
Cillas E 46 B2
Cilleros E 43 B3
Cilleruelo de Arriba E 37 C3
Cilleruelo de Bezana E . . .37 B3
Cimalmotto CH 27 A5
Cimanes del Tejar E 35 B5
Cinctorres E 47 B3
Ciney B 7 B5
Cinfães P 42 A1
Cinq-Mars-la-Pile F 16 B2
Cintegabelle F 40 A2
Cintruénigo E 38 B2
Ciperez E 47 B3
Cirat E 47 B3
Cirey-sur-Vezouze F 12 C2
Ciria E 46 A2
Ciriè I 27 B4
Ciry-le-Noble F 18 C3
Cisneros E 36 B2
Cissac-Médoc F 28 A2
Cistérniga E 44 A3
Cistierna E 36 B1
Ciudadela de Menorca
  E 61 B3
Ciudad Real E 51 B4
Ciudad Rodrigo E 43 B3
Ciutadilla E 41 C2
Civray F 23 B4
Cizur Mayor E 38 B2
Clairvaux-les-Lacs F 19 C4
Clamecy F 18 B2
Claye-Souilly F 10 C2
Cléder F 14 A1
Clefmont F 19 A4
Cléguérec F 14 A2
Clelles F 26 C2
Cléon-d'Andran F 25 C4
Cléré-les-Pins F 16 B2
Clères F 9 A5
Clermont F 10 B2
Clermont-en-Argonne F . .11 B4
Clermont-Ferrand F 24 B3
Clermont-l'Hérault F 30 B2
Clerval F 19 B5
Clervaux L 12 A2
Cléry-St André F 17 B3
Clisson F 15 B4
Clohars-Carnoët F 14 B2
Cloyes-sur-le-Loir F 17 C3
Cluis F 17 C3
Cluny F 25 A4
Cluses F 26 A3
Coaña E 35 A4
Cobas E 34 A2
Cobertelade E 45 A5
Cobeta E 46 B1
Cóbreces E 36 A2
Coca E 44 A3
Cocentaina E 53 C3
Codos E 46 A2
Coelhoso P 43 A3
Cofrentes E 53 B2
Cogeces del Monte E 44 A3
Cognac F 23 C3
Cogne I 27 B4
Cogolin F 32 B2
Cogollos de Guadix E 58 B1
Cogollos-Vega E 57 A4
Cogolludo E 45 B4
Coimbra P 42 B1
Coin E 57 B3
Coirós E 34 A2
Colares P 48 C1
Colera E 40 B4
Coligny F 26 A2
Colindres E 37 A3
Collado-Mediano E 45 B3
Collado Villalba E 45 B4
Collanzo E 36 A1
Collat F 25 B3
Coll de Nargó E 41 B2
Collinée F 15 A3
Collobrières F 32 B2
Colmar F 20 A2
Colmars F 32 A2
Colmenar E 57 B3
Colmenar de la Sierra E . .45 B4
Colmenar de Oreja E 45 B4
Colmenar Viejo E 45 B4
Cologne F 29 C3
Colombey-les-Belles F . . .12 C1
Colombey-les-deux-Églises
  F 19 A3
Colombres E 36 A2
Colomera E 57 A4
Colomers E 41 B3
Colomiers F 29 C4
Colònia de Sant Jordi E . .61 B3
Colos P 54 B1
Colunga E 36 A1
Coma-ruga E 41 C2

Combarros E 35 B4
Combeaufontaine F . . .19 B4
Combloux F 26 B3
Combourg F 8 B2
Combronde F 24 B3
Comillas E 36 A2
Comines F 6 B3
Commensacq F 28 B2
Commentry F 24 A2
Commercy F 12 C1
Cómpeta E 57 B4
Compiègne F 10 B2
Comporta P 48 C2
Comps-sur-Artuby F . .32 B2
Conceição P 54 B1
Conches-en-Ouche F . . .9 B4
Concots F 29 B4
Condat F 24 B2
Condé-en-Brie F 11 C3
Condeixa P 42 B1
Condemios de Abajo E .45 A4
Condemios de Arriba E .45 A4
Condé-sur-l'Escaut F . . .7 B3
Condé-sur-Marne F . . .11 B4
Condé-sur-Noireau F . . .8 B3
Condom F 29 C3
Condove I 27 B4
Condrieu F 25 B4
Conflans-sur-Lanterne
  F 19 B5
Confolens F 23 B4
Conforto E 35 A3
Congosto E 35 B4
Congosto de Valdavia E 36 B2
Congostrina E 45 A4
Conil de la Frontera E . .56 B1
Conlie F 16 A1
Conliège F 19 C4
Connantre F 11 C3
Connerré F 16 A2
Connaux F 31 A3
Conques F 24 C2
Conques-sur-Orbiel F . .40 A3
Conquista E 51 B3
Conquista de la Sierra
  E 50 A2
Consenvoye F 11 B5
Consolação P 48 B1
Constancia P 48 B2
Constanco E 34 A2
Constanti E 41 C2
Constantina E 56 A2
Consuegra E 51 A4
Contay F 10 B2
Conthey CH 27 A4
Contis-Plage F 28 B1
Contres F 17 B3
Contrexéville F 19 A4
Conty F 10 B2
Coole F 11 C4
Cope E 59 B3
Coray F 14 A2
Corbeil-Essonnes F . . .10 C2
Corbeny F 11 B3
Corbera E 53 B3
Corbie F 10 B2
Corbigny F 18 B2
Corbion B 11 B4
Corconte E 37 A3
Corcubión E 34 B1
Cordes-sur-Ciel F 29 B4
Córdoba E 50 C3
Cordobilla de Lácara E .49 B4
Corella E 38 B2
Coreses E 44 A2
Corga de Lobão P 42 B1
Coria E 49 B4
Coria del Río E 56 A1
Cório I 27 B4
Coripe E 56 B2
Corlay F 14 A2
Cormainville F 17 A3
Cormatin F 18 C3
Cormeilles F 9 A4
Cormery F 16 B2
Cormoz F 26 A2
Cornago E 38 B1
Cornellana E 35 A4
Cornimont F 20 B1
Cornudella de Montsant
  E 41 C1
Cornudilla E 37 B3
Cornus F 30 B2
Corps F 26 C2
Corps Nuds F 15 B4
Corral de Almaguer E .51 A4
Corral de Ayllon E 45 A4
Corral de Calatrava E . .51 B3
Corrales E 43 A4
Corral-Rubio E 52 C2
Corredoiras E 34 A2
Corrèze F 24 B1
Corrubedo E 34 B1
Corte F 62 A2
Corteconceptión E 55 B3
Corte de Peleas E 49 C4
Cortegaca P 42 B1
Cortegada E 34 B2
Cortegana E 55 B3
Cortemilia I 33 A4
Corte Pinto P 54 B2
Cortes E 38 C2
Cortes de Aragón E . . .47 B3
Cortes de Arenoso E . .47 B3
Cortes de Baza E 58 B2
Cortes de la Frontera E .56 B2
Cortes de Pallás E 53 B3
Cortiçadas P 48 C2
Cortico P 42 A2
Cortijo de Arriba E 51 B3
Cortijos Nuevos E 58 A2
Coruche P 48 C2
Corullón E 35 B4
Corvera E 59 B3
Coslada E 45 B4
Cosne-Cours-sur-Loire
  F 18 B1
Cosne d'Allier F 17 C4
Cospeito E 34 A3
Cossato I 27 B5
Cossaye F 18 C2
Cossé-le-Vivien F 15 B5
Cossonay CH 19 C5
Costa da Caparica P . .48 C1

Costa de Santo André
  P 54 A1
Costa Nova P. 42 B1
Costaros F 25 C3
Costigliole d'Asti I 27 C5
Costigliole Saluzzo I . . .33 A3
Coublanc F 19 B4
Couches F 18 C3
Couço P 48 C2
Coucouron F 25 C3
Coucy-le-Château-Auffrique
  F 10 B3
Couëron F 15 B4
Couflens F 40 B2
Couhé F 23 B4
Couiza F 40 B3
Coulanges F 18 C2
Coulanges-la-Vineuse F 18 B2
Coulanges-sur-Yonne F 18 B2
Coulmier-le-Sec F 18 C1
Coulmier-le-Sec F 18 B3
Coulombiers F 10 C3
Coulonges-sur-l'Autize
  F 22 B3
Coulounieix-Chamiers
  F 29 A3
Coupéville F 11 C4
Couptrain F 9 B3
Coura P 34 C2
Courcelles B 7 B4
Courcelles-Chaussy F . .12 B2
Courchevel F 26 B3
Cour-Cheverny F 17 B3
Courcôme F 23 C4
Courçon F 22 B3
Cour-et-Buis F 25 B4
Courgenay CH 20 B2
Courmayeur I 27 B3
Courniou F 30 B1
Cournon-d'Auvergne F .24 B3
Cournonterral F 30 B2
Courpière F 25 B3
Coursan F 30 B2
Courseulles-sur-Mer F . .9 A3
Cours-la-Ville F 25 A4
Courson-les-Carrières
  F 18 B2
Courtalain F 17 A3
Courtenay F 18 A2
Courtomer F 9 B4
Courville
  Eure-et-Loire F 9 B5
  Marne F 11 B3
Coussac-Bonneval F . .23 C5
Coutances F 8 A2
Couterne F 9 B3
Coutras F 28 A2
Couvet CH 20 C1
Couvin B 11 A4
Couzon F 18 C2
Covadonga E 36 A1
Covaleda E 37 C4
Covarrubias E 37 B3
Covas E 42 A1
Covilhã P 42 B2
Cox F 29 C4
Cozes F 22 C3
Cozzano F 62 B2
Craon F 15 B5
Craonne F 11 B3
Crápone F 25 B4
Craponne-sur-Arzon F .25 B3
Crato P 49 B3
Crecente E 34 B2
Crèches-sur-Saône F . .25 A4
Crécy-en-Ponthieu F . . .6 B1
Crécy-la-Chapelle F . . .10 C2
Crécy-sur-Serre F 11 B3
Creil F 10 B2
Creissels F 30 A2
Cremeaux F 25 B3
Crémenes E 36 B1
Crémieu F 26 B2
Creney F 11 C4
Créon F 28 B2
Crépey F 12 C1
Crépy F 11 B3
Crépy-en-Valois F 10 B2
Crescentino I 27 B5
Crespos E 44 B3
Cressensac F 29 A4
Cressia F 19 C4
Crest F 25 C5
Cresta CH 21 C4
Créteil F 10 C2
Creully F 8 A3
Creutzwald F 12 B2
Crèvecoeur-le-Grand F .10 B2
Crevillente E 59 A4
Crévola d'Ossola I 27 A5
Criales E 37 B3
Criel-sur-Mer F 10 A1
Crillon F 10 B1
Cripán E 37 B4
Criquetot-l'Esneval F . . .9 A4
Crissolo I 27 C4
Cristóbal E 43 B4
Crocq F 24 B2
Crodo I 27 A5
Cronat F 18 C2
Crouy F 10 B3
Crozon F 14 A1
Cruas F 25 C4
Cruis F 32 A1
Cruseilles F 26 A3
Cruz de Incio E 35 B3
Cuacos de Yuste E 44 B2
Cualedro E 34 C3
Cuanca de Campos E . .36 B1
Cuba P 54 A2
Cubel E 46 A2
Cubelles E 41 C2
Cubillos E 37 C4
Cubillos del Sil E 35 B4
Cubjac F 29 A3
Cubo de la Solana E . . .46 A1
Cucuron F 31 B4
Cudillero E 35 A4
Cuéllar E 45 A3
Cuenca E 46 B1
Cuers F 32 B2
Cuerva E 51 A3
Cueva de Agreda E . . .38 C2
Cuevas Bajas E 57 A3

Cuevas del Almanzora
  E 58 B3
Cuevas del Becerro E . .56 B2
Cuevas del Campo E . .58 B2
Cuevas del Valle E 44 B2
Cuevas de San Clemente
  E 37 B3
Cuevas de San Marcos
  E 57 A3
Cuges-les-Pins F 32 B1
Cugnaux F 29 C4
Cuinzier F 25 A4
Cuiseaux F 19 C4
Cuisery F 19 C4
Culan F 17 C4
Culemborg NL 7 A5
Cúllar E 58 B2
Cullera E 53 B3
Cully CH 20 C1
Culoz F 26 B2
Cumbres de San Bartolomé
  E 55 A3
Cumbres Mayores E . . .55 A3
Cumiana I 27 C4
Cúneo I 33 A3
Cunlhat F 25 B3
Cuntis E 34 B2
Cuorgnè I 27 B4
Currelos E 34 B3
Curtis E 34 A2
Curtis Santa Eulalia E . .34 A2
Cusset F 25 A3
Cussy-les-Forges F . . .18 B3
Custines F 12 C2
Cutanda E 46 B2
Cuts F 10 B3
Cuvilly F 10 B2

D

Dabo F 12 C3
Dagmersellen CH 20 B3
Dahn D 13 B3
Daimiel E 51 A4
Dalaas A 21 B5
Dalheim L 12 B2
Dalias E 58 C2
Daluis F 32 A2
Damazan F 29 B3
Damgan F 15 B3
Dammarie-les-Lys F . . .10 C2
Dammartin-en-Goële F .10 B2
Dampierre F 19 B4
Dampierre-sur-Salon F .19 B4
Damüls A 21 B4
Damville F 9 B5
Damvillers F 12 B1
Dangers F 9 B5
Dangé-St Romain F . . .16 C2
Dangeul F 9 B4
Danjoutin F 20 B1
Dannemarie F 20 B2
Daoulas F 14 A1
Darmstadt D 13 B4
Darney F 19 A5
Daroca E 46 A2
Darque F 42 A1
Daumeray F 16 B1
Davos CH 21 C4
Dax F 28 C1
Deauville F 9 A4
Deba E 37 A4
Decazeville F 30 A1
Decize F 18 C2
Degaña E 35 B4
Dego I 33 A4
Degolados P 49 B3
De Haan B 6 A3
Dehesas de Guadix E . .58 B3
Dehesas Viejas E 57 A4
Deia E 60 B2
Deinze B 7 B3
Deleitosa E 50 A2
Delémont CH 20 B2
Delle F 20 B2
Delme F 12 C2
Demigny F 19 C3
Demonte I 33 A3
Denain F 6 B3
Dender-monde B 7 A4
Denia E 53 C4
Déols F 17 C3
De Panne B 6 A2
Derval F 15 B4
Desana I 27 B5
Descartes F 16 C2
Destriana E 35 B4
Desvres F 6 B1
Dettingen D 21 B4
Dettwiller F 13 C3
Deza E 46 A1
Diano d'Alba I 27 C5
Diano Marina I 33 B4
Die F 26 C2
Diebling F 12 B2
Dieburg D 13 B4
Diego del Carpio E 44 B2
Diekirch L 12 B2
Diélette F 8 A2
Diémoz F 26 B2
Diepenbeck B 7 B5
Dieppe F 9 A5
Diest B 7 B5
Dietikon CH 20 B3
Dietzenbach D 13 A4
Dieue-sur-Meuse F . . .12 B1
Dieulefit F 31 A4
Dieulouard F 12 C2
Dieuze F 12 C2
Diezma E 57 A4
Differdange L 12 B1
Dignac F 23 C4
Digne-les-Bains F 32 A2
Digny F 9 B5
Dijon F 19 B4
Diksmuide B 6 A2
Dilar E 57 A4
Dillingen D 12 B2
Dinan F 15 A3
Dinant B 7 B4
Dinard F 15 A3
Diou F 18 C2
Dirksland NL 7 A4
Disentis CH 21 C3

Ditzingen D 13 C5
Dives-sur-Mer F 9 A3
Divion F 6 B2
Divonne les Bains F . . .26 A3
Dixmont F 18 A2
Dizy-le-Gros F 11 B4
Doade E 35 B3
Dobro E 37 B3
Dogliani I 33 A3
Dogueno P 54 B2
Doische B 11 A4
Dois Portos P 48 B1
Dolancourt F 18 A3
Dolceácqua I 33 B3
Dol-de-Bretagne F 8 B2
Dole F 19 B4
Dollot F 18 A2
Dolores E 59 A4
Domaine F 12 C2
Domène F 26 B2
Domérat F 24 A2
Domfessel F 12 C3
Domfront F 8 B3
Domfront-en-Champagne
  F 16 A2
Domingão P 48 B2
Domingo Pérez
  Granada E 57 A4
  Toledo E 44 C3
Dommartin F 11 C4
Dommartin-le-Franc F . .11 C4
Domme F 29 B4
Domodóssola I 27 A5
Dompaire F 19 A5
Dompierre-du-Chemin F .8 B2
Dompierre-sur-Besbre
  F 18 C2
Dompierre-sur-Mer F . .22 B2
Domrémy-la-Pucelle F .12 C1
Domsure F 26 A2
Donado E 35 B4
Don Alvaro E 49 C4
Don Benito E 50 B2
Donestebe-Santesteban
  E 38 A2
Donzenac F 29 A4
Donzère F 31 A3
Donzy F 18 B2
Dor E 34 A1
Dordrecht NL 7 A4
Dormans F 11 B3
Dornbirn A 21 B4
Dornecy F 18 B2
Dornes F 18 C2
Dornhan D 13 C4
Dortan F 26 A2
Dos Aguas E 53 B3
Dosbarrios E 45 C4
Dos Hermanas E 56 A2
Dos-Torres E 50 B3
Dottignies B 6 B3
Döttingen CH 20 B3
Douai F 6 B3
Douarnenez F 14 A1
Douchy F 18 B2
Douchy-les-Mines F . . .6 B3
Doucier F 19 C4
Doudeville F 9 A4
Doué-la-Fontaine F . . .16 B1
Doulaincourt-Saucourt
  F 11 C5
Doulevant-le-Château F 11 C4
Doullens F 10 A2
Dour B 7 B3
Dourdan F 10 C2
Dourgne F 40 A3
Dournazac F 23 C4
Douro Calvo P 42 B2
Douvaine F 26 A3
Douvres-la-Délivrande F .9 A3
Douzy F 11 B5
Doyet F 24 A2
Dozule F 9 A3
Draguignan F 32 B2
Dreieich D 13 A4
Dreisen D 13 B4
Dreux F 9 B5
Dronero I 33 A3
Droué F 17 A3
Drulingen F 12 C3
Drunen NL 7 A5
Duas Igrejas P 43 A3
Dübendorf CH 21 B3
Ducey F 8 B2
Duclair F 9 A4
Dueñas E 36 C2
Duffel B 7 A4
Dugny-sur-Meuse F . . .12 B1
Duingt F 26 B3
Dun-le-Palestel F 24 A1
Dun-les-Places F 18 B3
Dunningen D 21 A3
Dun-sur-Auron F 17 C4
Dun-sur-Meuse F 11 B5
Durach D 21 B5
Durana E 37 B4
Durance F 28 B3
Durango E 37 A4
Duras F 28 B3
Durban-Corbières F . . .40 B3
Dürbheim D 21 A3
Durbuy B 7 B5
Dúrcal E 57 B4
Durtol F 24 B3
Durrö I 33 C4
Dürrboden CH 21 C4
Dürrenboden CH 21 C3
Durtal F 16 B1
Dusslingen D 13 C5

E

Ea E 37 A4
Eaux-Bonnes F 39 B3
Eauze F 28 C3
Eberbach D 13 B4

Ebnat-Kappel CH 21 B4
Ebreuil F 24 A3
Echallens CH. 20 C1
Echauri E 38 B2
Echiré F 22 B3
Echirolles F 26 B2
Echourgnac F 28 A3
Echternach L 12 B2
Ecija E 56 A2
Eclaron F 11 C4
Écommoy F 16 B2
Écouché F 9 B3
Ecouis F 10 B1
Écueillé F 17 B3
Edenkoben D. 13 B4
Edesheim D 13 B4
Eekloo B 7 A3
Eersel NL 7 A5
Effiat F 24 A3
Egg
  A 21 B4
  D 21 A5
Éghezée B 7 B4
Égletons F 24 B2
Eglisau CH 21 B3
Égliseneuve-d'Entraigues
  F 24 B2
Eglofs D 21 B4
Eguilles F 31 B4
Eguilly-sous-Bois F . . .18 A3
Éguzon-Chantôme F . . .17 C3
Ehrang D 12 B2
Eibar E 37 A4
Eindhoven NL 7 A5
Einsiedeln CH 21 B3
Einville-au-Jard F 12 C2
Eisenberg D 13 B4
Eivissa = Ibiza E 60 C1
Eixo P 42 B1
Ejea de los Caballeros
  E 38 B2
Ejulve E 47 B3
Eke B 7 B3
El Alamo
  Madrid E 45 B4
  Sevilla E 55 B3
El Algar E 59 B4
El Almendro E 55 B2
El Alquián E 58 C2
El Arahal E 56 A2
El Arenal E 44 B2
El Arguellite E 58 A2
El Astillero E 37 A3
El Ballestero E 52 C1
El Barco de Ávila E 44 B2
El Berrón E 36 A1
El Berrueco E 45 B3
El Bodón E 43 B3
El Bonillo E 52 C1
El Bosque E 56 B2
El Bullaque E 51 A3
El Burgo E 56 B3
El Burgo de Ebro E . . .47 A3
El Burgo de Osma E . . .45 A4
El Burgo Ranero E 36 B1
El Buste E 38 C2
El Cabaco E 43 B3
El Callejo E 37 A3
El Campillo E 55 B3
El Campillo de la Jara E .50 A2
El Cañavete E 52 B1
El Carpio E 51 C3
El Carpio de Tajo E . . .44 C3
El Casar E 45 B4
El Casar de Escalona E .44 B3
El Castillo de las Guardas
  E 55 B3
El Centenillo E 51 B4
El Cerro E 43 B4
El Cerro de Andévalo E .55 B3
Elche E 59 A4
Elche de la Sierra E . . .52 C1
El Comenar E 56 B2
El Coronil E 56 A2
El Crucero E 35 A4
El Cubo de Tierra del Vino
  E 43 A4
El Cuervo E 56 B1
Elda E 53 C3
El Ejido E 58 C2
El Escorial E 45 B3
El Espinar E 45 B3
El Frago E 38 B3
El Franco E 35 A4
El Frasno E 46 A2
El Garrobo E 55 B3
El Gastor E 56 B2
Elgoibar E 37 A4
El Gordo E 44 C2
El Grado E 39 B4
El Granado E 55 B2
El Grao de Castelló E . .53 B4
El Grau E 53 C3
El Higuera E 57 A3
El Hijate E 58 B2
El Hontanar E 46 B2
El Hoyo E 51 B4
Elizondo E 38 A2
Ellezelles B 7 B3
Elm CH 21 C4
El Madroño E 55 B3
El Maillo E 43 B3
El Masnou E 41 C3
El Mirón E 44 B2
El Molar E 45 B4
El Molinillo E 51 A3
El Morell E 41 C2
Elmstein D 13 B3
El Muyo E 45 A4
El Olmo E 45 A4
Elorrio E 37 A4
Éloyes F 19 A5
El Palo E 57 B3
El Pardo E 45 B4
El Payo E 43 B3
El Pedernoso E 52 B1
El Pedroso E 56 A2
El Peral E 52 B2
El Perelló
  Tarragona E 47 C4
  Valencia E 53 B3
El Picazo E 52 B1
El Pinell de Bray E 47 A4

El Piñero E 44 A2
El Pla de Santa Maria E .41 C2
El Pobo E 47 B3
El Pobo de Dueñas E . .46 B2
El Pont d'Armentera E . .41 C2
El Port de la Selva E . . .41 B4
El Port de Llançà E 40 B4
El Port de Sagunt E . . .53 B3
El Prat de Llobregat E . .41 C3
El Provencio E 52 B1
El Puente E 37 A3
El Puente del Arzobispo
  E 44 C2
El Puerto E 35 A4
El Puerto de Santa María
  E 56 B1
El Real de la Jara E . . .55 B3
El Real de San Vicente
  E 44 B3
El Robledo E 51 A3
El Rocio E 55 B3
El Rompido E 55 B3
El Ronquillo E 55 B3
El Royo E 37 C4
El Rubio E 56 A3
El Sabinar E 58 A2
El Saler E 53 B3
El Salobral E 52 C2
El Saucejo E 56 A2
Els Castells E 41 B2
Elsenfeld D 13 B5
El Serrat AND. 40 B2
El Temple E 38 C3
El Tiemblo E 44 B3
El Toboso E 51 A5
El Tormillo E 39 C3
El Torno E 43 B4
Eltville D 13 A4
El Valle de las Casas E .36 B1
Elvas P 49 C3
El Vellón E 45 B4
Elven F 15 B3
El Vendrell E 41 C2
El Villar de Arnedo E . .38 B1
El Viso E 50 B3
El Viso del Alcor E 56 A2
Elzach D 20 A3
Embrun F 32 A2
Embún E 38 B3
Emmen CH 20 B3
Emmendingen D 20 A2
Encamp AND 40 B2
Encarnaçao P 48 C1
Encinas de Abajo E . . .44 B2
Encinas de Esgueva E . .36 C2
Encinasola E 55 A3
Encinas Reales E 57 A3
Encio E 37 B3
Endingen D 20 A2
Endrinal E 43 B4
Engelberg CH 20 C3
Engen D 21 B3
Enghien B 7 B4
Enguera E 53 C3
Enguidanos E 52 B2
Enkenbach D. 13 B3
Ennezat F 24 B3
Ensisheim F 20 B2
Entlebuch CH 20 B3
Entrácque I 33 A3
Entradas P 54 B1
Entrains-sur-Nohain F . .18 B2
Entrambasaguas E 37 A3
Entrambasmestas E . . .37 A3
Entraygues-sur-Truyère
  F 24 C2
Entre-os-Rios P 42 A1
Entrevaux F 32 B2
Entrin Bajo E 49 C4
Entroncamento P 48 B2
Entzheim F 13 C3
Envermeu F 9 A5
Enzklösterle D 13 C4
Épagny F 10 B3
Epalinges CH 20 C1
Epannes F 22 B3
Épernay F 11 B3
Épernon F 10 C1
Epfig F 13 C3
Épierre F 26 B3
Épila E 46 A2
Épinac F 18 C3
Épinal F 19 A5
Epoisses F 18 B3
Eppenbrunn D 13 B3
Eppingen D 13 B4
Erbach D 13 B4
Erbalunga F 62 A2
Ericeira P 48 C1
Eriswil CH 20 B2
Erla E 38 B3
Erli I 33 A4
Ermenonville F 10 B2
Ermezinde P 42 A1
Ermidas P 54 A1
Ernée F 8 B3
Erolzheim D 21 A5
Erquy F 15 A3
Erra P 48 C2
Erratzu E 38 A2
Erro E 38 B2
Ersa F 62 A2
Erstein F 13 C3
Erstfeld CH 21 C3
Ertingen D 21 A4
Ervedal
  Coimbra P 42 B1
  Portalegre P. 48 B3
Ervidel P 54 B1
Ervy-le-Châtel F 18 A2
Esbly F 10 C2
Escacena del Campo E .55 B3
Escairón E 34 B3
Escalada E 37 B3
Escalante E 37 A3
Escalona E 44 B3
Escalona del Prado E . .45 A3
Escalonilla E 44 C3
Escalos de Baixo P 49 B3
Escalos de Cima P 49 B3
Escamilla E 46 B1

Es Caná E 60 B1
Escañuela E 51 C3
Es Castell E 61 B4
Escatrón E 47 A3
Eschach D 21 B4
Eschenz CH 21 B3
Esch-sur-Alzette L 12 B1
Esch-sur-Sûre L 12 B1
Escobasa de Almazán
E 46 A1
Escoeuilles F 6 B1
Escombreras E 59 B4
Escos F 38 A2
Escource F 28 B1
Escragnolles F 32 B2
Escurial E 50 A2
Escurial de la Sierra E 43 B4
Esgos E 34 B3
Eslava E 38 B2
Eslida E 53 B3
Es Mercadal E 61 B4
Es Migjorn Gran E 61 B4
Espalion F 30 A1
Esparragalejo E 49 C4
Esparragosa del Caudillo
E 50 B2
Esparragossa de la Serena
E 50 B2
Esparreguera E 41 C2
Esparron F 32 B1
Espejo
Alava E 37 B3
Córdoba E 57 A3
Espeluche F 31 A3
Espeluy E 51 B4
Espera E 56 B2
Esperança P 49 B3
Espéraza F 40 B3
Espiel E 50 B2
Espinama E 36 A2
Espiñaredo E 34 A3
Espinasses F 32 A2
Espinelves E 41 C3
Espinhal P 48 A2
Espinho P 42 A1
Espinilla E 36 A2
Espinosa de Cerrato E 37 C3
Espinosa de los Monteros
E 37 A3
Espinoso del Rey E 50 A3
Espirito Santo P 54 B2
Espluga de Francolí E 41 C2
Esplús E 39 C4
Espolla E 40 B3
Esporles E 60 B2
Es Port d'Alcúdia E 61 B3
Esposende P 42 A1
Espot E 40 B2
Es Pujols E 60 C1
Esquedas E 39 B3
Esquivias E 45 B4
Essay F 9 B4
Essen B 7 A4
Essertaux F 10 B2
Es Soleràs E 47 A4
Essoyes F 18 A3
Estacas E 34 B2
Estadilla E 39 B4
Estagel F 40 B3
Estaires F 6 B2
Estang F 28 C2
Estarreja P 42 B1
Estartit E 41 B4
Estavayer-le-Lac CH 20 C1
Esteiro E 34 A2
Estela P 42 A1
Estella E 38 B1
Estellencs E 60 B2
Estepa E 56 A3
Estépar E 37 B3
Estepona E 56 B2
Esternay F 11 C3
Esterri d'Aneu E 40 B2
Estissac F 18 A2
Estivadas E 34 B3
Estivareilles F 24 A2
Estivella E 53 B3
Estói P 54 B2
Estopiñán E 39 C4
Estoril P 48 C1
Estoublon F 32 B2
Estrée-Blanche F 6 B2
Estrées-St Denis F 10 B2
Estrela P 49 C3
Estremera E 45 B4
Estremoz P 49 C3
Esyres F 16 B2
Etables-sur-Mer F 14 A3
Étain F 12 B1
Étalans F 19 B5
Etalle B 12 B1
Étampes F 10 C2
Etang-sur-Arroux F 18 C3
Étaples F 6 B1
Etauliers F 28 A2
Etoges F 11 C3
Etréaupont F 11 B3
Étréchy F 10 C2
Étrépagny F 10 B1
Étretat F 9 A4
Étroeungt F 11 A3
Étroubles I 27 B4
Ettelbruck L 12 B2
Etten NL 7 A4
Ettenheim D 20 A2
Ettlingen D 13 C4
Etuz F 19 B4
Etxarri-Aranatz E 38 B1
Eu F 10 A1
Eulate E 38 B1
Europoort NL 7 A4
Évaux-les-Bains F 24 A2
Evergem B 7 A3
Évian-les-Bains F 26 A3
Evisa F 62 A1
Evolène CH 27 A4
Évora P 48 C3
Evoramonte P 49 C3
Evran F 15 A4
Evrecy F 9 A3
Évreux F 9 A5
Évron F 16 A1
Évry F 10 C2
Excideuil F 23 C5
Exmes F 9 B4
Eyguians F 32 A1
Eyguières F 31 B4
Eygurande F 24 B2
Eylie F 39 B4
Eymet F 29 B3
Eymoutiers F 24 B1
Ezaro E 34 B1
Ezcaray E 37 B4
Ezcároz E 38 B2
Ezmoriz P 42 B1

F

Fabara E 47 A4
Fabero E 35 B4
Fabrègues F 30 B2
Facha P 42 A1
Facinas E 56 B2
Fadagosa P 49 B3
Fafe P 42 A1
Fagnières F 11 C4
Faido CH 21 C3
Fains-Véel F 11 C5
Falaise F 9 B3
Falces E 38 B2
Falset E 41 C1
Fanjeaux F 40 A3
Faramontanos de Tábara
E 43 A4
Fara Novarese I 27 B5
Farasdues E 38 B2
Fariza E 43 A3
Farlete E 47 A3
Faro P 54 B2
Fátima P 48 B2
Faucogney-et-la-Mer F 19 B5
Fauguerolles F 28 B3
Faulquemont F 12 B2
Fauquembergues F 6 B2
Fauville-en-Caux F 9 A4
Fauvillers B 12 B1
Favara E 53 B3
Faverges F 26 B3
Faverney F 19 B5
Fay-aux-Loges F 17 B4
Fayence F 32 B2
Fayet F 30 B1
Fayl-Billot F 19 B4
Fayón E 47 A4
Fécamp F 9 A4
Felanitx E 61 B3
Feldkirch A 21 B4
Felgueiras P 42 A1
Félix E 58 C2
Felizzano I 27 C5
Felletin F 24 B2
Fene E 34 A2
Fenestrelle I 27 B4
Fénétrange F 12 C3
Feneu F 16 B1
Fère-Champenoise F 11 C3
Fère-en-Tardenois F 11 B3
Feria E 49 C4
Fermil P 42 A2
Fermoselle E 43 A3
Fernancabellero E 51 A4
Fernán Nuñéz E 57 A3
Fernán Peréz E 58 C2
Fernão Ferro P 48 C1
Fernay-Voltaire F 26 A3
Ferpécle CH 27 A4
Ferrals-les-Corbières F 40 A3
Ferreira E 35 A3
Ferreira do Alentejo P 54 A1
Ferreira do Zêzere P 48 B2
Ferreras de Abajo E 35 C4
Ferreras de Arriba E 35 C4
Ferreries E 61 B4
Ferreruela E 46 A2
Ferreruela de Tabara E 43 A3
Ferret CH 27 B4
Ferrette F 20 B2
Ferrière-la-Grande F 7 B3
Ferrières
Hautes-Pyrénées F 39 A3
Loiret F 17 A4
Oise F 10 B2
Ferrières-sur-Sichon F 25 A3
Ferrol E 34 A2
Festieux F 11 B3
Feuges F 11 C4
Feuquières F 10 B1
Feurs F 25 B4
Fiano I 27 B4
Fiesch CH 27 A5
Figari F 62 B2
Figeac F 24 C2
Figols E 39 B4
Figueira da Foz P 42 B1
Figueira de Castelo Rodrigo
P 43 B3
Figueira dos Caveleiros
P 54 A1
Figueiredo P 48 B3
Figueiredo de Alva P 42 B2
Figueiródos Vinhos P 48 B2
Figueres E 41 B3
Figueroles E 47 B3
Figueruela de Arriba E 35 C4
Filisur CH 21 C4
Finale Lígure I 33 A4
Fiñana E 58 B2
Firmi F 30 A1
Firminy F 25 B4
Fischbach D 13 B3
Fischen D 21 B5
Fismes F 11 B3
Fisterra E 34 B1
Fitero E 38 B2
Flaça E 41 B3
Flace F 25 A4
Flaine F 26 A3
Flamatt CH 20 C2
Flassans-sur-Issole F 32 B2
Flavigny-sur-Moselle F 12 C2
Flavy-le-Martel F 10 B3
Flawil CH 21 B4
Flayosc F 32 B2
Flehingen D 13 B4
Flers F 8 B3
Fleurance F 29 C3
Fleuré F 23 B4
Fleurier CH 19 C5
Fleurus B 7 B4
Fleury
Hérault F 30 B2
Yonne F 18 B2
Fleury-les-Aubrais F 17 B3
Fleury-sur-Andelle F 9 A5
Fleury-sur-Orne F 9 A3
Flims CH 21 C4
Flines-lèz-Raches F 6 B3
Flirey F 12 C1
Flix E 47 A4
Flixecourt F 10 A2
Flize F 11 B4
Flobecq B 7 B3
Flogny-la-Chapelle F 18 B2
Flonheim D 13 B4
Florac F 30 A2
Floreffe B 7 B4
Florennes B 7 B4
Florensac F 30 B2
Florentin F 29 C5
Florenville B 11 B5
Flores de Avila E 44 B2
Flörsheim D 13 A4
Flühli CH 20 C3
Flumet F 26 B3
Flums CH 21 B4
Foix F 40 B2
Folelli F 62 A2
Folgosinho P 42 B2
Folgoso de la Ribera E 35 B4
Folgoso do Courel E 35 B3
Foncebadón E 35 B4
Foncine-le-Bas F 19 C5
Fondevila E 34 C2
Fonelas E 58 B1
Fonfría
Teruel E 46 B2
Zamora E 43 A3
Fontaine F 11 C4
Fontainebleau F 10 C2
Fontaine de Vaucluse F 31 B4
Fontaine-Française F 19 B4
Fontaine-le-Dun F 9 A4
Fontan F 33 A3
Fontanarejo E 51 A3
Fontane I 33 A3
Fontanières F 24 A2
Fontanosas E 51 B3
Fontenay-le-Comte F 22 B3
Fontenay-Trésigny F 10 C2
Fontevrault-l'Abbaye F 16 B2
Fontiveros E 44 B3
Fontoy F 12 B1
Fontpédrouse F 40 B3
Font-Romeu F 40 B3
Fonz E 39 B4
Forbach
D 13 C4
F 12 B2
Forcall E 47 B3
Forcalquier F 32 B1
Forcarei E 34 B2
Forges-les-Eaux F 10 B1
Forjães P 42 A1
Formazza I 27 A5
Formerie F 10 B1
Formigliana I 27 B5
Formiguères F 40 B3
Fornalutx E 60 B2
Fornells E 61 A4
Fornelos de Montes E 34 B2
Fornes E 57 B4
Forno
Piemonte I 27 B4
Piemonte I 27 B5
Forno Alpi-Gráie I 27 B4
Fornos de Algodres P 42 B2
Foros do Arrão P 48 B2
Forriolo E 34 B3
Fortanete E 47 B3
Fort-Mahon-Plage F 6 B1
Fortuna E 59 A3
Fos F 39 B4
Fossano I 33 A3
Fosse-la-Ville B 7 B4
Fos-sur-Mer F 31 B3
Fouchères F 18 A3
Fouesnant F 14 B1
Foug F 12 C1
Fougères F 8 B2
Fougerolles F 19 B5
Foulain F 19 A4
Fouras F 22 C2
Fourchambault F 18 B2
Fourmies F 11 A4
Fournels F 24 C3
Fournols F 25 B3
Fourques F 40 B3
Fourquevaux F 40 A2
Fours F 18 C2
Foz E 35 A3
Foz do Arelho P 48 B1
Foz do Giraldo P 49 B3
Frabosa Soprana I 33 A3
Frades de la Sierra E 43 B4
Fraga E 47 A4
Frailes E 57 A4
Fraire B 7 B4
Fraize F 20 A1
França P 35 C4
Francaltroff F 12 C2
Francescas F 29 B3
Franco P 42 A2
Francos E 45 A4
Frangy F 26 A2
Frankenthal D 13 B4
Frasne F 19 C5
Frasnes-lez-Anvaing B 7 B3
Frasseto F 62 B2
Frastanz A 21 B4
Fratel P 49 B3
Frauenfeld CH 21 B3
Frayssinet F 29 B4
Frayssinet-le-Gélat F 29 B4
Frechas P 43 A2
Frechilla E 36 B2
Fregenal de la Sierra E 55 A3
Freiburg D 20 B2
Freisen D 12 B3
Freixedas P 43 B2
Freixo de Espada à Cinta
P 43 A3
Fréjus F 32 B2
Fresnay-sur-Sarthe F 9 B4
Fresneda de la Sierra E 46 B1
Fresneda de la Sierra Tiron
E 37 B3
Fresnedillas E 45 B3
Fresnes-en-Woevre F 12 B1
Fresne-St Mamès F 19 B4
Fresno Alhandiga E 44 B2
Fresno de la Ribera E 44 A2
Fresno de la Vega E 36 B1
Fresno de Sayago E 43 A4
Fresnoy-Folny F 10 B1
Fresnoy-le-Grand F 11 B3
Fressenville F 10 A1
Fréteval F 17 B3
Fretigney F 19 B4
Freudenstadt D 13 C4
Freux B 12 B1
Frévent F 6 B2
Freyming-Merlebach F 12 B2
Frias de Albarracin E 46 B2
Fribourg CH 20 C2
Frick CH 20 B3
Friedrichshafen D 21 B4
Friesenheim D 13 C3
Frigiliana E 57 B4
Friol E 34 A3
Froges F 26 B2
Froissy F 10 B2
Frómista E 36 B2
Fronsac F 28 B2
Front I 27 B4
Fronteira P 49 B3
Frontenay-Rohan-Rohan
F 22 B3
Frontignan F 30 B2
Fronton F 29 C4
Frouard F 12 C2
Fruges F 6 B2
Frutigen CH 20 C2
Fuencaliente
Ciudad Real E 51 A4
Ciudad Real E 51 B3
Fuencemillán E 45 B4
Fuendejalón E 38 C2
Fuengirola E 57 B3
Fuenlabrada E 45 B4
Fuenlabrada de los Montes
E 50 A3
Fuensalida E 45 B3
Fuensanta E 58 B3
Fuensanta de Martos E 57 A4
Fuente-Alamo E 52 C2
Fuente-Álamo de Murcia
E 59 B3
Fuentealbilla E 52 B2
Fuente al Olmo de Iscar
E 44 A3
Fuentecén E 45 A4
Fuente Dé E 36 A2
Fuente de Cantos E 49 C4
Fuente del Arco E 50 B2
Fuente del Conde E 57 A3
Fuente del Maestre E 49 C4
Fuente de Santa Cruz E 44 A3
Fuente el Fresno E 51 A4
Fuente el Saz de Jarama
E 45 B4
Fuente el Sol E 44 A3
Fuenteguinaldo E 43 B3
Fuentelapeña E 44 A2
Fuentelcésped E 45 A4
Fuentelespino de Haro
E 52 B1
Fuentelespino de Moya
E 52 B2
Fuentenovilla E 45 B4
Fuente Obejuna E 50 B2
Fuente Palmera E 56 A2
Fuentepelayo E 45 A3
Fuentepinilla E 45 A5
Fuenterroble de Salvatierra
E 44 B2
Fuenterrobles E 52 B2
Fuentes E 52 B1
Fuentesauco E 45 A3
Fuentesaúco E 44 A2
Fuentes de Andalucía E 56 A2
Fuentes de Ebro E 47 A3
Fuentes de Jiloca E 46 A2
Fuentes de la Alcarria E 45 B5
Fuentes de León E 55 A3
Fuentes de Nava E 36 B2
Fuentes de Oñoro E 43 B3
Fuentes de Ropel E 36 B1
Fuentespalda E 47 B4
Fuentespina E 45 A4
Fuente-Tójar E 57 A3
Fuente Vaqueros E 57 A4
Fuentidueña E 45 A4
Fuentidueña de Tajo E 45 B4
Fuerte del Rey E 51 C4
Fully CH 27 A4
Fumay F 11 B4
Fumel F 29 B3
Fundão P 42 B2
Furadouro P 42 B1
Fürth D 13 B4
Furtwangen D 20 A3
Fusio CH 21 C3
Fustiñana E 38 B2

G

Gabaldón E 52 B2
Gabarret F 28 C2
Gabriac F 30 A1
Gaby I 27 B4
Gacé F 9 B4
Gadmen CH 20 C3
Gádor E 58 C2
Gael F 15 A3
Gafanhoeira P 48 C2
Gaggenau D 13 C4
Gaillac F 29 C4
Gaillefontaine F 10 B1
Gaillon F 9 A5
Gaja-la-Selve F 40 A2
Gajanejos E 45 B5
Galan F 39 A4
Galapagar E 45 B3
Galápagos E 45 B4
Galaroza E 55 B3
Galdakao E 37 A4
Galende E 35 B4
Galera E 58 B2
Galéria F 62 A1
Galgon F 28 B2
Galices P 42 B2
Galinduste E 44 B2
Galisteo E 49 B4
Gallardon F 10 C1
Gallegos de Argañán E 43 B3
Gallegos del Solmirón
E 44 B2
Galleguillos de Campos
E 36 B1
Gallocanta E 46 B2
Gallur E 38 C2
Galtür A 21 C5
Galve de Sorbe E 45 A4
Galveias P 48 B2
Gálvez E 51 A3
Gamaches F 10 B1
Gammertingen D 21 A4
Gams CH 21 B4
Gan F 39 A3
Gáname E 43 A3
Gandarela P 42 A1
Gandesa E 47 A4
Gandía E 53 C3
Ganges F 30 B2
Gannat F 24 A3
Gannay-sur-Loire F 18 C2
Gap F 32 A2
Garaballa E 52 B2
Garbayuela E 50 A2
Garciaz E 50 A2
Garcihernández E 44 B2
Garcillán E 45 B3
Garcinarro E 45 B5
Garcisobaco E 56 B2
Gardanne F 31 B4
Gardouch F 40 A2
Garein F 28 B2
Garéoult F 32 B2
Garéssio I 33 A4
Gargaligas E 50 A2
Gargallo E 47 B3
Garganta la Olla E 44 B2
Gargantiel E 50 B3
Gargellen A 21 C4
Gargilesse-Dampierre F 17 C3
Gárgoles de Abajo E 46 B1
Garlin F 28 C2
Garlitos E 50 B2
Garnat-sur-Engièvre F 18 C2
Garray E 37 C4
Garriguella E 40 B4
Garrovillas E 49 B4
Garrucha E 58 B3
Garvão P 54 B1
Gaschurn A 21 C5
Gascueña E 46 B1
Gasny F 10 B1
Gastes F 28 B1
Gata E 43 B3
Gata de Gorgos E 53 C4
Gátova E 53 B3
Gattinara I 27 B5
Gaucín E 56 B2
Gava E 41 C3
Gavarnie F 39 B3
Gavião P 48 B3
Gavray F 8 B2
Gea de Albarracin E 46 B2
Géaudot F 11 C4
Geaune F 28 C2
Gedinne B 11 B4
Gèdre F 39 B4
Geel B 7 A4
Geetbets B 7 B5
Geinsheim D 13 B4
Geisenheim D 13 B4
Geisingen D 21 B3
Geldermalsen NL 7 A5
Gelida E 41 C2
Gelsa E 47 A3
Gelterkinden CH 20 B2
Gelves E 56 A1
Gembloux B 7 B4
Gemeaux F 19 B4
Gémenos F 32 B1
Gémozac F 22 C3
Gemünden D 13 B3
Genappe B 7 B4
Génave E 58 A2
Gençay F 23 B4
Genelard F 18 C3
Geneva = Genève CH 26 A3
Genève = Geneva CH 26 A3
Genevriéres F 19 B4
Gengenbach D 13 C4
Genillé F 17 B3
Genlis F 19 B4
Gennes F 16 B1
Genola I 33 A3
Gensingen D 13 B3
Gent = Ghent B 7 A3
Gentioux F 24 B1
Geraards-bergen B 7 B3
Gérardmer F 20 A1
Gerbéviller F 12 C2
Gerena E 55 B3
Gérgal E 58 B2
Gergy F 19 C3
Gerindote E 44 C3
Germay F 12 C1
Germersheim D 13 B4
Gernika-Lumo E 37 A4
Gernsbach D 13 C4
Gernsheim D 13 B4
Gerpinnes B 7 B4
Gerri de la Sal E 41 B2
Gerzat F 24 B3
Gespunsart F 11 B4
Gesté F 15 B4
Getafe E 45 B4
Getxo E 37 A4
Gevora del Caudillo E 49 C4
Gevrey-Chambertin F 19 B3
Gex F 26 A3
Ghent = Gent B 7 A3
Ghigo I 27 C4
Ghisonaccia F 62 A2
Ghisoni F 62 A2
Giat F 24 B2
Giaveno I 27 B4
Gibraleón E 55 B3
Gibraltar GBZ 56 B2
Gien F 17 B4
Giens F 32 B2
Giffaumont-Champaubert
F 11 C4
Gignac F 30 B2
Gijón = Xixón E 36 A1
Gilena E 56 A3
Gilley F 19 B5
Gilley-sur-Loire F 18 C2
Gilocourt F 10 B2
Gilze NL 7 A4
Gimont F 29 C3
Ginasservis F 32 B1
Gingelom B 7 B5
Giões P 54 B2
Giromagny F 20 B1
Girona E 41 C3
Gironcourt-sur-Vraine F 12 C1
Gironella E 41 B2
Gironville-sous-les-Côtes
F 12 C1
Gisors F 10 B1
Gistel B 6 A2
Giswil CH 20 C3
Givet F 11 A4
Givors F 25 B4
Givry
B 7 B4
F 18 C3
Givry-en-Argonne F 11 C4
Gizeux F 16 B2
Gland CH 19 C5
Glarus CH 21 B4
Gletsch CH 20 C3
Glomel F 14 A2
Gloria P 48 B2
Goderville F 9 A4
Goes NL 7 A3
Goetzenbrück F 13 C3
Góglio I 27 A5
Goirle NL 7 A5
Góis P 42 B1
Goizueta E 38 A2
Goldach CH 21 B4
Goldbach D 13 A5
Golegã P 48 B2
Gómara E 46 A1
Gomaringen D 13 C5
Gomes Aires P 54 B1
Gómezserracin E 44 A3
Goncelin F 26 B2
Gondomar
E 34 B2
P 42 A1
Gondrecourt-le-Château
F 12 C1
Gondrin F 28 C3
Gonfaron F 32 B2
Goñi E 38 B2
Gooik B 7 B4
Goppenstein CH 27 A4
Gor E 58 B2
Gorafe E 58 B1
Gordaliza del Pino E 36 B1
Gordoncillo E 36 B1
Gorey GB 8 A1
Gorinchem NL 7 A4
Górliz E 37 A4
Gorron F 8 B3
Gossau CH 21 B4
Götzis A 21 B4
Gouarec F 14 A2
Gourdon F 29 B4
Gourgançon F 11 C4
Gourin F 14 A2
Gournay-en-Bray F 10 B1
Gouveia P 42 B2
Gouzeacourt F 10 A3
Gouzon F 24 A2
Gozee B 7 B4
Grabs CH 21 B4
Graçay F 17 B3
Gradefes E 36 B1
Gradil P 48 C1
Grado E 35 A4
Graja de Iniesta E 52 B2
Grajera E 45 A4
Gramat F 29 B4
Granada E 57 A4
Grañas E 34 A3
Granátula de Calatrava
E 51 B4
Grancey-le-Château F 19 B4
Grandas de Salime E 35 A4
Grandcamp-Maisy F 8 A2
Grand-Champ F 14 B3
Grand Couronne F 9 A5
Grand-Fougeray F 15 B4
Grândola P 54 A1
Grandpré F 11 B4
Grandrieu
B 7 B4
F 25 C3
Grandson CH 20 C1
Grandvillars F 20 B1
Grandvilliers F 10 B1
Grañén E 39 C3
Granges-de Crouhens F 39 B4
Granges-sur-Vologne F 20 A1
Granja
Évora P 49 C3
Porto P 42 A1
Granja de Moreruela E 36 C1
Granja de Torrehermosa
E 50 B2
Granollers E 41 C3
Granville F 8 B2
Grasse F 32 B2
Graulhet F 29 C4
Graus E 39 B4
Grávalos E 38 B2
Gravelines F 6 A2
Gravellona Toce I 27 B5
Graveson F 31 B3
Gray F 19 B4
Grazalema E 56 B2
Grenade F 29 C4
Grenade-sur-l'Adour F 28 C2
Grenchen CH 20 B2
Grenoble F 26 B2
Gréoux-les-Bains F 32 B1
Gressoney-la-Trinité I 27 B4
Gressoney-St.-Jean I 27 B4
Grevenmacher L 12 B2
Grez-Doiceau B 7 B4
Grèzec F 29 B4
Grez-en-Bouère F 16 B1
Griesheim D 13 B4

Grignan F 31 A3
Grignols F 28 B2
Grignon F 26 B3
Grijota E 36 B2
Grimaud F 32 B2
Grimbergen B 7 B4
Grimmialp CH 20 C2
Grindelwald CH 20 C3
Griñón E 45 B4
Grisolles F 29 C4
Groix F 14 B2
Grönenbach D 21 B5
Gross-Gerau D 13 B4
Grosshöchstetten CH 20 C2
Grossostheim D 13 B5
Gross Umstadt D 13 B4
Grostenquin F 12 C2
Grove E 34 B2
Gruissan F 30 B2
Grullos E 35 A4
Grünstadt D 13 B4
Gruyères CH 20 C2
Gstaad CH 20 C2
Gsteig CH 27 A4
Guadahortuna E 57 A4
Guadalajara E 45 B4
Guadalaviar E 46 B2
Guadalcanal E 50 B2
Guadalcázar E 56 A3
Guadalix de la Sierra E 45 B4
Guadálmez E 50 B3
Guadalupe E 50 A2
Guadamur E 45 C3
Guadarrama E 45 B3
Guadiaro E 56 B2
Guadix E 58 B1
Guagno F 62 A1
Guajar-Faragüit E 57 B4
Gualchos E 57 B4
Guarda P 43 B2
Guardamar del Segura E 59 A4
Guardão P 42 B1
Guardias Viejas E 58 C2
Guardiola de Bergueda E 41 B2
Guardo E 36 B2
Guareña E 50 B1
Guaro E 56 B3
Guarromán E 51 B4
Guebwiller F 20 B2
Guéjar-Sierra E 57 A4
Guémené-Penfao F 15 B4
Guémené-sur-Scorff F 14 A2
Güeñes E 37 A3
Guer F 15 B3
Guérande F 15 B3
Guéret F 24 A1
Guérigny F 18 B2
Guesa E 38 B2
Gueugnon F 18 C3
Guia P 48 B2
Guichen F 15 B4
Guignes F 10 C2
Guijo E 50 B3
Guijo de Coria E 43 B3
Guijo de Santa Bábera E 44 B2
Guijuelo E 44 B2
Guillaumes F 32 A2
Guillena E 56 A1
Guillestre F 26 C3
Guillos F 28 B2
Guilvinec F 14 B1
Guimarães P 42 A1
Guincho P 48 C1
Guînes F 6 B1
Guingamp F 14 A2
Guipavas F 14 A1
Guiscard F 10 B3
Guiscriff F 14 A2
Guise F 11 B3
Guisona E 41 C2
Guitiriz E 34 A3
Guîtres F 28 A2
Gujan-Mestras F 28 B1
Gumiel de Hizán E 37 C3
Gundel-fingen D 20 A2
Gundelsheim D 13 B5
Gunderschoffen F 13 C3
Guntersblum D 13 B4
Guntín E 34 B3
Gurrea de Gállego E 38 B3
Guttannen CH 20 C3
Güttingen CH 21 B4
Gy F 19 B4
Gyé-sur-Seine F 18 A3
Gypsera CH 20 C2

H

Haacht B 7 B4
Haamstede NL 7 A3
Habas F 28 C2
Habay B 12 B1
Habsheim F 20 B2
Hacinas E 37 C3
Hagenbach D 13 B4
Hagetmau F 28 C2
Hagondange F 12 B2
Haguenau F 13 C3
Haigerloch D 13 C4
Halle B 7 B4
Halluin F 6 B3
Ham F 10 B3
Hambach F 12 B3
Hamme B 7 A4
Hannut B 7 B5
Hardelot Plage F 6 B1
Hardt D 20 A3
Harfleur F 9 A4
Hargicourt F 10 B3
Hargnies F 11 A4
Haro E 37 B4
Haroué F 12 C2
Hartennes F 10 B3
Haslach D 20 A3
Hasparren F 38 A2
Hasselt B 7 B5
Hassloch D 13 B4
Hastière-Lavaux B 7 B4
Hatten F 13 C3
Hattstadt F 20 A2
Haudainville F 12 B1
Hausach D 20 A3
Hautefort F 29 A4
Hauterives F 25 B5
Hauteville-Lompnès F 26 B2
Haut-Fays B 11 A5
Hautmont F 7 B3
Hautrage B 7 B3
Havelange B 7 B5
Hayange F 12 B2
Hazebrouck F 6 B2
Héas F 39 B4
Hechingen D 13 C4
Hecho E 38 B3
Hechtel B 7 A5
Hédé F 15 A4
Heidelberg D 13 B4
Heilbronn D 13 B5
Heinerscheid L 12 A2
Heist-op-den-Berg B 7 A4
Helchteren B 7 A5
Helechosa E 50 A3
Hellevoetsluis NL 7 A4
Hellín E 52 C2
Héming F 12 C2
Hendaye F 38 A2
Hénin-Beaumont F 6 B2
Hennebont F 14 B2
Henrichemont F 17 B4
Heppenheim D 13 B4
Herbault F 17 B3
Herbeumont B 11 B5
Herbignac F 15 B3
Herbisse F 11 C4
Herbitzheim F 12 B3
Herbolzheim D 20 A2
Herencia E 51 A4
Herent B 7 B4
Herentals B 7 A4
Hérépian F 30 B2
Herguijuela E 50 A2
Héric F 15 B4
Héricourt F 20 B1
Héricourt-en-Caux F 9 A4
Hérimoncourt F 20 B1
Herisau CH 21 B4
Hérisson F 17 C4
Herk-de-Stad B 7 B5
Herment F 24 B2
Hermeskeil D 12 B2
Hermisende E 35 C4
Hermonville F 11 B3
Hernani E 38 A2
Hernansancho E 44 B3
Herramelluri E 37 B3
Herrenberg D 13 C4
Herrera E 56 A3
Herrera de Alcántara E 49 B3
Herrera del Duque E 50 A2
Herrera de los Navarros E 46 A2
Herrera de Pisuerga E 36 B2
Herreros del Suso E 44 B2
Herrlisheim F 13 C3
Herselt B 7 A4
Hervás E 43 B4
Herxheim D 13 B4
Herzogenbuchsee CH 20 B2
Hesdin F 6 B2
Hettange-Grande F 12 B2
Heuchin F 6 B2
Heudicourt-sous-les-Côtes F 12 C1
Heunezel F 19 A5
Heuqueville F 9 A4
Hiendelaencina E 45 A5
Hiersac F 23 C4
Higuera de Arjona E 51 C4
Higuera de Calatrava E 57 A3
Higuera de la Serena E 50 B2
Higuera de la Sierra E 55 B3
Higuera de Vargas E 49 C4
Higuera la Real E 55 A3
Higuers de Llerena E 50 B1
Higueruela E 52 C2
Híjar E 47 A3
Hilvarenbeek NL 7 A5
Hindelbank CH 20 B2
Hinjosa del Valle E 50 B1
Hinojal E 49 B4
Hinojales E 55 B3
Hinojos E 55 B3
Hinojosa del Duque E 50 B2
Hinojosas de Calatrava E 51 B3
Hinterweidenthal D 13 B3
Hinwil CH 21 B3
Hirschhorn D 13 B4
Hirsingue F 20 B2
Hirson F 11 B4
Hittisau A 21 B4
Hobscheid L 12 B1
Hochdorf CH 20 B3
Hochfelden F 13 C3
Hochspeyer D 13 B3
Höchst im Odenwald D 13 B5
Hockenheim D 13 B4
Hoedekenskerke NL 7 A3
Hoegaarden B 7 B4
Hoek van Holland NL 7 A4
Hofheim D 13 A4
Hohenems A 21 B4
Hohentengen D 20 B3
Holguera E 49 B4
Homburg D 13 B3
Hondarribia E 38 A2
Hondón de los Frailes E 59 A4
Hondschoote F 6 B2
Honfleur F 9 A4
Honrubia E 52 B1
Hontalbilla E 45 A3
Hontheim D 12 A2
Hontoria de la Cantera E 37 B3
Hontoria del Pinar E 37 C3
Hontoria de Valdearados E 37 C3
Hoogerheide NL 7 A4
Hoogstraten B 7 A4
Horb am Neckar D 13 C4
Horcajada de la Torre E 52 A1
Horcajo de los Montes E 50 A3
Horcajo de Santiago E 45 C4
Horcajo-Medianero E 44 B2
Horche E 45 B4
Horgen CH 21 B3
Horna E 52 C2
Hornachos E 50 B1
Hornachuelos E 56 A2
Hornberg D 20 A3
Hornos E 58 A2
Hornoy-le-Bourg F 10 B1
Horta P 42 A2
Hortezuela E 45 A5
Hortiguela E 37 B3
Hösbach D 13 A5
Hosingen L 12 A2
Hospental CH 21 C3
Hossegor F 28 C1
Hostal de Ipiés E 39 B3
Hostalric E 41 C3
Hostens F 28 B2
Hotton B 7 B5
Houdain F 6 B2
Houdan F 10 C1
Houdelaincourt F 12 C1
Houeillès F 28 B3
Houffalize B 12 A1
Houlgate F 9 A3
Hourtin F 28 A1
Hourtin-Plage F 28 A1
Houthalen B 7 A5
Houyet B 7 B4
Hoya de Santa Maria E 55 B3
Hoya-Gonzalo E 52 C2
Hoyocasero E 44 B3
Hoyo de Manzanares E 45 B4
Hoyo de Pinares E 44 B3
Hoyos E 43 B3
Hoyos del Espino E 44 B2
Hucqueliers F 6 B1
Huélago E 57 A4
Huélamo E 46 B2
Huelgoat F 14 A2
Huelma E 57 A4
Huelva E 55 B3
Huéneja E 58 B2
Huércal de Almeria E 58 C2
Huércal-Overa E 58 B3
Huerta de Abajo E 37 B3
Huerta del Rey E 37 C3
Huerta de Valdecarabanos E 45 C4
Huertahernando E 46 B1
Huesa E 58 B1
Huesca E 39 B3
Huéscar E 58 B2
Huete E 45 B5
Huétor Tájar E 57 A3
Hüfingen D 20 B3
Hulst NL 7 A4
Humanes E 45 B4
Humilladero E 57 A3
Hürbel D 21 A4
Huttwil CH 20 B2
Huy B 7 B5
Hyères F 32 B2
Hyères Plage F 32 B2

I

Ibahernando E 50 A2
Ibarranguelua E 37 A4
Ibeas de Juarros E 37 B3
Ibi E 53 C3
Ibiza = Eivissa E 60 C1
Ibros E 51 B4
Ichtegem B 6 A3
Idanha-a-Novo P 49 B3
Idar-Oberstein D 13 B3
Idiazábal E 38 B1
Ieper = Ypres B 6 B2
Igea E 38 B1
Iglesias E 37 B3
Igny-Comblizy F 11 B3
Igorre E 37 A4
Igries E 39 B3
Igualada E 41 C2
Igüeña E 35 B4
Iguerande F 25 A4
Ihringen D 20 A2
IJzendijke NL 7 A3
Ilanz CH 21 C4
Ilche E 39 C4
Ílhavo P 42 B1
Illana E 45 B5
Illano E 35 A4
Illar E 58 C2
Illas E 35 A5
Illats F 28 B2
Illescas E 45 B4
Ille-sur-Têt F 40 B3
Illfurth F 20 B2
Illiers-Combray F 9 B5
Illkirch-Graffenstaden F 13 C3
Íllora E 57 A4
Illueca E 46 A2
Immenstadt D 21 B5
Imon E 45 A5
Impéria I 33 B4
Imphy F 18 C2
Inca E 61 B2
Incinillas E 37 B3
Inerthal CH 21 B3
Infiesto E 36 A1
Ingelheim D 13 B4
Ingelmunster B 6 B3
Ingrandes
  Maine-et-Loire F 15 B5
  Vienne F 16 C2
Ingwiller F 13 C3
Iniesta E 52 B2
Innertkirchen CH 20 C3
Ins CH 20 B2
Interlaken CH 20 C2
Irrel D 12 B2
Iruela E 35 B4
Irún E 38 A2
Irurita E 38 A2
Irurzun E 38 B2
Isaba E 38 B3
Isabela E 51 B4
Íscar E 44 A3
Ischgl A 21 B5
Isdes F 17 B4
Iselle I 27 A5
Iseltwald CH 20 C2
Isigny-sur-Mer F 8 A2
Isla Canela E 55 B2
Isla Cristina E 55 B2
Islares E 37 A3
Isna P 48 B3
Isny D 21 B5
Isoba E 36 A1
Isola F 32 A3
Isola d'Asti I 27 C5
Isona E 41 B2
Ispagnac F 30 A2
Issigeac F 29 B3
Issogne I 27 B4
Issoire F 24 B3
Issoncourt F 11 C5
Issoudun F 17 C4
Is-sur-Tille F 19 B4
Issy-l'Evêque F 18 C2
Istán E 56 B3
Istres F 31 B3
Itoiz E 38 B2
Ítrabo E 57 B4
Ivoz Ramet B 7 B5
Ivrea I 27 B4
Ivry-en-Montagne F 18 B3
Ivry-la-Bataille F 10 C1
Iwuy F 6 B3
Izarra E 37 B4
Izeda P 43 A3
Izegem B 6 B3
Izernore F 26 A2
Iznájar E 57 A3
Iznalloz E 57 A4
Iznatoraf E 58 A1

J

Jabalquinto E 51 B4
Jabugo E 55 B3
Jaca E 39 B3
Jadraque E 45 B5
Jaén E 57 A4
Jalance E 53 B2
Jaligny-sur-Besbre F 25 A3
Jallais F 16 B1
Jalón E 53 C3
Jâlons F 11 C4
Jamilena E 57 A4
Jamoigne B 12 B1
Janville F 17 A3
Janzé F 15 B4
Jarafuel E 53 B2
Jaraicejo E 50 A2
Jaraíz de la Vera E 44 B2
Jarandilla de la Vera E 44 B2
Jaray E 46 A1
Jard-sur-Mer F 22 B2
Jargeau F 17 B4
Jarnac F 23 C3
Jarny F 12 B1
Jarzé F 16 B1
Jasseron F 26 A2
Játar E 57 B4
Jaun CH 20 C2
Jausiers F 32 A2
Jávea E 53 C4
Javerlhac F 23 C4
Javier E 38 B2
Javron F 9 B3
Jayena E 57 B4
Jegun F 29 C3
Jenaz CH 21 C4
Jeres del Marquesado E 58 B1
Jerez de la Frontera E 56 B1
Jerez de los Caballeros E 49 C4
Jerica E 53 B3
Jerte E 44 B2
Jeumont F 7 B4
Jijona E 53 C3
Jimena E 57 A4
Jimena de la Frontera E 56 B2
Jimera de Libar E 56 B2
João da Loura P 48 C2
Jódar E 57 A4
Jodoigne B 7 B4
Joeuf F 12 B1
Joigny F 18 B2
Joinville F 11 C5
Jonchery-sur-Vesle F 11 B3
Jonzac F 22 C3
Jorba E 41 C2
Jorquera E 52 B2
Josselin F 15 B3
Jou P 42 A2
Jouarre F 10 C3
Joué-lès-Tours F 16 B2
Joué-sur-Erdre F 15 B4
Joux-la-Ville F 18 B2
Jouy F 10 C1
Jouy-le-Châtel F 10 C3
Jouy-le-Potier F 17 B3
Joyeuse F 31 A3
Joze F 24 B3
Juan-les-Pins F 32 B3
Jubera E 38 B1
Jubrique E 56 B2
Jugon-les-Lacs F 15 A3
Juillac F 29 A4
Juillan F 39 A4
Jullouville F 8 B2
Jumeaux F 25 B3
Jumièges F 9 A4
Jumilhac-le-Grand F 23 C5
Jumilla E 53 C2
Juncosa E 47 A4
Juneda E 41 C1
Jungingen D 13 C5
Junglingster L 12 B2
Juniville F 11 B4
Junqueira P 43 A2
Juromenha P 49 C3
Jussac F 24 C2
Jussey F 19 B4
Jussy F 10 B3
Juvigny-le-Terte F 8 B2
Juvigny-sous-Andaine F 9 B3
Juzennecourt F 19 A3

K

Kaatscheuvel NL 7 A5
Kahl D 13 A5
Kaiserslautern D 13 B3
Kalmthout B 7 A4
Kaltbrunn CH 21 B4
Kandel D 13 B4
Kandern D 20 B2
Kandersteg CH 20 C2
Kapellen B 7 A4
Kappel D 13 C3
Kappl A 21 B5
Karlsruhe D 13 B4
Kastellaun D 13 A3
Kasterlee B 7 A4
Kaub D 13 A3
Kaysersberg F 20 A2
Keerbergen B 7 A4
Kehl D 13 C3
Kell D 12 B2
Kelsterbach D 13 A4
Kempten D 21 B5
Kemptthal CH 21 B3
Kenzingen D 20 A2
Kérien F 14 A2
Kerlouan F 14 A1
Kernascléden F 14 A2
Kerns CH 20 C3
Kerzers CH 20 C2
Kimratshofen D 21 B5
Kirchberg
  CH 20 B2
  Rheinland-Pfalz D 13 B3
Kirchheimbolanden D 13 B4
Kirchzarten D 20 B2
Kirn D 13 B3
Kisslegg D 21 B4
Klingenberg D 13 B5
Klingenmunster D 13 B4
Kloosterzande NL 7 A4
Klösterle A 21 B5
Klosters CH 21 C4
Kloten CH 21 B3
Kluisbergen B 7 B3
Klundert NL 7 A4
Knesselare B 6 A3
Knokke-Heist B 6 A3
Koblenz CH 20 B3
Koekelare B 6 A2
Koksijde B 6 A2
Köniz CH 20 C2
Konstanz D 21 B4
Kontich B 7 A4
Konz D 12 B2
Kopstal L 12 B2
Kortrijk B 6 B3
Kressbronn D 21 B4
Kreuzlingen CH 21 B4
Kriegsfeld D 13 B3
Kriens CH 20 B3
Krimpen aan de IJssel NL 7 A4
Kruishoutem B 7 B3
Küblis CH 21 C4
Kuppenheim D 13 C4
Kusel D 13 B3
Küsnacht CH 20 B3
Küttingen CH 20 B3
Kyllburg D 12 A2

L

La Adrada E 44 B3
La Alameda E 51 B4
La Alberca E 43 B3
La Alberca de Záncara E 52 B1
La Albergueria de Argañán E 43 B3
La Albuera E 49 C4
La Aldea del Portillo del Busto E 37 B3
La Algaba E 56 A1
La Aliseda de Tormes E 44 B2
La Almarcha E 52 B1
La Almolda E 47 A3
La Almunia de Doña Godina E 46 A2
La Antillas E 55 B2
La Arena E 35 A4
La Aulaga E 55 B3
La Balme-de-Sillingy F 26 B3
La Bañeza E 35 B5
La Barca de la Florida E 56 B2
La Barre-de-Monts F 22 B1
La Barre-en-Ouche F 9 B4
La Barrosa E 56 B1
La Barthe-de-Neste F 39 A4
La Bassée F 6 B2
La Bastide-de-Sèrou F 40 A2
La Bastide-des-Jourdans F 32 B1
Labastide-Murat F 29 B4
La Bastide-Puylaurent F 25 C3
Labastide-Rouairoux F 30 B1
Labastide-St Pierre F 29 C4
La Bathie F 26 B3
La Baule-Escoublac F 15 B3
La Bazoche-Gouet F 16 A2
La Bégude-de-Mazenc F 31 A3
Labenne F 28 C1
La Bernerie-en-Retz F 22 A1
La Bisbal d'Empordà E 41 C4
Lablachère F 31 A3
La Boissière F 9 A4
Labouheyre F 28 B2
La Bourboule F 24 B2
La Bóveda de Toro E 44 A2
La Brède F 28 B2
La Bresse F 20 A1
La Bridoire F 26 B2
La Brillanne F 32 B1
Labrit F 28 B2
Labros E 46 A2
La Bruffière F 22 A2
Labruguière F 30 B1
Labrujo P 42 A1
L'Absie F 22 B3
La Bussière F 17 B4
La Caillère F 22 B3
Lacalahorra E 58 B1
La Calmette F 31 B3
La Calzada de Oropesa E 44 C2
La Campana E 56 A2
La Cañada E 44 B3
Lacanau F 28 B1
Lacanau-Océan F 28 A1
Lacanche F 18 B3
La Canourgue F 30 A2
La Capelle F 11 B3
Lacapelle-Marival F 29 B4
La Cardanchosa E 50 B2
La Caridad E 35 A4
La Carlota E 56 A3
La Carolina E 51 B4
Lacaune F 30 B1
La Cava E 47 B4
La Cavalerie F 30 A2
La Celle-en-Moravan F 18 B3
La Celle-St Avant F 16 B2
La Cerca E 37 B3
La Chaise-Dieu F 25 B3
La Chaize-Giraud F 22 B2
La Chaize-le-Vicomte F 22 B2
La Chambre F 26 B3
La Chapelaude F 24 A2
La Chapelle-d'Angillon F 17 B4
La Chapelle-en-Aalgaudémar F 26 C3
La Chapelle-en-Vercors F 26 C2
La Chapelle-Glain F 15 B4
La Chapelle-la-Reine F 10 C2
La Chapelle-Laurent F 24 B3
La Chapelle-St Luc F 11 C4
La Chapelle-sur-Erdre F 15 B4
La Chapelle-Vicomtesse F 17 B3
La Charce F 32 A1
La Charité-sur-Loire F 18 B2
La Chartre-sur-le-Loir F 16 B2
La Châtaigneraie F 22 B3
La Châtre F 17 C3
La Chaussée-sur-Marne F 11 C4
La Chaux-de-Fonds CH 20 B1
Lachen CH 21 B3
La Cheppe F 11 B4
La Chèze F 15 A3
La Ciotat F 32 B1
La Clayette F 25 A4
La Clusaz F 26 B3
La Codosera E 49 B3
La Concha E 37 A3
La Condamine-Châtelard F 32 A2
La Contienda E 55 A3
La Coquille F 23 C4
La Coronada E 50 B2
La Côte-St André F 26 B2
La Cotinière F 22 C2
La Courtine F 24 B2
Lacq F 39 A3
La Crau F 32 B2
La Crèche F 23 B3
La Croix F 16 B2
Lacroix-Barrez F 24 C2
Lacroix-St Ouen F 10 B2
Lacroix-sur-Meuse F 12 C1
La Croix-Valmer F 32 B2
La Cumbre E 50 A2
Ladignac-le-Long F 23 C5
Ladoeiro P 49 B3
Ladon F 17 B4
La Douze F 29 A3
La Espina E 35 A4
La Estrella E 50 A2
La Farga de Moles E 40 B2
La Fatarella E 47 A4
La Felipa E 52 B2
La Fère F 10 B3
La Ferrière
  Indre-et-Loire F 16 B2
  Vendée F 22 B2
La Ferrière-en-Parthenay F 23 B3
La-Ferté-Alais F 10 C2
La Ferté-Bernard F 16 A2
La Ferté-Frênel F 9 B4
La Ferté-Gaucher F 10 C3
La Ferté-Imbault F 17 B3
La Ferté-Macé F 9 B3
La Ferté-Milon F 10 B3
La Ferté-sous-Jouarre F 10 C3
La Ferté-St-Aubin F 17 B3
La Ferté-St-Cyr F 17 B3
La Ferté-Vidame F 9 B4
La Ferté Villeneuil F 17 B3
La Feuillie F 10 B1
La Flèche F 16 B1
La Flotte F 22 B2
La Font de la Figuera E 53 C3
La Fouillade F 30 A1
Lafrançaise F 29 B4
La Fregeneda E 43 B3
La Fresneda E 47 B4
La Fuencubierta E 56 A3
La Fuente de San Esteban E 43 B3
La Fulioala E 41 C2
La Gacilly F 15 B3
La Galera E 47 B4
Lagarde F 40 A2
La Garde-Freinet F 32 B2
Lagares
  Coimbra P 42 B2
  Porto P 42 A1
La Garnache F 22 B2
La Garriga E 41 C3
La Garrovilla E 49 C4
Lagartera E 44 C2
La Gaubretière F 22 B2
La Gineta E 52 B1
Lagnieu F 26 B2
Lagny-sur-Marne F 10 C2
Lagôa P 54 B1
Lagoaça P 43 A3
Lagos P 54 B1
La Granadella
  Alicante E 53 C4
  Lleida E 47 A4
La Grand-Combe F 31 A3
La Grande-Croix F 25 B4
La Grande-Motte F 31 B3
La Granja d'Escarp E 47 A4
La Granjuela E 50 B2
Lagrasse F 40 A3
La Grave F 26 B3
La Gravelle F 15 A4
Laguardia E 37 B4

La Guardia E . . . 45 C4
La Guardia de Jaén E . 57 A4
Laguarres E . . . 39 B4
Laguenne F . . . 24 B1
Laguépie F . . . 29 B4
La Guerche-de-Bretagne
  F . . . 15 B4
La Guerche-sur-l'Aubois
  F . . . 18 C1
La Guérinière F . . 22 B1
Laguiole F . . . 24 C2
Laguna de Duera E . 44 A3
Laguna del Marquesado
  E . . . 46 B2
Laguna de Negrillos E . 36 B1
Lagunilla E . . . 43 B3
La Haba E . . . 50 B2
Laharie F . . . 28 B1
La Haye-du-Puits F . 8 A2
La Haye-Pesnel F . . 8 B2
La Herlière F . . . 6 B2
La Hermida E . . . 36 A2
La Herrera E . . . 52 C1
Laheycourt F . . . 11 C5
La Higuera E . . . 52 C2
La Hiniesta E . . . 43 A4
La Horcajada E . . 44 B2
La Horra E . . . 37 C3
Lahr D . . . 13 C3
La Hulpe B . . . 7 B4
La Hutte F . . . 9 B4
L'Aigle F . . . 9 B4
La Iglesuela E . . 44 B3
La Iglesuela del Cid E . 47 B3
Laignes F . . . 18 B3
Laiguéglia I . . . 33 B4
L'Aiguillon-sur-Mer F . 22 B2
Laina E . . . 46 A1
La Iruela E . . . 58 B2
Laissac F . . . 30 A1
La Javie F . . . 32 A2
La Jonchère-St Maurice
  F . . . 24 A1
La Jonquera E . . 40 B3
La Lantejuela E . . 56 A2
L'Albagès E . . . 47 A4
Lalbenque F . . . 29 B4
L'Alcudia E . . . 53 B3
L'Aldea E . . . 47 B4
Lalin E . . . 34 B2
Lalinde F . . . 29 B3
La Línea de la Concepción
  E . . . 56 B2
Lalizolle F . . . 24 A3
La Llacuna E . . . 41 C2
Lalley F . . . 26 C2
La Londe-les-Maures F . 32 B2
La Loupe F . . . 9 B5
La Louvière B . . . 7 B4
L'Alpe-d'Huez F . . 26 B3
La Luisiana E . . . 56 A2
Laluque F . . . 28 C1
La Machine F . . . 18 C2
Lamadrid E . . . 36 A2
Lamagistére F . . 29 B3
La Mailleraye-sur-Seine
  F . . . 9 A4
La Malène F . . . 30 A2
La Mamola E . . . 57 B4
La Manresana dels Prats
  E . . . 41 C2
Lamarche F . . . 19 A4
Lamarche-sur-Saône F . 19 B4
Lamargelle F . . . 19 B3
Lamarosa P . . . 48 B2
Lamarque F . . . 28 A2
Lamas P . . . 42 B1
La Masadera E . . 37 C3
Lamas de Moaro P . 34 B2
Lamastre F . . . 25 C4
La Mata E . . . 44 C3
La Mata de Ledesma E . 43 A4
La Mata de Monteagudo
  E . . . 36 B1
Lamballe F . . . 15 A3
Lambesc F . . . 31 B4
Lamego P . . . 42 A2
La Meilleraye-de-Bretagne
  F . . . 15 B4
La Ménitré F . . . 16 B1
L'Ametlla de Mar E . 47 B4
La Mojonera E . . 58 C2
La Mole F . . . 32 B2
La Molina E . . . 41 B2
La Monnerie-le-Montel
  F . . . 25 B3
La Morera E . . . 49 C4
La Mothe-Achard F . 22 B2
Lamothe-Cassel F . 29 B4
Lamothe-Montravel F . 28 B3
La Mothe-St Héray F . 23 B3
Lamotte-Beuvron F . 17 B4
La Motte-Chalançon F . 31 A4
La Motte-du-Caire F . 32 A2
La Motte-Servolex F . 26 B2
Lampertheim D . . 13 B4
L'Ampolla E . . . 47 B4
La Mudarra E . . . 36 C2
La Muela E . . . 46 A2
La Mure F . . . 26 C2
Lamure-sur-Azergues F 25 A4
Lanaja E . . . 39 C3
Lanarce F . . . 25 C3
La Nava E . . . 55 B3
La Nava de Ricomalillo
  E . . . 50 A3
La Nava de Santiago E . 49 B4
Lançon-Provence F . 31 B4
Landau D . . . 13 B4
Landen B . . . 7 B5
Landerneau F . . . 14 A1
Landete E . . . 52 B2
Landévant F . . . 14 B3
Landévennec F . . 14 A1
Landivisiau F . . . 14 A1
Landivy F . . . 8 B2
Landos F . . . 25 C3
Landouzy-le-Ville F . 11 B4
Landquart CH . . . 21 C4
Landrecies F . . . 11 A3
Landreville F . . . 18 A3
Landscheid D . . . 12 B2
Landstuhl D . . . 13 B3

Lanester F . . . 14 B2
Lanestosa E . . . 37 A3
La Neuve-Lyre F . . 9 B4
La Neuveville CH . . 20 B2
Langa de Duero E . 45 A4
Langeac F . . . 25 B3
Langeais F . . . 16 B2
Langemark-Poelkapelle
  B . . . 6 B2
Langen D . . . 13 B4
Langenbruck CH . . 20 B2
Langenlonsheim D . 13 B3
Langenthal CH . . 20 B2
Langnau CH . . . 20 C2
Langogne F . . . 25 C3
Langon F . . . 28 B2
Langreo E . . . 36 A1
Langres F . . . 19 B4
Langueux F . . . 15 A3
Languidic F . . . 14 B2
Langwies CH . . . 21 C4
Lanheses P . . . 42 A1
Lanildut F . . . 14 A1
Lanjarón E . . . 57 B4
Lanmeur F . . . 14 A2
Lannéanou F . . . 14 A2
Lannemezan F . . 39 A4
Lanneuville-sur-Meuse
  F . . . 11 B5
Lannilis F . . . 14 A1
Lannion F . . . 14 A2
La Nocle-Maulaix F . 18 C2
Lanouaille F . . . 23 C5
Lanslebourg-Mont-Cenis
  F . . . 27 B3
Lanta F . . . 29 C4
Lantadilla E . . . 36 B2
Lanton F . . . 28 B1
Lantosque F . . . 33 B3
La Nuez de Arriba E . 37 B3
Lanvollon F . . . 14 A3
Lanza E . . . 34 A2
Lanzada E . . . 34 B2
Lanzahíta E . . . 44 B3
Lanzo Torinese I . . 27 B4
Laon F . . . 11 B3
Laons F . . . 9 B5
La Paca E . . . 58 B3
La Pacaudière F . . 25 A3
Lapalisse F . . . 25 A3
La Palma d'Ebre E . 47 A4
La Palma del Condado
  E . . . 55 B3
La Palme F . . . 40 B4
La Palmyre F . . . 22 C2
La Parra E . . . 49 C4
La Pedraja de Portillo E 44 A3
La Peraleja E . . . 46 B1
La Petit-Pierre F . . 13 C3
Lapeyrade F . . . 28 B2
Lapeyrouse F . . . 24 A2
La Pinilla E . . . 59 B3
La Plagne F . . . 26 B3
La Plaza E . . . 35 A4
Laplume F . . . 29 B3
La Pobla de Lillet E . 41 B2
La Pobla de Vallbona E . 53 B3
La Pobla Llarga E . 53 B3
La Pola de Gordón E . 36 B1
la Porta F . . . 62 A2
La Pouèze F . . . 16 B1
Lapoutroie F . . . 20 A2
La Póveda de Soria E . 37 B4
La Preste F . . . 40 B3
La Primaube F . . 30 A1
La Puebla de Almoradie
  E . . . 51 A4
La Puebla de Cazalla E . 56 A2
La Puebla de los Infantes
  E . . . 56 A2
La Puebla del Río E . 56 A1
La Puebla de Montalbán
  E . . . 44 C3
La Puebla de Roda E . 39 B4
La Puebla de Valdavia
  E . . . 36 B2
La Puebla de Valverde
  E . . . 46 B3
La Pueblanueva E . . 44 C3
La Puerta de Segura E . 58 A2
La Punt CH . . . 21 C4
La Quintana E . . 56 A3
La Quintera E . . 56 A2
La Rábita
  Granada E . . . 58 C1
  Jaén E . . . 57 A3
Laracha E . . . 34 A2
Laragne-Montéglin F . 32 A1
La Rambla E . . . 57 A3
l'Arboç E . . . 41 C2
L'Arbresle F . . . 25 B4
Larceveau F . . . 38 A2
Larche
  Alpes-de-Haute-Provence
  F . . . 32 A2
  Corrèze F . . . 29 A4
Lardosa P . . . 49 B3
Laredo E . . . 37 A3
La Redondela E . . 55 B2
La Réole F . . . 28 B2
Largentière F . . . 31 A3
L'Argentière-la-Bessée
  F . . . 26 C3
La Riera E . . . 35 A4
La Riera de Gaià E . 41 C2
La Rinconada E . . 56 A1
Lariño E . . . 34 B1
La Rivière-Thibouville F . 9 A4
Larmor-Plage F . . 14 B2
La Robla E . . . 36 B1
La Roca de la Sierra E . 49 B4
La Roche F . . . 20 C2
La Rochebeaucourt-
  Argentine F . . . 23 C4
La Roche-Bernard F . 15 B3
La Roche-Canillac F . 24 B1
La Roche-Chalais F . 28 A3
La Roche Derrien F . 14 A2
La Roche-des-Arnauds
  F . . . 32 A1
La Roche-en-Brénil F . 18 B3
La Rochefoucauld F . 23 C4
La Roche-Guyon F . 10 B1
La Rochelle F . . . 22 B2
La Roche-Posay F . 23 B4
La Roche-sur-Foron F . 26 A3

La Roche-sur-Yon F . 22 B2
Larochette L . . . 12 B2
La Rochette F . . . 31 A4
La Roda
  Albacete E . . . 52 B1
  Oviedo E . . . 35 A4
La Roda de Andalucía E 56 A3
Laroquebrou F . . 24 C2
La Roquebrussanne F . 32 B1
Laroque d'Olmes F . 40 B2
La Roque-Gageac F . 29 B4
La Roque-Ste Marguerite
  F . . . 30 A2
Laroque-Timbaut F . 29 B3
Larouco E . . . 35 B3
Larraga E . . . 38 B2
Larrau F . . . 38 A3
Larrazet F . . . 29 C4
La Rubia E . . . 37 C4
Laruns F . . . 39 A3
Larva E . . . 58 B1
La Sagrada E . . . 43 B3
La Salceda E . . . 45 A4
Lasalle F . . . 31 A2
La Salle F . . . 26 C3
La Salvetat-Peyralés F . 30 A1
La Salvetat-sur-Agout F 30 B1
Las Arenas E . . . 36 A2
La Sarraz CH . . . 19 C5
Lasarte E . . . 38 A1
Las Cabezadas E . 45 A4
Las Cabezas de San Juan
  E . . . 56 B2
Las Correderas E . 51 B4
Las Cuevas de Cañart
  E . . . 47 B3
La Seca E . . . 44 A3
La Selva del Camp E . 41 C2
La Senia E . . . 47 B4
La Serra E . . . 41 C2
La Seu d'Urgell F . . 40 B2
La Seyne-sur-Mer F . 32 B1
Las Gabias E . . . 57 A4
Las Herencias E . . 44 C3
Las Herrerías E . . 55 B3
Las Labores E . . . 51 A4
Las Mesas E . . . 52 B1
Las Minas E . . . 58 A3
Las Navas E . . . 57 A3
Las Navas de la
  Concepción E . . 50 C2
Las Navas del Marqués
  E . . . 44 B3
Las Navillas E . . . 51 A3
Las Negras E . . . 58 C3
La Solana E . . . 51 B4
La Souterraine F . . 24 A1
Las Pajanosas E . . 55 B3
Laspaules E . . . 39 B4
Las Pedroñas E . . 52 B1
Las Planes d'Hostoles
  E . . . 41 B3
Laspuña E . . . 39 B4
Las Rozas
  Cantabria E . . . 36 B2
  Madrid E . . . 45 B3
Lassay-les-Châteaux F . 9 B3
Lasseube F . . . 39 A3
Lassigny F . . . 10 B2
Lastras de Cuéllar E . 45 A3
Las Uces E . . . 43 A3
La Suze-sur-Sarthe F . 16 B2
Las Veguillas E . . 43 B4
Las Ventas con Peña
  Aguilera E . . . 51 A3
Las Ventas de San Julián
  E . . . 44 B2
Las Villes E . . . 47 B4
Latasa E . . . 38 B2
La Teste F . . . 28 B1
La Thuile I . . . 27 B3
La Toba E . . . 46 B2
La Toledana E . . . 51 A3
La Torre de Cabdella E . 40 B1
La Torre de Esteban
  Hambrán E . . . 45 B3
La Torre del l'Espanyol
  E . . . 47 A4
La Torresaviñán E . 46 B1
La Tour d'Aigues F . 32 B1
La Tour de Peilz CH . 20 C1
La Tour-du-Pin F . . 26 B2
La Tranche-sur-Mer F . 22 B2
La Tremblade F . . 22 C2
La Trimouille F . . 23 B5
La Trinité F . . . 14 B2
La Trinité-Porhoët F . 15 A3
Latronquière F . . 24 C2
La Turballe F . . . 15 B3
Laubert F . . . 25 C3
Laufen CH . . . 20 B2
Lauffen D . . . 13 B5
Laujar de Andarax E . 58 C2
La Uña E . . . 36 A1
La Unión E . . . 59 B4
Launois-sur-Vence F . 11 B4
Laurière F . . . 24 A1
Lausanne CH . . . 20 C1
Laussonne F . . . 25 C4
Lauterach A . . . 21 B4
Lauterbrunnen CH . 20 C2
Lauterecken D . . . 13 B3
Lautrec F . . . 30 B1
Lauzerte F . . . 29 B4
Lauzès F . . . 29 B4
Lauzun F . . . 29 B3
Laval F . . . 16 A1
La Vall d'Uixó E . . 53 B3
Lavardac F . . . 29 B3
Lavaris P . . . 42 B1
Lavau F . . . 18 B1
Lavaur F . . . 29 C4
La Vecilla de Curueño
  E . . . 36 B1
La Vega
  Asturias E . . . 35 A5
  Asturias E . . . 36 A1
  Cantabria E . . . 36 A2
Lavelanet F . . . 40 B2
La Velilla E . . . 45 A4
La Velles E . . . 44 A2
La Victoria E . . . 56 A3
La Vid E . . . 45 A4
La Vilavella E . . . 53 B3

La Vilella Baixa E . . 41 C1
La Villa de Don Fadrique
  E . . . 51 A4
Lavilledieu F . . . 31 A3
La Villedieu F . . . 23 B3
La Ville Dieu-du-Temple
  F . . . 29 B4
Lavit F . . . 29 C3
Lavoncourt F . . . 19 B4
Lavos P . . . 42 B1
La Voulte-sur-Rhône F . 25 C4
Lavoûte-Chilhac F . 25 B3
Lavradio P . . . 48 C1
Lavre P . . . 48 C2
La Wantzenau F . . 13 C3
Laxe E . . . 34 A2
La Yesa E . . . 53 B3
Laza E . . . 35 B3
Lazkao E . . . 38 A1
La Zubia E . . . 57 A4
Lebach D . . . 12 B2
Le Barp F . . . 28 B2
Le Bar-sur-Loup F . 32 B2
Le Béage F . . . 25 C4
Le Beausset F . . . 32 B1
Lebekke B . . . 7 A4
Le Bessat F . . . 25 B4
Le Blanc F . . . 23 B5
Le Bleymard F . . 30 A2
Leboreiro E . . . 34 B3
Le Boullay-Mivoye F . 9 B5
Le Boulou F . . . 40 B3
Le Bourg F . . . 29 B4
Le Bourg-d'Oisans F . 26 B3
Le Bourget-du-Lac F . 26 B2
Le Bourgneuf-la-Forêt
  F . . . 15 A5
Le Bousquet d'Orb F . 30 B2
Le Brassus CH . . 19 C5
Le Breuil F . . . 25 A3
Le Breuil-en-Auge F . 9 A4
Lebrija E . . . 56 B1
Le Brusquet F . . . 32 A2
Le Bry CH . . . 20 C2
Le Bugue F . . . 29 B3
Le Buisson F . . . 29 B3
Leca da Palmeira P . 42 A1
Le Caloy F . . . 28 C2
Le Cap d'Agde F . . 30 B2
Le Cateau Cambrésis F . 11 A3
Le Caylar F . . . 30 B2
Le Cayrol F . . . 24 C2
Lécera E . . . 47 A3
Lech A . . . 21 B5
Le Chambon-Feugerolles
  F . . . 25 B4
Le Chambon-sur-Lignon
  F . . . 25 B4
Le Château d'Oléron F . 22 C2
Le Châtelard F . . 26 B3
Le Châtelet F . . . 17 C4
Le Châtelet-en-Brie F . 10 C2
Le Chesne F . . . 11 B4
Le Cheylard F . . . 25 C4
Leciñena E . . . 39 C3
Le Collet-de-Deze F . 31 A2
Le Conquet F . . . 14 A1
Le Creusot F . . . 18 C3
Le Croisic F . . . 15 B3
Le Crotoy F . . . 6 B1
Lectoure F . . . 29 C3
Ledaña E . . . 52 B2
Lede B . . . 7 B3
Le Deschaux F . . 19 C4
Ledesma E . . . 43 A3
Lédignan F . . . 31 B3
Lédigos E . . . 36 B2
Leerdam NL . . . 7 A5
Le Faou F . . . 14 A1
Le Faouët F . . . 14 A2
Le Folgoet F . . . 14 A1
Le Fossat F . . . 40 A2
Le Fousseret F . . 40 A2
Le Fugeret F . . . 32 A2
Leganés E . . . 45 B4
Legau D . . . 21 B5
Le Gault-Soigny F . 11 C3
Legé F . . . 22 B2
Lège-Cap-Ferret F . 28 B1
Léglise B . . . 12 B1
Le Grand-Bornand F . 26 B3
Le-Grand-Bourg F . 24 A1
Le Grand-Lucé F . . 16 B2
Le Grand-Pressigny F . 16 C2
Le Grand-Quevilly F . 9 A5
Le Grau-du-Roi F . . 31 B3
Léguevin F . . . 29 C4
Legutiano E . . . 37 B4
Le Havre F . . . 9 A4
Le Hohwald F . . . 13 C3
Le Houga F . . . 28 C2
Leignon B . . . 7 B5
Leimen D . . . 13 B4
Leiria P . . . 48 B2
Leitza E . . . 38 A2
Lekeitio E . . . 37 A4
Lekunberri E . . . 38 A2
Le Lardin-St Lazare F . 29 A4
Le Lauzet-Ubaye F . 32 A2
Le Lavandou F . . 32 B2
Le Lion-d'Angers F . 16 B1
Le Locle CH . . . 20 B1
Le Loroux-Bottereau F . 15 B4
Le Louroux-Béconnais
  F . . . 15 B5
Le Luc F . . . 32 B2
Le Lude F . . . 16 B2
Le Malzieu-Ville F . 24 C3
Le Mans F . . . 16 A2
Le Mas-d'Azil F . . 40 A2
Le Massegros F . . 30 A2
Le Mayet-de-Montagne
  F . . . 25 A3
Le May-sur-Evre F . 15 B5
Lembach F . . . 13 B3
Lemberg F . . . 13 B3
Lembèye F . . . 39 A3
Le Mêle-sur-Sarthe F . 9 B4
Le Ménil F . . . 19 A5
Le Merlerault F . . 9 B4
Le Mesnil-sur-Oger F . 11 C4
Le Miroir F . . . 19 C4
Le Molay-Littry F . . 8 A3

Le Monastier-sur-Gazeille
  F . . . 25 C3
Le Monêtier-les-Bains
  F . . . 26 C3
Le Mont-Dore F . . 24 B2
Le Montet F . . . 24 A3
Le Mont-St Michel F . 8 B2
Lempdes F . . . 24 B3
Le Muret F . . . 28 B2
Le Muy F . . . 32 B2
Lencloître F . . . 16 C2
Le Neubourg F . . 9 A4
Lenk CH . . . 20 C2
Le Nouvion-en-Thiérache
  F . . . 11 A3
Lens
  B . . . 7 B3
  F . . . 6 B2
Lens Lestang F . . 25 B5
Lentellais E . . . 35 B3
Lenzburg CH . . . 20 B3
Lenzerheide CH . . 21 C4
León E . . . 36 B1
Léon F . . . 28 C1
Leonberg D . . . 13 C5
Léoncel F . . . 26 C2
Leopoldsburg B . . 7 A5
Le Palais F . . . 14 B2
Le Parcq F . . . 6 B2
Lepe E . . . 55 B2
Le Péage-de-Roussillon
  F . . . 25 B4
Le Pellerin F . . . 15 B4
Le Perthus F . . . 40 B3
Le Pertuis F . . . 25 B4
Le Petit-Bornand F . 26 B3
L'Epine F . . . 32 A1
Le Poët F . . . 32 A1
Le Poirè-sur-Vie F . 22 B2
Le Pont CH . . . 19 C5
Le Pont-de-Montvert F . 30 A2
Le Porge F . . . 28 B1
Le Porge-Océan F . 28 B1
Le Portel F . . . 6 B1
Le Pouldu F . . . 14 B2
Le Pouliguen F . . 15 B3
Le Puy-en-Velay F . 25 B3
Le Puy-Ste Réparade F . 31 B4
Le Quesnoy F . . . 7 B3
Le Rayol F . . . 32 B2
Le Rozier F . . . 30 A2
Le Russey F . . . 20 B1
Lés E . . . 39 B4
Les Abrets F . . . 26 B2
Les Aix-d'Angillon F . 17 B4
Lesaka E . . . 38 A2
Les Ancizes-Comps F . 24 B2
Les Andelys F . . . 10 B1
Les Arcs
  Savoie F . . . 27 B3
  Var F . . . 32 B2
Les-Aubiers F . . . 16 C1
Les Baux-de-Provence
  F . . . 31 B3
Les Bézards F . . . 17 B4
Les Bois CH . . . 20 B1
Les Bordes F . . . 17 B4
Les Borges Blanques E 41 C1
Les Borges del Camp E 41 C2
Les Brunettes F . . 18 C2
Les Cabannes F . . 40 B2
L'Escala E . . . 41 B4
Lescar F . . . 39 A3
L'Escarène F . . . 33 B3
Lescheraines F . . 26 B3
Lesconil F . . . 14 B1
Les Contamines-Montjoie
  F . . . 27 B3
les Coves de Vinroma E 47 B4
Les Déserts F . . . 26 B2
Les Deux-Alpes F . 26 C3
Les Diablerets CH . 27 A4
Lesdins F . . . 10 B3
Les Echelles F . . . 26 B2
Le Sel-de-Bretagne F . 15 B4
Le Sentier CH . . . 19 C5
Les Escaldes AND . 40 B2
Les Essarts F . . . 22 B2
Les Estables F . . 25 C4
Les Eyzies-de-Tayac F . 29 B4
Les Gets F . . . 26 A3
Les Grandes-Ventes F . 9 A5
Les Haudères CH . . 27 A4
Les Herbiers F . . 22 B2
Les Hôpitaux-Neufs F . 19 C5
Les Lucs-sur-Boulogne
  F . . . 22 B2
Les Mages F . . . 31 A3
Les Mazures F . . . 11 B4
Les Mées F . . . 32 A1
Lesmont F . . . 11 C4
Les Mureaux F . . 10 C1
Lesneven F . . . 14 A1
Les Omergues F . . 32 A1
Les Ormes-sur-Voulzie
  F . . . 10 C3
Les Orres F . . . 32 A2
Le Souquet F . . . 28 C1
Lesparre-Médoc F . 28 A2
l'Espérance F . . . 11 B3
l'Esperou F . . . 30 A2
Les Pieux F . . . 8 A2
Lesponne F . . . 39 A4
Les Ponts-de-Cé F . 16 B1
Les Ponts-de-Martel CH 20 C1
Les Praz F . . . 27 B3
L'Espunyola E . . . 41 B2
Les Riceys F . . . 18 B3
Les Roches F . . . 25 B4
Les Rosaires F . . . 15 A3
Les Rosiers F . . . 16 B1
Les Rousses F . . . 19 C5
Les Sables-d'Olonne F . 22 B2
Lessay F . . . 8 A2
Les Settons F . . . 18 B3
Lessines B . . . 7 B3
L'Estany E . . . 41 C3
Les Ternes F . . . 24 B2
Lesterps F . . . 23 B4

Les Thilliers en-Vexin F . 10 B1
Les Touches F . . . 15 B4
Les Trois Moûtiers F . 16 C1
Les Vans F . . . 31 A3
Les Verrières CH . . 19 C5
Les Vignes F . . . 30 A2
Le Teil F . . . 31 A3
Le Teilleul F . . . 8 B3
Le Temple-de-Bretagne
  F . . . 15 B4
Le Theil F . . . 9 B4
Le Thillot F . . . 20 B1
Le Touquet-Paris-Plage
  F . . . 6 B1
Le Touvet F . . . 26 B2
Le Translay F . . . 10 B1
Le Tréport F . . . 10 A1
Letur E . . . 58 A2
Letux E . . . 47 A3
Leucate F . . . 40 B4
Leuglay F . . . 19 B3
Leuk CH . . . 27 A4
Leukerbad CH . . . 27 A4
Leutkirch D . . . 21 B5
Leuven B . . . 7 B4
Leuze-en-Hainaut B . 7 B3
Le Val F . . . 32 B2
Le Val-André F . . 15 A3
Le Val-d'Ajol F . . 19 B5
Levare F . . . 8 B3
Le Verdon-sur-Mer F . 22 C2
Le Vernet F . . . 32 A2
Levet F . . . 17 C4
Levie F . . . 62 B2
Levier F . . . 19 C5
Le Vigan F . . . 30 B2
Lévignen F . . . 10 B2
Le Vivier-sur-Mer F . 8 B2
Levroux F . . . 17 C3
Leysin CH . . . 27 A4
Lézardrieux F . . . 14 A2
Lézat-sur-Léze F . . 40 A2
Lezay F . . . 23 B3
Lézignan-Corbières F . 30 B1
Lezignan-la-Cèbe F . 30 B2
Lézinnes F . . . 18 B3
Lezoux F . . . 25 B3
Lezuza E . . . 52 C1
Lherm F . . . 40 A2
Lhommaizé F . . . 23 B4
L'Hospitalet F . . . 40 B2
L'Hospitalet de l'Infant
  E . . . 47 D1
L'Hospitalet de Llobregat
  E . . . 41 C3
L'Hospitalet-du-Larzac
  F . . . 30 B2
Lhuître F . . . 11 C4
Liancourt F . . . 10 B2
Liart F . . . 11 B4
Liber E . . . 35 B3
Libourne F . . . 28 B2
Libramont B . . . 12 B1
Librilla E . . . 59 B3
Libros E . . . 46 B2
Liceros E . . . 45 A4
Lichères-près-Aigremont
  F . . . 18 B2
Lichtensteig CH . . 21 B4
Lichtervelde B . . . 6 A3
Licques F . . . 6 B1
Lier B . . . 7 A4
Liernais F . . . 18 B3
Liestal CH . . . 20 B2
Liétor E . . . 52 C2
Lieurac F . . . 40 B2
Lieurey F . . . 9 A4
Liévin F . . . 6 B2
Liffol-le-Grand F . . 12 C1
Liffré F . . . 15 A4
Ligardes F . . . 29 B3
Ligne F . . . 15 B4
Lignières F . . . 17 C4
Ligny-en-Barrois F . 12 C1
Ligny-le-Châtel F . . 18 B2
Liguiell F . . . 16 B2
Lille-Bouchard F . . 16 B2
l'Île-Rousse F . . . 62 A1
Lille
  B . . . 7 A4
  F . . . 6 B3
Lillebonne F . . . 9 A4
Lillers F . . . 6 B2
Lillo E . . . 51 A4
Limésy F . . . 9 A4
Limoges F . . . 23 C5
Limogne-en-Quercy F . 29 B4
Limoise F . . . 18 C2
Limone Piemonte I . 33 A3
Limons F . . . 25 B3
Limours F . . . 10 C2
Limoux F . . . 40 A3
Linares E . . . 51 B4
Linares de Mora E . 47 B3
Linares de Riofrío E . 43 B4
Linas de Broto E . . 39 B3
Lindau D . . . 21 B4
Lindenberg im Allgäu D 21 B4
Lindoso P . . . 42 A1
Linkenheim D . . . 13 B4
Linthal CH . . . 21 C4
Linyola E . . . 41 C1
Lion-sur-Mer F . . 9 A3
Liposthey F . . . 28 B2
Liré F . . . 15 B4
Lisboa = Lisbon P . . 48 C1
Lisbon = Lisboa P . . 48 C1
L'Isle CH . . . 19 C5
L'Isle-Adam F . . . 10 B2
L'Isle-de-Noé F . . 29 C3
L'Isle-Jourdain
  Gers F . . . 29 C4
  Vienne F . . . 23 B4
L'Isle-sur-la-Sorgue F . 31 B4
L'Isle-sur-le Doubs F . 19 B5
L'Isle-sur-Serein F . 18 B3
Lisle-sur-Tarn F . . 29 C4
Listrac-Médoc F . . 28 A2
Lit-et-Mixe F . . . 28 B1
Livarot F . . . 9 B4
Livernon F . . . 29 B4
Livigno I . . . 21 C5
Livorno Ferraris I . . 27 B5
Livron-sur-Drôme F . 25 C4

Livry-Louvercy F 11 B4
Lixheim F 12 C3
Lizy-sur-Ourcq F 10 B3
Lladurs E 41 B2
Llafranc E 41 C4
Llagostera E 41 C3
Llançà E 40 B4
Llandudec F 14 A1
Llanes E 36 A2
Llanteno E 37 A3
Llavorsi E 40 B2
Lleida E 47 A4
Llera E 50 B1
Llerena E 50 B1
Lles E 40 B2
Llessui E 40 B2
Llinars E 41 B2
Lliria E 53 B3
Llivia E 40 B2
Llodio E 37 A4
Lloret de Mar E 41 C3
Llosa de Ranes E 53 B3
Lloseta E 61 B2
Llucena del Cid E 47 B3
Llucmajor E 61 B2
Llutxent E 53 C3
Loano I 33 A4
Loarre E 39 B3
Lobón E 49 C4
Locana I 27 B4
Lochau A 21 B4
Loches F 16 B2
Locmaria F 14 B2
Locmariaquer F 14 B3
Locminé F 14 B3
Locquirec F 14 A2
Locronan F 14 A1
Loctudy F 14 B1
Lodares de Osma E 45 A4
Lodève F 30 B2
Lodosa E 38 B1
Loeches E 45 B4
Logroño E 37 B4
Logrosán E 50 A2
Loivos P 42 A2
Loivos do Monte P 42 A2
Loja E 57 A3
Lokeren B 7 A3
L'Olleria E 53 C3
Lombez F 40 A1
Lommel B 7 A5
Londerzeel B 7 A4
Londinières F 9 A5
Longares E 46 A2
Longchamp-sur-Aujon
  F 19 A3
Longchaumois F 26 A2
Longeau F 19 B4
Longecourt-en-Plaine F 19 B4
Longeville-les-St Avold
  F 12 B2
Longeville-sur-Mer F 22 B2
Longny-au-Perche F 9 B4
Longré F 23 B3
Longroiva P 43 B2
Longueau F 10 B2
Longué-Jumelles F 16 B1
Longuyon F 12 B1
Longvic F 19 B4
Longvilly B 12 A1
Longwy F 12 B1
Lons-le-Saunier F 19 C4
Loone-Plage F 6 A2
Lo Pagán E 59 B4
Lopera E 51 C3
Lopigna F 62 A1
Lor F 11 B4
Lora de Estepa E 56 A3
Lora del Río E 56 A2
Loranca del Campo E 45 B5
Lorca E 58 B3
Lorch D 13 A3
Lorgues F 32 B2
Lorient F 14 B2
Lorignac F 22 C3
Loriol-sur-Drôme F 25 C4
Lormes F 18 B2
Lorqui E 59 A3
Lörrach D 20 B2
Lorrez-le-Bocage F 17 A4
Lorris F 17 B4
Losacino E 43 A3
Los Alcázares E 59 B4
Los Arcos E 38 B1
Losar de la Vera E 44 B2
Los Barios de Luna E 35 B5
Los Barrios E 56 B2
Los Caños de Meca E 56 B1
Los Cerricos E 58 B2
Los Corrales E 56 A1
Los Corrales de Buelna
  E 36 A2
Los Dolores E 59 B3
Los Gallardos E 58 B3
Losheim D 12 B2
Los Hinojosos E 52 B1
Los Isidros E 53 B2
Los Molinos E 45 B3
Los Morales E 56 A2
Los Navalmorales E 50 A3
Los Navalucillos E 50 A3
Losne F 19 B4
Los Nietos E 59 B4
Los Palacios y Villafranca
  E 56 A2
Los Pozuelos de Calatrava
  E 51 B3
Los Rábanos E 37 C4
Los Santos E 43 B4
Los Santos de la Humosa
  E 45 B4
Los Santos de Maimona
  E 49 C4
Lossburg D 13 C4
Losse F 28 B2
Los Tijos E 36 A2
Los Villares E 57 A4
Los Yébenes E 51 A4
Louargat F 14 A2
Loudéac F 15 A3
Loudun F 16 B2
Loué F 16 B1
Louhans F 19 C4
Loulay F 22 B3
Loulé P 54 B1

Lourdes F 39 A3
Lourenzá E 35 A3
Loures P 48 C1
Loures-Barousse F 39 A4
Louriçal P 48 A2
Lourinhã P 48 B1
Lourmarin F 31 B4
Loury F 17 B4
Lousa
  Bragança P 43 A2
  Castelo Branco P 49 B3
Lousã P 42 B1
Lousa E 48 C1
Lousada
  E 34 B3
  P 42 A1
Louverné F 16 A1
Louvie-Juzon F 39 A3
Louviers F 9 A5
Louvigné-du-Désert F 8 B2
Louvois F 11 B4
Lozoya E 45 B3
Lozoyuela E 45 B4
Luanco E 35 A5
Luarca E 35 A4
Lubersac F 23 C5
Lubia E 46 A1
Lubian E 35 B4
Lubrin E 58 B2
Luc F 25 C3
Lucainena de las Torres
  E 58 B2
Lúcar E 58 B2
Luçay-le-Mâle F 17 B3
Lucciana F 62 A2
Lucé F 10 C1
Lucena
  Córdoba E 57 A3
  Huelva E 55 B3
Lucenay-les-Aix F 18 C2
Lucenay-l'Evéque F 18 B3
Luc-en-Diois F 26 C2
Luceni E 38 C2
Lucens CH 20 C1
Luceram F 33 B3
Luciana E 51 B3
Lucon F 22 B2
Luc-sur-Mer F 9 A3
Ludweiler Warndt D 12 B2
Ludwigshafen D 13 B4
Luesia E 38 B2
Lugny F 19 C3
Lugo E 34 A3
Lugones E 35 A5
Lugros E 57 A4
Luintra E 34 B3
Lújar E 57 B4
Lumbier E 38 B2
Lumbrales E 43 B3
Lumbreras E 37 B4
Lumbres F 6 B2
Lummen B 7 B5
Lumpiaque E 46 A2
Lunas F 30 B2
Lunas F 30 B2
Lunel F 31 B3
Lunéville F 12 C2
Lungern CH 20 C3
Lupión E 51 B4
Luque E 57 A3
Lurcy-Lévis F 18 C1
Lure F 19 B5
Luri F 62 A2
Lury-sur-Arnon F 17 B4
Lusignan F 23 B4
Lusigny-sur-Barse F 18 A3
Luso P 42 B1
Lussac F 28 B2
Lussac-les-Châteaux F . . .23 B4
Lussac-les-Eglises F 23 B5
Lussan F 31 A3
Lustenau A 21 B4
Lutry CH 20 C1
Luxembourg L 12 B2
Luxeuil-les-Bains F 19 B5
Luxey F 28 B2
Luz
  Évora P 49 C3
  Faro P 54 B1
  Faro P 54 B2
Luzarches F 10 B2
Luzech F 29 B4
Luzern CH 20 B3
Luz-St Sauveur F 39 B3
Luzy F 18 C2
Lyon F 25 B4
Lyons-la-Forêt F 10 B1
Lyss CH 20 B2

M

Mably F 25 A4
Macael E 58 B2
Maçanet de Cabrenys E 40 B3
Mação P 48 B2
Macau F 28 A2
Maceda E 34 B3
Macedo de Cavaleiros
  P 43 A3
Maceira
  Guarda P 42 B2
  Leiria P 48 B2
Machault F 11 B4
Machecoul F 22 B2
Maceira P 42 A1
Macinaggio F 62 A2
Macon B 11 A4
Mâcon F 25 A4
Macotera E 44 B2
Macugnaga I 27 B4
Made NL 7 A4
Maderuelo E 45 A4
Madrid E 45 B4
Madridejos E 51 A4
Madrigal de las Altas Torres
  E 44 A2
Madrigal de la Vera E 44 B2
Madrigalejo E 50 A2
Madrigalejo de Monte E 37 B3
Madriguera E 45 A4
Madrigueras E 52 B2
Madroñera E 50 A2
Maël-Carhaix F 14 A2
Maella E 47 A4
Maello E 44 B3

Mafra P 48 C1
Magacela E 50 B2
Magallon E 38 C2
Magaluf E 60 B2
Magán E 45 C4
Magaña E 38 C1
Magaz E 36 C2
Magescq F 28 C1
Magioto P 48 C1
Magnac-Bourg F 23 C5
Magnac-Laval F 23 B5
Magnieres F 12 C2
Magny-Cours F 18 C2
Magny-en-Vexin F 10 B1
Maguilla E 50 B2
Mahide E 35 C4
Mahora E 52 B2
Maia
  E 38 A2
  P 42 A1
Maiaelrayo E 45 A4
Maials E 47 A4
Maîche F 20 B1
Maienfeld CH 21 B4
Maignelay Montigny F . . .10 B2
Maillezais F 22 B3
Mailly-le-Camp F 11 C4
Mailly-le-Château F 18 B2
Mainar E 46 A2
Maintenon F 10 C1
Mainvilliers F 10 C1
Mainz D 13 A4
Maiorca P 42 B1
Mairena de Aljarafe E . . .56 A1
Mairena del Alcor E 56 A2
Maison-Rouge F 10 C3
Maisse F 10 C2
Maizières-lès-Vic F 12 C2
Majadahonda E 45 B4
Majadas E 44 C2
Málaga E 57 B3
Malagón E 51 A4
Malaguilla E 45 B4
Malaucène F 31 A4
Malaunay F 9 A5
Malborn D 12 B2
Malbuisson F 19 C5
Malcocinado E 50 B2
Maldegem B 7 A3
Malemort F 29 A4
Malesherbes F 10 C2
Malestroit F 15 B3
Malgrat de Mar E 41 C3
Malhadas P 43 A3
Malicorne-sur-Sarthe F 16 B1
Malijai F 32 A2
Mallemort F 31 B4
Mallén E 38 C2
Malléon F 40 A2
Malpartida E 49 B4
Malpartida de la Serena
  E 50 B2
Malpartida de Plasencia
  E 44 C1
Malpas E 39 B4
Malpica P 49 B3
Malpica de Bergantiños
  E 34 A2
Malpica de Tajo E 44 C3
Malsch D 13 C4
Maltat F 18 C2
Malva E 36 C1
Malveira P 48 C1
Mamarrosa P 42 B1
Mamer L 12 B2
Mamers F 9 B4
Mamirolle F 19 B5
Manacor E 61 B3
Mancera de Abajo E 44 B2
Mancha Real E 57 A4
Manchita E 50 B1
Manciet F 28 C2
Mandayona E 45 B5
Mandelieu-la-Napoule F 32 B2
Mane
  Alpes-de-Haute-Provence
    F 32 B1
  Haute-Garonne F 39 A4
Mañeru E 38 B2
Manganeses de la
  Lampreana E 43 A4
Manganeses de la
  Polvorosa E 35 B5
Mangiennes F 12 B1
Mangualde P 42 B2
Manilva E 56 B2
Manises E 53 B3
Manlleu E 41 C3
Männedorf CH 21 B3
Mannheim D 13 B4
Manosque F 32 B1
Manresa E 41 C2
Mansilla de Burgos E 37 B3
Mansilla de las Mulas E 36 B1
Mansle F 23 C4
Manso F 62 A1
Manteigas P 42 B2
Mantes-la-Jolie F 10 C1
Mantes-la-Ville F 10 C1
Manthelan F 16 B2
Manuel E 53 B3
Manzanal de Arriba E 35 B4
Manzanares E 51 A4
Manzanares el Real E 45 B4
Manzaneda
  León E 35 B4
  Orense E 35 B3
Manzanedo E 37 B3
Manzaneque E 51 A4
Manzanera E 47 B3
Manzanilla E 55 B3

Marche-en-Famenne B . . .7 B5
Marchena E 56 A2
Marchenoir F 17 B3
Marcheprime F 28 B2
Marciac F 28 C3
Marcigny F 25 A4
Marcilla E 38 B2
Marcillac-la-Croisille F . . .24 B2
Marcillac-Vallon F 30 A1
Marcillat-en-Combraille
  F 24 A2
Marcille-sur-Seine F 11 C3
Marcilloles F 26 B2
Marcilly-le-Hayer F 11 C3
Marck F 6 B1
Marckolsheim F 20 A2
Marco de Canevezes P . .42 A1
Marennes F 22 C2
Maresquel F 6 B1
Mareuil F 23 C4
Mareuil-en-Brie F 11 C3
Mareuil-sur-Arnon F 17 C4
Mareuil-sur-Lay F 22 B2
Mareuil-sur-Ourcq F 10 B3
Margaux F 28 A2
Margerie-Hancourt F 11 C4
Margès F 25 B5
Margone I 27 B4
Marguerittes F 31 B3
Margut F 11 B5
Maria E 58 B2
Mariana E 46 B1
Mariembourg B 11 A4
Marieux F 10 A2
Marignane F 31 B4
Marigny
  Jura F 19 C4
  Manche F 8 A2
Marigny-le-Châtel F 11 C3
Marin E 34 B2
Marinaleda E 56 A3
Marine de Sisco F 62 A2
Marines F 10 B1
Maringues F 24 B3
Marinha das Ondas P 48 A2
Marinha Grande P 48 B2
Marinhas P 42 A1
Marjaliza E 51 A4
Markdorf D 21 B4
Marolles-les-Braults F 9 B4
Maromme F 9 A5
Marquion F 6 B3
Marquise F 6 B1
Marratxi E 60 B2
Marrupe E 44 B3
Marsac F 29 C5
Marsac-en-Livradois F . . .25 B3
Marseillan F 30 B2
Marseille = Marseilles F 31 B4
Marseille en Beauvaisis
  F 10 B1
Marseilles = Marseille F 31 B4
Mars-la-Tours F 12 B1
Marson F 11 C4
Martel F 29 B4
Martelange B 12 B1
Marthon F 23 C4
Martiago E 43 B3
Martigné-Briand F 16 B1
Martigné-Ferchaud F 15 B4
Martigne-sur-Mayenne
  F 16 A1
Martigny CH 27 A4
Martigny-les-Bains F 19 A4
Martigues F 31 B4
Martim-Longo P 54 B2
Martin de la Jara E 56 A3
Martin Muñoz de las
  Posadas E 44 A3
Martinshöhe D 13 B3
Martinszell D 21 B5
Martorell E 41 C2
Martos E 57 A4
Martres Tolosane F 40 A1
Marugán E 44 B3
Marvão P 49 B3
Marvejols F 30 A2
Marville F 12 B1
Masa E 37 B3
Mas-Cabardès F 40 A3
Mascaraque E 51 A4
Mascarenhas P 43 A2
Mas de Barberáns E 47 B4
Mas de las Matas E 47 B3
Masegoso E 52 C1
Masegoso de Tajuña E . . .45 B5
Masera I 27 A5
Masevaux F 20 B1
Masloc E 38 A3
Masone I 33 A4
Massamagrell E 53 B3
Massanassa E 53 B3
Massat F 40 B2
Massay F 17 B3
Masseret F 24 B1
Masseube F 39 A4
Massiac F 24 B3
Massignac F 23 C4
Massongex E 43 A3
Mata de Alcántara E 49 B4
Matalebreras E 38 C1
Matallana de Torio E 36 B1
Matamala E 45 A5
Mataporquera E 36 B2
Matapozuelos E 44 A3
Mataró E 41 C3
Matet E 53 B3
Mathay F 20 B1
Matignon F 15 A3
Matilla de los Caños del Rio
  E 43 B4
Matosinhos P 42 A1

Matour F 25 A4
Maubert-Fontaine F 11 B4
Maubeuge F 7 B3
Maubourguet F 39 A4
Mauguio F 31 B3
Maulbronn D 13 C4
Maule F 10 C1
Mauléon F 22 B3
Mauléon-Barousse F 39 B4
Mauléon-Licharre F 38 A3
Maulévrier F 22 A3
Maureilhan F 30 B2
Maure-de-Bretagne F 15 B4
Mauriac F 24 B2
Mauron F 15 A3
Maurs F 24 C2
Maury F 40 B3
Maussane-les-Alpilles F 31 B3
Mauvezin F 29 C3
Mauzé-sur-le-Mignon F 22 B3
Maxent F 15 B3
Maxey-sur-Vaise F 12 C1
Maxial P 48 B1
Maxieira P 48 B2
Mayalde E 43 A4
Mayals E 8 B3
Mayenne F 16 B2
Mayorga E 36 B1
Mayres F 25 C4
Mayrhofen A 55 B3
Mazagón E 47 A4
Mazaleón E 30 B1
Mazamet F 31 A4
Mazan F 51 A3
Mazarambroz E 46 B1
Mazarete E 34 B2
Mazarrón E 34 B2
Mazères F 40 A2
Mazères-sur-Salat F 39 A4
Mazières-en-Gâtine F 23 B3
Mazuelo E 37 B3
Méan B 7 B5
Meaulne F 17 C4
Meaux F 10 C2
Mecerreyes E 37 B3
Mechelen B 7 A4
Mecina-Bombarón E 58 C1
Meckenbeuren D 21 B4
Meckenheim D 13 B4
Meckesheim D 13 B4
Meda P 43 B2
Medelim P 49 A3
Medina de las Torres E . . .49 C4
Medina del Campo E 44 A3
Medina de Pomar E 37 B3
Medina de Ríoseco E 36 C1
Medina Sidonia E 56 B2
Medinilla E 44 B2
Medzev SK . . . . .65 B6 [not present]
Meek B 7 A4
Meerssen NL . . . . .7 A6 [not present]
Megève F 26 B3
Mehun-sur-Yèvre F 17 B4
Meilen CH 21 B3
Meilhan F 28 C2
Meimôa P 43 B2
Meina I 27 B5
Meira E 35 A3
Meiringen CH 20 C3
Meisenheim D 13 B3
Meix-devant-Virton B 12 B1
Melgaço P 34 B2
Melgar de Arriba E 36 B1
Melgar de Fernamental
  E 36 B2
Melgar de Yuso E 36 B2
Meliana E 53 B3
Melide E 34 B2
Melides P 54 A1
Melisey F 19 B5
Melle
  B 7 A3
  F 23 B3
Melón E 34 B2
Mels CH 21 B4
Melun F 10 C2
Membrilla E 51 B4
Membrio E 49 B3
Memer F 29 B4
Memmingen D 21 B5
Memoria P 48 B2
Menasalbas E 51 A3
Menat F 24 A2
Mendavia E 38 B1
Mendaza E 38 B1
Mende F 30 A2
Mendiga P 48 B2
Ménéac F 15 A3
Menen B 6 B3
Menetou-Salon F 17 B4
Mengamuñoz E 44 B3
Mengen D 21 A4
Mengíbar E 51 C4
Menou F 18 B2
Mens F 26 C2
Menton F 33 B3
Méntrida E 45 B3
Méobecq F 23 B5
Méounes-les-Montrieux
  F 32 B1
Mequinenza E 47 A4
Mer F 17 B3
Mera
  Coruña E 34 A2
  Coruña E 34 A2
Mercadillo E 37 A3
Merchtem B 7 A4
Merdrignac F 15 A3
Meré E 36 A2
Méréville F 10 C2
Méribel F 26 B3
Méribel Motraret F 26 B3
Mérida E 49 C4
Mérignac F 28 B2
Merksplas B 7 A4
Merlimont Plage F 6 B1
Mersch L 12 B2
Mers-les-Bains F 10 A1
Mértola P 54 B2
Méru F 10 B2
Merufe P 34 B2
Mervans F 19 C4
Merville F 6 B2

Méry-sur-Seine F 11 C3
Merzig D 12 B2
Mesão Frio P 42 A2
Mesas de Ibor E 50 A2
Meschers-sur-Gironde
  F 22 C3
Meslay-du-Maine F 16 B1
Messac F 15 B4
Messancy B 12 B1
Messei F 8 B3
Messejana P 54 B1
Messkirch D 21 B4
Messstetten D 21 A3
Mestanza E 51 B3
Mesvres F 18 C3
Mettendorf D 12 B2
Mettet B 7 B4
Mettlach D 12 B2
Mettlen CH 20 C2
Metz F 12 B2
Metzervisse F 12 B2
Meulan F 10 B1
Meung-sur-Loire F 17 B3
Meuzac F 23 C5
Meximieux F 26 B2
Meylan F 26 B2
Meymac F 24 B2
Meyrargues F 32 B1
Meyrueis F 30 A2
Meyssac F 29 A4
Meysse F 25 C4
Meyzieu F 25 B4
Mèze F 30 B2
Mézériat F 25 A5
Mézidon-Canon F 9 A3
Mézières-en-Brenne F . . .23 B5
Mézières-sur-Issoire F . . .23 B4
Mézilhac F 25 C4
Mézilles F 18 B2
Mézin F 28 B3
Mézos F 28 B1
Mezquita de Jarque E 47 B3
Miajadas E 50 A2
Michelstadt D 13 B5
Middelburg NL 7 A3
Middelharnis NL 7 A4
Middelkerke B 6 A2
Miedes de Aragón E 46 A2
Miedes de Atienza E 45 A4
Miélan F 39 A4
Miengo E 37 A3
Mieres
  Asturias E 35 A5
  Girona E 41 B3
Miesau D 13 B3
Migennes F 18 B2
Migné F 23 B5
Miguel Esteban E 51 A4
Miguelturra E 51 B4
Mijares E 44 B3
Mijas E 57 B3
Milagro E 38 B2
Milhão P 43 A3
Millançay F 17 B3
Millares E 53 B3
Millas F 40 B3
Millau F 30 A2
Millesimo I 33 A4
Millevaches F 24 B2
Milly-la-Forêt F 10 C2
Milmarcos E 46 A2
Mimizan F 28 B1
Mimizan-Plage F 28 B1
Mina de Juliana E 54 B1
Mina de São Domingos
  P 54 B2
Minas de Riotinto E 55 B3
Minatedâ E 52 C2
Minaya E 52 B1
Minde P 48 B2
Minglanilla E 52 B2
Mingorria E 44 B3
Miño E 34 A2
Miño de San Esteban E . .45 A4
Mios F 28 B2
Mira
  E 52 B2
  P 42 B1
Mirabel E 44 B1
Mirabel-aux-Baronnies
  F 31 A4
Miradoux F 29 B3
Miraflores de la Sierra E 45 B4
Miralrio E 45 B5
Miramar P 42 A1
Miramas F 31 B3
Mirambeau F 22 C3
Miramont-de-Guyenne
  F 29 B3
Miranda de Arga E 38 B2
Miranda de Ebro E 37 B4
Miranda do Corvo P 42 B1
Miranda do Douro P 43 A3
Mirande F 29 C3
Mirandela P 43 A2
Mirandilla E 49 C4
Miravet E 47 A4
Miré F 16 B1
Mirebeau F 16 C2
Mirebeau-sur-Bèze F 19 B4
Mirecourt F 19 A5
Mirepoix F 40 A2
Miribel F 25 B4
Missillac F 15 B3
Mittelberg A 21 B5
Mittersheim F 12 C2
Mitton F 23 B5
Moaña E 34 B2
Mocejón E 45 C4
Mochales E 46 A1
Moclin F 57 A4
Modane F 26 B3
Moëlan-sur-Mer F 14 B2
Moerbeke B 7 A3
Móes P 42 B2
Mogadouro P 43 A3
Mogor E 34 B2
Moguer E 55 B3
Mohedas E 43 B3
Mohedas de la Jara E 50 A2
Möhlin CH 20 B2
Moià E 41 C3
Moimenta da Beira P 42 B2

Moirans F 26 B2
Moirans-en-Montagne F .26 A2
Moisdon-la-Rivière F . . .15 B4
Moissac F 29 B4
Moita
  Coimbra P 42 B1
  Guarda P 43 B2
  Santarém P 48 B2
  Setúbal P 48 C1
Moita dos Ferreiros P . .48 B1
Moixent E 53 C3
Mojacar E 58 B3
Mojados E 44 A3
Mol B 7 A5
Molare I 33 A4
Molaretto I 27 B4
Molas F 39 A4
Moledo do Minho P 42 A1
Molières F 29 B4
Molina de Aragón E 46 B2
Molina de Segura E 59 A3
Molinar F 37 A3
Molinaseca E 35 B4
Molinet F 18 C2
Molinicos E 52 C1
Molinos de Duero E 37 C4
Molins de Rei E 41 C3
Molledo E 36 A2
Mollerussa E 41 C1
Mollet de Perelada E . . .40 B3
Mollina E 57 A3
Molló E 40 B3
Molompize F 24 B3
Moloy F 19 B3
Molsheim F 13 C3
Molvizar E 57 B4
Mombeltrán E 44 B2
Mombris D 13 A5
Mombuey E 35 B4
Momo I 27 B5
Monasterio de Rodilla E 37 B3
Monbahus F 29 B3
Monbazillac F 29 B3
Moncada E 53 B3
Moncalieri I 27 B4
Moncalvo I 27 B5
Monção P 34 B2
Moncarapacho P 54 A1
Moncel-sur-Seille F 12 C2
Monchique P 54 B1
Monclar-de-Quercy F . .29 C4
Moncofa E 53 B3
Moncontour F 15 A3
Moncoutant F 22 B3
Monda E 56 B3
Mondariz E 34 B2
Mondéjar E 45 B4
Mondim de Basto P 42 A2
Mondoñedo E 35 A3
Mondorf-les-Bains L . . .12 B2
Mondoubleau F 16 B2
Mondovì I 33 A3
Mondragon F 31 A3
Monein F 39 A3
Mónesi I 33 A3
Monesiglio I 33 A4
Monesterio E 55 B3
Monestier-de-Clermont
  F 26 C2
Monestiés F 30 A1
Monéteau F 18 B2
Monfero E 34 A2
Monflanquin F 29 B3
Monflorite E 39 B3
Monforte P 49 B3
Monforte da Beira
  E 49 B3
  P 49 B3
Monforte d'Alba I 33 A3
Monforte del Cid E 59 A4
Monforte de Lemos E . .34 B3
Monforte de Moyuela E .46 A2
Monistrol-d'Allier F 25 C3
Monistrol de Montserrat
  F 41 C2
Monistrol-sur-Loire F . .25 B4
Monnaie F 16 B2
Monnerville F 10 C2
Monóvar E 53 C3
Monpazier F 29 B3
Monreal E 38 B2
Monreal del Campo E . .46 B2
Monroy E 49 B4
Monroyo E 47 B3
Mons B 7 B3
Monsaraz P 49 C3
Monségur F 28 B3
Montafia I 27 C5
Montagnac F 30 B2
Montaigu F 22 B2
Montaigu-de-Quercy F .29 B4
Montaiguët-en-Forez F .25 A3
Montaigut F 24 A2
Montaigut-sur-Save F . .29 C4
Montainville F 10 C1
Montalbán E 47 B3
Montalbán de Córdoba
  E 57 A3
Montalbo E 52 B1
Montalegre P 42 A2
Montalieu-Vercieu F . . .26 B2
Montalivet-les-Bains F . .22 C2
Montalvão P 49 B3
Montamarta E 43 A4
Montana-Vermala CH . .27 A4
Montánchez E 50 A1
Montanejos E 47 B3
Montans F 29 C4
Montargil P 48 B2
Montargis F 17 B4
Montastruc-la-Conseillère
  F 29 C4
Montauban F 29 B4
Montauban-de-Bretagne
  F 15 A3
Montbard F 18 B3
Montbarrey F 19 B4
Montbazens F 30 A1
Montbazon F 16 B2
Montbéliard F 20 B1
Montbenoit F 19 C5
Montbeugny F 18 C2

Montblanc E 41 C2
Montbozon F 19 B5
Montbrison F 25 B4
Montbron F 23 C4
Montbrun-les-Bains F . .31 A4
Montceau-les-Mines F . .18 C3
Montcenis F 18 C3
Montchanin F 18 C3
Montcornet F 11 B4
Montcuq F 29 B4
Montdardier F 30 B2
Mont-de-Marsan F 28 C2
Montdidier F 10 B2
Monteagudo E 52 B2
Monteagudo de las Vicarias
  E 46 A1
Montealegre E 36 C2
Montealegre del Castillo
  E 53 C2
Montebourg F 8 A2
Monte-Carlo MC 33 B3
Montech F 29 C4
Montechiaro d'Asti I . . .27 B5
Monte Clara P 49 B3
Monte Clérigo P 54 B1
Monte da Pedra P 49 B3
Monte de Goula P 49 B3
Montederramo E 35 B3
Monte do Trigo P 49 C3
Montefrio E 57 A4
Monte Gordo P 54 B2
Montehermoso E 43 B3
Montejicar E 57 A4
Montejo de la Sierra E . .45 A4
Montejo de Tiermes E . .45 A4
Monte Juntos P 49 C3
Montel-de-Gelat F 24 B2
Montelier F 25 C5
Montélimar F 31 A3
Montella E 40 B2
Montellano E 56 A2
Montemagno I 27 C5
Montemayor E 57 A3
Montemayor de Pinilla
  E 44 A3
Montemolin E 55 A3
Montemor-o-Novo P . . .48 C2
Montemor-o-Velho P . . .42 B1
Montendre F 28 A2
Montenegro de Cameros
  E 37 B4
Monteneuf F 15 B3
Monte Real P 48 B2
Montereau-Faut-Yonne
  F 10 C2
Monte Redondo P 48 B2
Monterosso Grana I 33 A3
Monterrey E 35 C3
Monterroso E 34 B3
Monterrubio de la Serena
  E 50 B2
Montesa E 53 C3
Montesalgueiro E 34 A2
Montesclaros E 44 B3
Montesquieu-Volvestre
  F 40 A2
Montesquiou F 29 C3
Montestruc-sur-Gers F .29 C3
Montes Velhos P 54 B1
Monte Vilar P 48 B1
Montfaucon F 15 B4
Montfaucon-d'Argonne
  F 11 B5
Montfaucon-en-Velay F .25 B4
Montferrat
  Isère F 26 B2
  Var F 32 B2
Montfort-en-Chalosse F 28 C2
Montfort-l'Amaury F . . .10 C1
Montfort-le-Gesnois F . .16 A2
Montfort-sur-Meu F 15 A4
Montfort-sur-Risle F 9 A4
Montgai E 41 C1
Montgaillard F 39 A4
Montgenèvre F 26 C3
Montgiscard F 40 A2
Montguyon F 28 A2
Monthermé F 11 B4
Monthey CH 27 A3
Monthois F 11 B4
Monthureux-sur-Saône
  F 19 A4
Montiel E 52 C1
Montier-en-Der F 11 C4
Montiglio I 27 B5
Montignac F 29 A4
Montigny-le-Roi F 19 B4
Montigny-lès-Metz F . . .12 B2
Montigny-sur-Aube F . .19 B3
Montijo
  E 49 C4
  P 48 C2
Montilla E 57 A3
Montillana E 57 A4
Montilly F 18 C2
Montivilliers F 9 A4
Montjaux F 30 A1
Montjean-sur-Loire F . . .16 B1
Montlhéry F 10 C2
Montlieu-la-Garde F . . .28 A2
Mont-Louis F 40 B3
Montlouis-sur-Loire F . .16 B2
Montluçon F 24 A2
Montluel F 25 B5
Montmarault F 24 A2
Montmartin-sur-Mer F . .8 B2
Montmédy F 12 B1
Montmélian F 26 B3
Montmeyan F 32 B2
Montmeyran F 25 C4
Montmirail
  Marne F 11 C3
  Sarthe F 16 A2
Montmiral F 26 B2
Montmirat F 31 B3
Montmirey-le-Château
  F 19 B4
Montmoreau-St Cybard
  F 23 C4
Montmorency F 10 C2
Montmorillon F 23 B4
Montmort-Lucy F 11 C3
Montoir-de-Bretagne F .15 B3
Montoire-sur-le-Loir F . .16 B2
Montoito P 49 C3
Montolieu F 40 A3

Montoro E 51 B3
Montpellier F 31 B2
Montpezat-de-Quercy F .29 B4
Montpezat-sous-Bouzon
  F 25 C4
Montpon-Ménestérol F .28 A3
Montpont-en-Bresse F . .19 C4
Montréal
  Aude F 40 A3
  Gers F 28 C3
Montredon-Labessonnié
  F 30 B1
Montréjeau F 39 A4
Montrésor F 17 B3
Montret F 19 C4
Montreuil
  Pas de Calais F 6 B1
  Seine St Denis F . . .10 C2
Montreuil-aux-Lions F . .10 B3
Montreuil-Bellay F 16 B1
Montreux CH 20 C1
Montrevault F 15 B4
Montricoux F 29 B4
Mont-roig del Camp E . .41 C1
Montrond-les-Bains F . .25 B4
Montroy E 53 B3
Montsalvy F 24 C2
Montsauche-les-Settons
  F 18 B3
Montseny E 41 C3
Montsoreau F 16 B2
Mont-sous-Vaudrey F . .19 C4
Monts-sur-Guesnes F . .16 C2
Mont-St Aignan F 9 A5
Mont-St Vincent F 18 C3
Montsûrs F 16 A1
Montuenga E 44 A3
Montuïri E 61 B3
Monturque E 57 A3
Monzón E 39 C4
Monzón de Campos E . .36 B2
Moorslede B 6 B2
Moos D 21 B3
Mora E 51 A4
Móra P 48 C2
Mòra d'Ebre E 47 A4
Mora de Rubielos E 47 B3
Moradillo de Roa E 45 A4
Moraime E 34 A1
Morais P 43 A3
Mòra la Nova E 47 A4
Moral de Calatrava E . . .51 B4
Moraleda de Zafayona
  E 57 A4
Moraleja E 43 B3
Moraleja del Vino E 44 A2
Morales del Vino E 44 A2
Morales de Toro E 44 A2
Morales de Valverde E . .43 A3
Moralina E 43 A3
Morasverdes E 43 B3
Morata de Jalón E 46 A2
Morata de Jiloca E 46 A2
Morata de Tajuña E 45 B4
Moratalla E 58 A3
Morbach D 12 B3
Morbier F 19 C5
Morcenx F 28 B2
Morcuera E 45 A4
Mordelles F 15 A4
Moréac F 14 B3
Moreda
  Granada E 57 A4
  Oviedo E 36 A1
Morée F 17 B3
Moreles de Rey E 35 B5
Morella E 47 B3
Moreruela de los Infanzones
  E 43 A4
Morés E 46 A2
Morestel F 26 B2
Moret-sur-Loing F 10 C2
Moretta I 27 C4
Moreuil F 10 B2
Morez F 19 C5
Mörfelden D 13 B4
Morgat F 14 A1
Morges CH 19 C5
Morgex I 27 B4
Morhange F 12 C2
Morhet B 12 B1
Morialmé B 7 B4
Moriani Plage F 62 A2
Moriles E 57 A3
Morille E 44 B2
Morlaàs F 39 A3
Morlaix F 14 A2
Morley F 11 C5
Mormant F 10 C2
Mornant F 25 B4
Mornay-Berry F 17 B4
Morón de Almazán E . . .46 A1
Morón de la Frontera E . .56 A2
Morozzo I 33 A3
Mörsch D 13 C4
Mortagne-au-Perche F . .9 B4
Mortagne-sur-Gironde
  F 22 C3
Mortagne-sur-Sèvre F . .22 B3
Mortágua P 42 B1
Mortain F 8 B3
Morteau F 19 B5
Mortemart F 23 B4
Mortrée F 9 B4
Mortsel B 7 A4
Morzine F 26 A3
Mosbach D 13 B5
Mosca P 43 A3
Moscavide P 48 C1
Mosqueruela E 47 B3
Mössingen D 13 C5
Móstoles E 45 B4
Mostuéjouls F 30 A2
Mota del Cuervo E 52 B1
Mota del Marqués E 44 A2
Motilla del Palancar E . .52 B2
Motril E 57 B4
Mouchard F 19 C4
Moudon CH 20 C1
Mougins F 32 B3
Mouilleron-en-Pareds F .22 B3
Mouliherne F 16 B2
Moulinet F 33 B3

Moulins F 18 C2
Moulins-Engilbert F 18 C2
Moulins-la-Marche F 9 B4
Moulismes F 23 B4
Moult F 9 A3
Moura P 54 A2
Mourão P 49 C3
Mourenx F 39 A3
Mouriés F 31 B3
Mourmelon-le-Grand F . .11 B4
Mouronho P 42 B1
Mouscron B 6 B3
Moussey F 31 B3
Moussey F 12 C2
Mousteru F 14 A2
Moustey F 28 B2
Moustiers-Ste Marie F . .32 B2
Mouthe F 19 C5
Mouthier-Haute-Pierre F 19 B5
Mouthoumet F 40 B3
Moutier CH 20 B2
Moûtiers F 26 B3
Moutiers-les-Mauxfaits
  F 22 B2
Mouy F 10 B2
Mouzon F 11 B5
Moyenmoutier F 12 C2
Moyenvic F 12 C2
Mózar E 35 C5
Mucientes E 36 C2
Muda P 54 B1
Mudau D 13 B5
Muel E 46 A2
Muelas del Pan E 43 A4
Mugardos E 34 A2
Muge P 48 B2
Mugron F 28 C2
Mugueimes E 34 C3
Mühlacker D 13 C4
Muhlberg CH 20 C2
Mühleim D 21 A3
Muirteira P 48 B1
Mula E 59 A3
Mulegns CH 21 C4
Mulhouse F 20 B2
Müllheim D 20 B2
Munana E 44 B2
Muñás E 35 A4
Mundaka E 37 A4
Munderkingen D 21 A4
Munera E 52 B1
Mungia E 37 A4
Muñico E 44 B2
Muniesa E 47 A3
Muñopepe E 44 B3
Muñotello E 44 B2
Münsingen CH 20 C2
Münster
  CH 20 C3
  Hessen D 13 B4
Munster F 20 A2
Muntibar E 37 A4
Muotathal CH 21 C3
Muras E 34 A3
Murat F 24 B2
Murato F 62 A2
Murat-sur-Vèbre F 30 B1
Murazzano I 33 A4
Murça P 42 A2
Murchante E 38 B2
Murcia E 59 B3
Mur-de-Barrez F 24 C2
Mur-de-Bretagne F 14 A2
Mur-de-Sologne F 17 B3
Muret F 40 A2
Murg CH 21 B4
Murguia E 37 B4
Muri CH 20 B3
Murias de Paredes E . . .35 B4
Muriedas E 37 A3
Muriel Viejo E 37 C4
Murillo de Rio Leza E . . .37 B4
Murillo el Fruto E 38 B2
Muro
  E 61 B3
  F 62 A1
Muro de Alcoy E 53 C3
Murol F 24 B2
Muron F 22 B3
Muros E 34 B1
Muros de Nalón E 35 A4
Mürren CH 20 C2
Murten CH 20 C2
Murtas E 58 C1
Murten CH 20 C2
Murtosa P 42 B1
Murviel-lès-Béziers F . .30 B2
Musculdy F 38 A3
Mussidan F 29 A3
Musson B 12 B1
Mussy-sur-Seine F 18 B3
Mutriku E 37 A4
Muxía E 34 A1
Muxika-Ugarte E 37 A4
Muzillac F 15 B3
Myennes F 18 B1

N

Naaldwijk NL 7 A4
Nabais P 42 B2
Näfels CH 21 B4
Nagold D 13 C4
Nagore E 38 B2
Naharros E 46 B1
Nailloux F 40 A2
Naintré F 23 B4
Najac F 29 B4
Nájera E 37 B4
Nalda E 37 B4
Nalliers F 22 B2
Nalzen F 40 B2
Namur B 7 B4
Nançay F 17 B4
Nanclares de la Oca E . .37 B4
Nancy F 12 C2
Nangis F 10 C3
Nant F 30 A2
Nanterre F 10 C2
Nantes F 15 B4
Nanteuil-le-Haudouin F .10 B2
Nantiat F 23 B5
Nantua F 26 A2
Naraval E 35 A4
Narbonne F 30 B1
Narbonne-Plage F 30 B2

Narón E 34 A2
Narros del Castillo E . . .44 B2
Narzole I 33 A3
Nasbinals F 24 C3
Naters CH 27 A5
Naucelle F 30 A1
Nava E 36 A1
Navacerrada E 45 B3
Navaconcejo E 43 B4
Nava de Arévalo E 44 B3
Nava de la Asunción E . .44 A3
Nava del Rey E 44 A2
Navafría E 45 A4
Navahermosa E 51 A3
Naval E 39 B4
Navalacruz E 44 B3
Navalcán E 44 B2
Navalcarnero E 45 B3
Navaleno E 37 C3
Navalmanzano E 45 A3
Navalmoral E 44 B3
Navalmoral de la Mata
  E 44 C2
Naválón E 53 C3
Navalonguilla E 44 B2
Navalperal de Pinares E 44 B3
Navalpino E 51 A3
Navaltalgordo E 44 B3
Navaltoril E 50 A3
Navaluenga E 44 B3
Navalvillar de Pela E . . .50 A2
Navaperal de Tormes E .44 B2
Navarclés E 41 C2
Navarredonda de Gredos
  E 44 B2
Navarrenx F 38 A3
Navarrés E 53 B3
Navarrete E 37 B4
Navarrevisca E 44 B3
Navàs E 41 C2
Navascués E 38 B2
Navas del Madroño E . .49 B4
Navas del Rey E 45 B3
Navas del Sepillar E 57 A3
Navas de Oro E 44 A3
Navas de San Juan E . .51 B4
Navasfrias E 43 B3
Nave de Haver P 43 B3
Navés E 41 C2
Navezuelas E 50 A2
Navia E 35 A4
Navia de Suarna E 35 B4
Navilly F 19 C4
Nay F 39 A3
Nazaré P 48 B1
Nebreda E 37 C3
Neckargemünd D 13 B4
Neda E 34 A2
Neerpelt B 7 A5
Negredo E 45 A5
Negreira E 34 B2
Nègrepelisse F 29 B4
Negueira de Muñiz E . . .35 A4
Neila E 37 B4
Néive I 27 C5
Nelas P 42 B2
Nemours F 17 A4
Nenzing A 21 B4
Nérac F 29 B3
Néré F 23 C3
Néris-les-Bains F 24 A2
Nerja E 57 B4
Néronde F 25 B4
Nérondes F 17 C4
Nerpio E 58 A2
Nerva E 55 B3
Nesle F 10 B2
Nesslau CH 21 B4
Netstal CH 21 B4
Nettancourt F 11 C4
Neuchâtel CH 20 C1
Neudorf D 13 C4
Neuenbürg D 13 C4
Neuerburg D 12 A2
Neuf-Brisach F 20 A2
Neufchâteau
  B 12 B1
  F 12 C1
Neufchâtel-en-Bray F . .10 B1
Neufchâtel-sur-Aisne F .11 B4
Neuflize F 11 B4
Neuhausen CH 21 B3
Neuhausen ob Eck D . .21 B3
Neuillé-Pont-Pierre F . .16 B2
Neuilly-en-Thelle F 10 B2
Neuilly-le-Réal F 18 C2
Neuilly-l'Évêque F 19 B4
Neuilly-St Front F 10 B3
Neu-Isenburg D 13 A4
Neulise F 25 B4
Neumagen D 12 B2
Neumarkt
  Luzern CH 20 B3
  Schaffhausen CH . . .21 B3
Neunkirchen D 12 B3
Neuravensburg D 21 B4
Neureut D 13 B4
Neussargues-Moissac
  F 24 B2
Neustadt D 13 B4
Neuves-Maisons F 12 C2
Neuvic
  Corrèze F 24 B2
  Dordogne F 29 A3
Neuville-aux-Bois F 17 A4
Neuville-de-Poitou F . . .23 B4
Neuville-les-Dames F . .25 B4
Neuville-sur-Saône F . .25 B4
Neuvy-le-Roi F 16 B2
Neuvy-Santour F 18 A2
Neuvy-St Sépulchre F . .17 C3
Neuvy-sur-Barangeon F 17 B4
Névache F 26 B3
Nevers F 18 C2
Névez F 14 B2
Nexon F 23 C5
Nice F 33 B3
Niebla E 55 B3
Niederbipp CH 20 B2
Niederbronn-les-Bains
  F 13 C3
Nieder-Olm D 13 B4
Niederurnen CH 21 B4
Nierstein D 13 B4
Nieul-le-Dolent F 22 B2

Nieul-sur-Mer F 22 B2
Nieuwerkerken B 7 B5
Nieuwpoort B 6 A2
Nigüelas E 57 B4
Nijar E 58 C2
Nijlen B 7 A4
Nîmes F 31 B3
Ninove B 7 B4
Niort F 22 B3
Nisa P 49 B3
Nissan-lez-Ensérune F .30 B2
Nitry F 18 B2
Nivelles B 7 B4
Nizza Monferrato I 27 C5
Noailles F 10 B2
Noain E 38 B2
Noalejo E 57 A4
Noblejas E 45 C4
Noceda E 35 B4
Nods F 19 B5
Noé F 40 A2
Noeux-les-Mines F 6 B2
Noez E 51 A3
Nogales E 49 C4
Nogarejas E 35 B4
Nogaro F 28 C2
Nogent F 19 A4
Nogent l'Artaud F 10 C3
Nogent-le-Roi F 10 C1
Nogent-le-Rotrou F 9 B4
Nogent-sur-Seine F 10 C3
Nogent-sur-Vernisson F 17 B4
Noguera E 46 B2
Noguerones E 57 A3
Nohfelden D 12 B3
Noia E 34 B2
Noirétable F 25 B3
Noirmoutier-en-l'Île F . .22 A1
Noja E 37 A3
Nolay F 18 C3
Noli I 33 A4
Nombela E 44 B3
Nomeny F 12 C2
Nomexy F 12 C2
Nonancourt F 9 B5
Nonant-le-Pin F 9 B4
Nonaspe E 47 A4
None I 27 C4
Nontron F 23 C4
Nonza F 62 A2
Nordausques F 6 B2
Noreña E 36 A1
Norrent-Fontes F 6 B2
Nort-sur-Erdre F 15 B4
Nossa Senhora do Cabo
  P 48 C1
Nouan-le-Fuzelier F . . .17 B4
Nouans-les-Fontaines F 17 B3
Nougaroulet F 29 C3
Nouvion F 6 B1
Nouzonville F 11 B4
Novalaise F 26 B2
Novales E 39 B3
Novelda E 59 A4
Novés E 45 B3
Noves F 31 B3
Novés de Segre E 41 B2
Noville B 12 A1
Novion-Porcien F 11 B4
Novy-Chevrières F 11 B4
Noyalo F 15 B3
Noyal-Pontivy F 14 A3
Noyant F 16 B2
Noyelles-sur-Mer F 6 B1
Noyen-sur-Sarthe F 16 B1
Noyers F 18 B2
Noyers-sur-Cher F 17 B3
Noyers-sur-Jabron F . . .32 A1
Noyon F 10 B2
Nozay F 15 B4
Nuaillé F 16 B1
Nuaillé-d'Aunis F 22 B3
Nuars F 18 B2
Nubledo E 35 A5
Nuéno E 38 B3
Nuestra Señora Sa Verge
  des Pilar E 60 C1
Nueva E 36 A2
Nueva Cartoya E 57 A3
Nuevalos E 46 A2
Nuits F 18 B3
Nuits-St Georges F 19 B3
Nules E 53 B3
Numansdorp NL 7 A4
Nuñomoral E 43 B3
Nus I 27 B4
Nusplingen D 21 A3
Nyon CH 26 A3
Nyons F 31 A4

O

O Barco E 35 B4
Obejo E 50 B3
Oberbruck F 20 B1
Oberdiessbach CH 20 C2
Oberdorf CH 20 B2
Oberkirch D 13 C4
Obernai F 13 C3
Obernburg D 13 B5
Oberndorf D 13 C4
Oberriet CH 21 B4
Oberstaufen D 21 B5
Oberstdorf D 21 B5
Oberwesel D 13 A3
Óbidos P 48 B1
Objat F 29 A4
O Bolo E 35 B3
Obrigheim D 13 B5
Ocaña E 45 C4
O Carballiño E 34 B2
Occimiano I 27 B5
Ochagavía E 38 B2
Ochsenhausen D 21 A4
O Corgo E 35 B3
Octeville F 8 A2
Odeceixe P 54 B1
Odeleite P 54 B2
Odemira P 54 B1
Odiáxere P 54 B1
Odivelas P 54 A1
Odón E 46 B2
Offenburg D 13 C3
Offranville F 9 A5
Ofir P 42 A1

Ofterschwang D 21 B5
Ogihares E 57 A4
Ohanes E 58 B2
Ohey B 7 B5
Oia E 34 B2
Oiã P 42 B1
Oiartzun E 38 A2
Oimbra E 42 A2
Oiselay-et-Grachoux F . .19 B4
Oisemont F 10 B1
Oisterwijk NL 7 A5
Ojén E 56 B3
Ojuelos Altos E 50 B2
Olagüe E 38 B2
Olargues F 30 B1
Olazagutia E 38 B1
Olea E 36 B2
Oledo P 49 B3
Oleiros
   Coruña E 34 A2
   Coruña E 34 B1
   P 48 B3
Olen B 7 A4
Olesa de Montserrat E .41 C2
Oletta I 62 A2
Olette F 40 B3
Olhão P 54 B2
Olhavo P 48 B1
Oliana E 41 B2
Olias del Rey E 45 C4
Oliete E 47 B3
Olite E 38 B2
Oliva E 53 C3
Oliva de la Frontera E . .49 C4
Oliva de Mérida E 50 B1
Oliva de Plasencia E . . .43 B3
Olival P 48 B2
Olivar E 57 B4
Olivares E 55 B3
Olivares de Duero E 36 C2
Olivares de Júcar E 52 B1
Oliveira de Azeméis P . .42 B1
Oliveira de Frades P . . .42 B1
Oliveira do Conde P 42 B2
Oliveira do Douro P 42 A1
Oliveira do Hospital P . .42 B2
Olivenza E 49 C3
Olivet F 17 B3
Olivone CH 21 C3
Olliergues F 25 B3
Olmedilla de Alarcón E . .52 B1
Olmedillo de Roa E 37 C3
Olmedo E 44 A3
Olmeto F 62 B1
Olmillos de Castro E . . .43 A3
Olmos de Ojeda E 36 B2
Olocau del Rey E 47 B3
Olonne-sur-Mer F 22 B2
Olonzac F 30 B1
Oloron-Ste Marie F 39 A3
Olost E 41 C3
Olot E 41 B3
Olsene B 7 B3
Olten CH 20 B2
Olula del Rio E 58 B2
Olvega E 38 C2
Olvera E 56 B2
Omegna I 27 B5
On B 7 B5
Oña E 37 B3
Oñati E 37 A4
Onda E 53 B3
Ondarroa E 37 A4
Onesse-et-Laharie F . . .28 B1
Onhaye B 7 B4
Onil E 53 C3
Onis E 36 A2
Ontinyent E 53 C3
Ontur E 52 C2
Onzain F 17 B3
Onzonilla E 36 B1
Oostburg NL 7 A3
Oostende B 6 A2
Oosterhout NL 7 A4
Oosterzele B 7 B3
Oostkamp B 6 A3
Oostmalle B 7 A4
Oostvoorne NL 7 A4
O Páramo E 34 B3
O Pedrouzo E 34 B2
Oper Thalkirchdorf D . . .21 B5
O Pino E 34 B2
O Porriño E 34 B2
Oppenau D 13 C4
Oppenheim D 13 B4
Orada P 49 C3
Oradour-sur-Glane F . . .23 C5
Oradour-sur-Vayres F . .23 C4
Oraison F 32 B1
Orange F 31 A3
Orba E 53 C3
Orbacém P 42 A1
Orbais F 11 C3
Orbassano I 27 B4
Orbe CH 19 C5
Orbec F 9 A4
Orbigny F 17 B3
Orce E 58 B2
Orcera E 58 A2
Orchamps-Vennes F . . .19 B5
Orches F 16 C2
Orchete E 53 C3
Orchies F 6 B3
Orcières F 26 C3
Ordes E 34 A2
Ordino AND 40 B2
Ordizia E 38 A1
Orduña E 37 B4
Orea E 46 B2
Orellana E 50 A2
Orellana de la Sierra E . .50 A2
Organyà E 41 B2
Orgaz E 51 A4
Orgelet F 19 C4
Orgères-en-Beauce F . .17 A3
Orgibet F 39 B4
Orgnac-l'Aven F 31 A3
Orgon F 31 B4
Oria E 58 B2
Origny-Ste Benoite F . . .11 B3
Orihuela E 59 A4
Orihuela del Tremedal
   E 46 B2
Oriola P 48 C3
Orjiva E 57 B4

Orléans F 17 B3
Ormea I 33 A3
Ormelle I 19 B5
Ornans F 19 B5
Oron-la-Ville CH 20 C1
Oropa I 27 B4
Oropesa
   Castellón de la Plana
   E 47 B4
   Toledo E 44 C2
O Rosal E 34 C2
Orozko E 37 A4
Orreaga-Roncesvalles
   E 38 A2
Orsay F 10 C2
Orscholz D 12 B2
Orsennes F 17 C3
Orsières CH 27 A4
Orthez F 28 C2
Ortigueira E 34 A3
Ortilla E 39 B3
Orusco E 45 B4
Orvalho P 49 A3
Orvault F 15 B4
Osann-Monzel D 12 B2
Oseja de Sajambre E . . .36 A1
Osera de Ebro E 47 A3
Osorno E 36 B2
Os Peares E 34 B3
Ospedaletti I 33 B3
Ossa de Montiel E 52 C1
Ossun F 39 A3
Ostheim F 20 A2
Osthofen D 13 B4
Ostiz E 38 B2
Ostrach D 21 B4
Osuna E 56 A2
Oteiza E 38 B2
Oteo E 37 A3
Otero de Herreros E 45 B3
Otero de O Bodas E 35 C4
Ottenhöfen D 13 C4
Otterbach D 13 B3
Otterberg D 13 B3
Ottersweier D 13 C4
Ottignies B 7 B4
Ottmarsheim F 20 B2
Ottobeuren D 21 B5
Ottweiler D 12 B3
Ouanne F 18 B2
Ouarville F 10 C1
Oucques F 17 B3
Oud-Beijerland NL 7 A4
Ouddorp NL 7 A3
Oudenaarde B 7 B3
Oudenbosch NL 7 A4
Oudenburg B 6 A3
Oude-Tonge NL 7 A4
Oud Gastel NL 7 A4
Oudon F 15 B4
Ouguela P 49 B3
Ouistreham F 9 A3
Oulchy-le-Château F . . .11 B3
Oullins F 25 B4
Oulmes F 22 B3
Oulx I 27 B3
Ourém P 48 B2
Ourense E 34 B3
Ourique P 54 B1
Ourol E 34 A3
Ouroux-en-Morvan F . . .18 B2
Oust F 40 B2
Outeiro P 42 B1
Outeiro de Rei E 34 A3
Outes E 34 B2
Outreau F 6 B1
Ouzouer-le-Marché F . . .17 B3
Ouzouer-sur-Loire F . . .17 B4
Ovada I 33 A4
Ovar P 42 B1
Overijse B 7 B4
Overpelt B 7 A5
Oviedo E 35 A5
Oviglio I 27 C5
Oyonnax F 26 A2
Ozaeta E 37 B4
Ozzano Monferrato I . . .27 B5

P

Paal B 7 A5
Paços de Ferreira P 42 A1
Pacy-sur-Eure F 9 A5
Paderne P 54 B1
Padornelo P 42 A1
Padron E 34 B2
Padul E 57 A4
Paesana I 27 C4
Pagny-sur-Moselle F . . .12 C2
Pailhès F 40 A2
Paimboeuf F 15 B3
Paimpol F 14 A2
Paimpont F 15 A3
Pajares E 35 A5
Pajares de los Oteros E .36 B1
Palacios de la Sierra E . .37 C3
Palaciòs de la Valduerna
   E 35 B5
Palacios del Sil E 35 B4
Palacios de Sanabria E . .35 B4
Palaciosrubios E 44 A2
Palafrugell E 41 C4
Palaiseau F 10 C2
Palamòs E 41 C4
Palas de Rei E 34 B3
Palavas-les-Flots F 31 B2
Palazuelos de la Sierra
   E 37 B3
Palencia E 36 B2
Palenciana E 57 A3
Palhaça P 42 B1
Palheiros da Tocha P . . .42 B1
Palheiros de Quiaios P . .42 B1
Paliseul B 11 B5
Pallanza I 27 B5
Pallaruelo de Monegros
   E 47 A3
Pallerols E 40 B2
Palluau F 22 B2
Palma del Rio E 56 A2
Palma de Mallorca E . . .60 B2
Palma Nova E 60 B2
Palmela P 48 C2
Palmerola E 41 B3

Palomares E 58 B3
Palomares del Campo E .52 B1
Palomas E 50 B1
Palos de la Frontera E . .55 B3
Pals E 41 C4
Pamiers F 40 A2
Pampaneira E 57 B4
Pamparato I 33 A3
Pampilhosa
   Aveiro P 42 B1
   Coimbra P 42 B2
Pampliega E 37 B3
Pamplona E 38 B2
Pancalieri I 27 C4
Pancey F 11 C5
Pancorvo E 37 B3
Pancrudo E 46 B2
Panes E 36 A2
Panissières F 25 B4
Pannes F 17 A4
Pantano de Cíjara E 50 A3
Panticosa E 39 B3
Pantin F 34 A2
Pantoja E 45 B4
Pantón E 34 B3
Panxon E 34 B2
Parada
   Bragança P 43 A3
   Viseu P 42 B1
Paradas E 56 A2
Paradela E 34 B3
Parades de Rubiales E . .44 A2
Paradinas de San Juan
   E 44 B2
Paramé F 8 B2
Páramo E 35 A4
Páramo del Sil E 35 B4
Parandaça P 42 A2
Paravadella E 35 A3
Paray-le-Monial F 18 C3
Parceiros P 48 B2
Parcey F 19 B4
Pardilla E 44 A3
Paredes
   E 45 B5
   P 42 A1
Paredes de Coura P 34 C2
Paredes de Nava E 36 B2
Paredes de Siguenza E . .45 A5
Pareja E 45 B5
Parennes F 16 A1
Parentis-en-Born F 28 B1
Pargny-sur-Saulx F 11 C4
Parigné-l'Évêque F 16 B2
Paris F 10 C2
Parisot F 29 B4
Parla E 45 B4
Parlavá E 41 B4
Parolis E 58 A2
Parthenay F 16 C1
Passais F 8 B3
Passegueiro P 42 B1
Passy F 26 B3
Pastrana E 45 B5
Patay F 17 A3
Paterna E 53 B3
Paterna del Campo E . . .55 B3
Paterna del Madera E . . .52 C1
Paterna de Rivera E 56 B2
Patrimonio F 62 A2
Pau F 39 A3
Pauillac F 28 A2
Paulhaguet F 25 B3
Paulhan F 30 B2
Pauva F 48 C2
Pavias E 53 B3
Pavilly F 9 A4
Payerne CH 20 C1
Paymogo E 55 B2
Payrac F 29 B4
Paziols F 40 B3
Peal de Becerro E 58 B1
Pechao P 54 B2
Pedrafita E 35 B3
Pedrajas de San Esteban
   E 44 A3
Pedralba E 53 B3
Pedralba de la Pradería
   E 35 B4
Pedreguer E 53 C4
Pedrera E 56 A3
Pedro Abad E 51 C3
Pedro Bernardo E 44 B3
Pedroche E 50 B3
Pedrógão P 54 A2
Pedrogao P 43 B2
Pedrógão P 48 B2
Pedrógão Grande P 48 B2
Pedrola E 38 C2
Pedro-Martínez E 58 B1
Pedro Muñoz E 52 B1
Pedrosa del Rey E 44 A2
Pedrosa del Rio Urbel E .37 B3
Pedrosa de Tobalina E . .37 B3
Pedrosillo de los Aires
   E 44 B2
Pedrosillo el Ralo E 44 A2
Peer B 7 A5
Pega P 43 B2
Pegalajar E 57 A4
Pegli I 33 A4
Pego E 53 C3
Pegões-Estação P 48 C2
Pegões Velhos P 48 C2
Peguera E 60 B2
Peisey-Nancroix F 26 B3
Pelahustán E 44 B3
Pélissanne F 31 B4
Pellegrue F 28 B3
Pellevoisin F 17 C3
Peloche E 50 A2
Pelussin F 25 B4
Penacerrada E 37 B4
Penacova P 42 B1
Peña de Cabra E 43 B4
Peñafiel E 45 A3
Penafiel P 42 A1
Peñaflor E 56 A2
Peñalba de Santiago E . .35 B4
Peñalsordo E 50 B2
Penalva do Castelo P . . .42 B2
Penamacôr P 43 B2
Peñaparda E 43 B3

Peñaranda de Bracamonte
   E 44 B2
Peñaranda de Duero E . .37 C3
Peñarroya de Tastavíns
   E 47 B4
Peñarroya-Pueblonuevo
   E 50 B2
Peñarrubia E 35 B3
Peñascosa E 52 C1
Peñas de San Pedro E . .52 C2
Peñausende E 43 A4
Pendueles E 36 A2
Penedono P 42 B2
Penela P 48 A2
Penha P 42 A2
Penhas Juntas P 43 A2
Peniche P 48 B1
Penilhos P 54 B2
Peñíscola E 47 B4
Penmarch F 14 B1
Penne-d'Agenais F 29 B3
Pera Boa P 42 B2
Perafita P 42 A1
Peraleda de la Mata E . .44 C2
Peraleda del Zaucejo E . .50 B2
Peraleda de San Román
   E 50 A2
Perales de Alfambra E . .46 B2
Perales del Puerto E 43 B3
Perales de Tajuña E 45 B4
Peralta E 38 B2
Peralta de la Sal E 39 C4
Peralva P 54 B2
Peralveche E 46 B1
Piornal E 44 B2
Percy F 8 B2
Perdiguera E 39 C3
Peredo P 43 A3
Pereiro
   Faro P 54 B2
   Guarda P 43 B2
   Santarém P 48 B2
Pereiro de Aguiar E 34 B3
Perelada E 41 B4
Perelejos de las Truchas
   E 46 B2
Pereña E 43 A3
Pereruela E 43 A4
Periana E 57 B3
Périers F 8 A2
Périgueux F 29 A3
Peris P 48 B2
Pernes-les-Fontaines F .31 A4
Peroguarda P 54 A1
Pérols F 31 B2
Peron F 26 B2
Péronnes B 7 B4
Pero Pinheiro P 48 C1
Perorrubio E 45 A4
Perosa Argentina I 27 C4
Perozinho P 42 A1
Perpignan F 40 B3
Perrecy-les-Forges F . . .18 C3
Perrero I 27 C4
Perrignier F 26 A3
Perros-Guirec F 14 A2
Persan F 10 B2
Pertuis F 31 B4
Péruwelz B 7 B3
Perwez B 7 B4
Pesadas de Burgos E . . .37 B3
Pesaguero E 36 A2
Pesmes F 19 B4
Peso da Régua P 42 A2
Pesquera de Duero E . . .36 C2
Pessac F 28 B2
Pétange L 12 B1
Petín E 35 B3
Petra E 61 B3
Petreto-Bicchisano F . . .62 B1
Pétrola E 52 C2
Peuntenansa E 36 A2
Peveragno I 33 A3
Peyrat-le-Château F 24 B1
Peyrehorade F 28 C1
Peyriac-Minervois F 40 A3
Peyrins F 25 B5
Peyrolles-en-Provence
   F 32 B1
Peyruis F 32 A1
Pézarches F 10 C2
Pézenas F 30 B2
Pezuls F 29 B3
Pfaffenhoffen F 13 C3
Pfäffikon CH 21 B3
Pfetterhouse F 20 B2
Pforzheim D 13 C4
Pfullendorf D 21 B4
Pfungstadt D 13 B4
Pfyn CH 21 B3
Phalsbourg F 12 C3
Philippeville B 7 B4
Piana F 62 A1
Piana Crixia I 33 A4
Pias
   E 35 B4
   P 54 A2
Picassent E 53 B3
Picón E 51 A3
Picquigny F 10 B2
Piedicroce F 62 A2
Piedimulera I 27 A5
Piedrabuena E 51 A3
Piedraescrita E 50 A3
Piedrafita E 36 A1
Piedrahita E 44 B2
Piedralaves E 44 B3
Piedras Albas E 49 B4
Piedras Blancas E 35 A5
Piera E 41 C2
Piere-Buffière F 23 C5
Pierrecourt F 19 B4
Pierre-de-Bresse F 19 C4
Pierrefeu-du-Var F 32 B2
Pierrefitte-Nestalas F . . .39 B3
Pierrefitte-sur-Aire F . . .12 C1
Pierrefonds F 10 B2
Pierrefontaine-les-Varans
   F 19 B5
Pierrefort F 24 C2
Pierrelatte F 31 A3
Pierrepont
   Aisne F 11 B3
   Meurthe-et-Moselle F . .12 B1
Pietra Ligure I 33 A4

Pieve di Teco I 33 A3
Pigna I 33 B3
Pignan F 30 B2
Pilar de la Horadada E . .59 B4
Pilas E 55 B3
Pina de Ebro E 47 A3
Piñar E 57 A4
Pinas F 39 A4
Pineda de la Sierra E . . .37 B3
Pineda de Mar E 41 C3
Pinerolo I 27 C4
Piney F 11 C4
Pinhal Novo P 48 C2
Pinhão P 42 A2
Pinheiro
   Aveiro P 42 A1
   Aveiro P 42 B1
Pinheiro Grande P 48 B2
Pinhel P 43 B2
Pinilla E 52 C2
Pinilla de Toro E 44 A2
Pino F 62 A2
Pino del Rio E 36 B2
Pino de Val E 34 B2
Pinofranqueado E 43 B3
Pinols F 25 B3
Piñor E 34 B2
Pinos del Valle E 57 B4
Pinoso E 53 C2
Pinos Puente E 57 A4
Pinzio P 43 B2
Pionsat F 24 A2
Piornal E 44 B2
Pipriac F 15 B4
Piré-sur-Seiche F 15 A4
Piriac-sur-Mer F 15 B3
Pirmasens D 13 B3
Pisany F 22 C3
Pissos F 28 B2
Pithiviers F 17 A4
Pitres E 57 B4
Pizarra E 57 B3
Plabennec F 14 A1
Placencia E 37 A4
Plaffeien CH 20 C2
Plaisance
   Gers F 28 C3
   Haute-Garonne F 29 C4
   Tarn F 30 B1
Plan E 39 B4
Planchez F 18 B3
Plancoët F 15 A3
Plancy-l'Abbaye F 11 C3
Plan-de-Baix F 26 C2
Plan-d'Orgon F 31 B3
Plasencia E 43 B3
Plasenzuela E 50 A1
Platja d'Aro E 41 C4
Playben F 14 A2
Pléaux F 24 B2
Pleine-Fougères F 8 B2
Plélan-le-Grand F 15 B3
Plémet F 15 A3
Pléneuf-Val-André F 15 A3
Plentzia E 37 A4
Plérin F 15 A3
Plescop F 15 B4
Plestin-les-Grèves F 14 A2
Pleubian F 14 A2
Pleumartin F 23 B4
Pleumeur-Bodou F 14 A2
Pleurs F 11 C3
Pleyber-Christ F 14 A2
Pliego E 59 B3
Ploemeur F 14 B2
Ploërmel F 15 B3
Ploeuc-sur-Lie F 15 A3
Plogastel St Germain F . .14 B1
Plogoff F 14 A1
Plombières-les-Bains F . .19 B5
Plonéour-Lanvern F 14 B1
Plouagat F 14 A2
Plouaret F 14 A2
Plouarzel F 14 A1
Plouay F 14 B2
Ploubalay F 15 A3
Ploubazlanec F 14 A2
Ploudalmézeau F 14 A1
Ploudiry F 14 A1
Plouénan F 14 A2
Plouescat F 14 A1
Plouézec F 14 A2
Plougasnou F 14 A2
Plougastel-Daoulas F . . .14 A1
Plougonven F 14 A2
Plougonver F 14 A2
Plougrescant F 14 A3
Plouguenast F 15 A3
Plouguerneau F 14 A1
Plouha F 14 A3
Plouhinec F 14 A1
Plouigneau F 14 A2
Ploumanach F 14 A2
Plounévez-Quintin F 14 A2
Plouray F 14 A2
Plouzévédé F 14 A1
Plozévet F 14 B1
Pluméliau F 14 B3
Pluvigner F 14 B2
Pobes E 37 B4
Pobla de Segur E 39 B4
Pobladura del Valle E . . .36 B1
Pobla-Tornesa E 47 B4
Pobra de Trives E 35 B3
Pobra do Brollón E 35 B3
Pobra do Caramiñal E . .34 B2
Poceirão P 48 C2
Pociano E 43 A3
Podensac F 28 B2
Podenzano I 27 C5
Poo E 36 A2
Poperinge B 6 B2
Poppel B 7 A5
Pópulo P 42 A2
Porcuna E 57 A3
Pordic F 14 A3
Pornic F 15 B3
Pornichet F 15 B3
Porquerolles F 32 C2
Porrentruy CH 20 B2
Porreres E 61 B3
Porspoder F 14 A1
Port-a-Binson F 11 B3
Portaje E 49 B4
Portalban CH 20 C1
Portale P 35 C4
Portemoure E 34 B2
Portela P 35 C4
Portelo P 35 C4
Port-en-Bessin F 8 A3
Portes-lès-Valence F . . .25 C4
Portets F 28 B2
Portezuelo E 49 B4
Porticcio F 62 B1
Portilla de la Reina E . . .36 A2
Portillo E 44 A3

Portimao P 54 B1
Portinatx E 60 B1
Portinho da Arrabida P 48 C1
Port-Joinville F 22 B1
Port-la-Nouvelle F 30 B2
Port Louis F 14 B2
Portman E 59 B4
Port Manech F 14 B2
Port-Navalo F 14 B3
Porto
F 62 A1
P 42 A1
Porto-Alto P 48 C2
Porto Colom E 61 B3
Porto Covo P 54 B1
Porto Cristo E 61 B3
Porto de Lagos P 54 B1
Porto de Mos P 48 B2
Porto de Rei P 48 C2
Porto do Son E 34 B2
Portomarin E 34 B3
Portonovo E 34 B2
Porto Petro E 61 B3
Porto-Vecchio F 62 B2
Portsall F 14 A1
Port-Ste Marie F 29 B3
Port-St-Louis-du-Rhône
F 31 B3
Port-sur-Saône F 19 B5
Portugalete E 37 A4
Port-Vendres F 40 B4
Porzuna E 51 A3
Posada
Oviedo E 35 A5
Oviedo E 36 A2
Posada de Valdeón E 36 A2
Posadas E 56 A2
Possesse F 11 C4
Potes E 36 A2
Potigny F 9 B3
Potries E 53 C3
Pouancé F 15 B4
Pougues-les-Eaux F 18 B2
Pouilly-en-Auxois F 18 B3
Pouilly-sous Charlieu F 25 A4
Pouilly-sur-Loire F 18 B1
Poujol-sur-Orb F 30 B2
Poullaouen F 14 A2
Pourcy F 11 B3
Pourrain F 18 B2
Pouyastruc F 39 A4
Pouy-de-Touges F 40 A2
Pouzauges F 22 B3
Pova de Santa Iria P 48 C1
Povedilla E 52 C1
Póvoa
Beja P 55 A2
Santarém P 48 B2
Póvoa de Lanhoso P 42 A1
Póvoa de Varzim P 42 A1
Póvoa e Meadas P 49 B3
Poyales del Hoyo E 44 B2
Poza de la Sal E 37 B3
Pozaldez E 44 A3
Pozán de Vero E 39 B4
Pozo Alcón E 58 B2
Pozoantiguo E 44 A2
Pozoblanco E 50 B3
Pozo Cañada E 52 C2
Pozo de Guadalajara E 45 B4
Pozo de la Serna E 51 B4
Pozohondo E 52 C2
Pozondón E 46 B2
Pozuel del Campo E 46 B2
Pozuelo de Alarcón E 45 B4
Pozuelo de Calatrava E 51 B4
Pozuelo del Páramo E 36 B1
Pozuelo de Zarzón E 43 B3
Prada E 35 B3
Pradelle F 26 C2
Pradelles F 25 C3
Prades
E 41 C1
F 40 B3
Prado
E 36 A1
P 42 A1
Prado del Rey E 56 B2
Pradoluengo E 37 B3
Pragelato I 27 B3
Prahecq F 23 B3
Praia P 48 B1
Praia da Rocha P 54 B1
Praia da Viera P 48 B2
Praia de Mira P 42 B1
Pralognan-la-Vanoise F 26 B3
Prat F 40 A1
Prat de Compte E 47 B4
Pratdip E 41 C1
Prats-de-Mollo-la-Preste
F 40 B3
Prauthoy F 19 B4
Pravia E 35 A4
Prayssac F 29 B4
Prazzo I 32 A3
Préchac F 28 B2
Précy-sur-Thil F 18 B3
Pré-en-Pail F 9 B3
Préfailles F 15 B3
Preignan F 29 C3
Prémery F 18 B2
Prémia I 27 A5
Premiàde Mar E 41 C3
Prémont F 11 A3
Presencio E 37 B3
Presly F 17 B4
Pressac F 23 B4
Preuilly-sur-Claise F 23 B4
Prevenchères F 31 A2
Préveranges F 24 A2
Priaranza del Bierzo E 35 B4
Priay F 26 A2
Priego E 46 B1
Priego de Córdoba E 57 A3
Primel-Trégastel F 14 A2
Primstal D 12 B2
Prioro E 36 B2
Privas F 25 C4
Proaza E 35 A4
Proença-a-Nova P 48 B3
Proença-a-Velha P 49 A3
Profondeville B 7 B4
Propriano F 62 B1
Provins F 10 C3
Pruna E 56 B2
Prunelli-di-Fiumorbo F 62 A2
Pruniers F 17 C4
Puchevillers F 10 A2
Puçol E 53 B3
Puebla de Albortón E 47 A3
Puebla de Alcocer E 50 B2
Puebla de Beleña E 45 B4
Puebla de Don Fadrique
E 58 B2
Puebla de Don Rodrigo
E 50 A3
Puebla de Guzmán E 55 B2
Puebla de la Calzada E 49 C4
Puebla de la Reina E 50 B1
Puebla de Lillo E 36 A1
Puebla del Maestre E 55 A3
Puebla del Principe E 52 C1
Puebla de Obando E 49 B4
Puebla de Sanabria E 35 B4
Puebla de Sancho Pérez
E 49 C4
Puente Almuhey E 36 B2
Puente de Domingo Flórez
E 35 B4
Puente de Génave E 58 A2
Puente del Congosto E 44 B2
Puente de Montañana E 39 B4
Puente Duero E 44 A3
Puente-Genil E 56 A3
Puente la Reina E 38 B2
Puente la Reina de Jaca
E 38 B3
Puentelarra E 37 B3
Puente Mayorga E 56 B2
Puente Viesgo E 37 A3
Puertas
Asturias E 36 A2
Salamanca E 43 A3
Puerto de Mazarrón E 59 B3
Puerto de Santa Cruz E 50 A2
Puerto de San Vicente
E 50 A2
Puerto-Lápice E 51 A4
Puertollano E 51 B3
Puerto Lumbreras E 58 B3
Puerto Moral E 55 B3
Puerto Real E 56 B1
Puerto Rey E 50 A2
Puerto Seguro E 43 B3
Puerto Serrano E 56 B2
Puget-Sur-Argens F 32 B2
Puget-Théniers F 32 B2
Puget-ville F 32 B2
Puigcerdà E 40 B2
Puigpunyent E 60 B2
Puig Reig E 41 C2
Puillon F 28 C2
Puimichel F 32 B2
Puimoisson F 32 B2
Puiseaux F 17 A4
Puisieux F 10 A2
Puisserguier F 30 B2
Puivert F 40 B3
Pujols F 28 B2
Pulgar E 51 A3
Pulpi E 58 B3
Punta Prima E 61 B4
Puntas de Calnegre E 59 B3
Punta Umbria E 55 B3
Purchena E 58 B2
Purullena E 58 B1
Putanges-Pont-Ecrepin F 9 B3
Putte B 7 A4
Puttelange-aux-Lacs F 12 B2
Püttlingen D 12 B2
Puy-Guillaume F 25 B3
Puylaroque F 29 B4
Puylaurens F 40 A3
Puy-l'Évêque F 29 B4
Puymirol F 29 B3
Puyôo F 28 C2
Puyrolland F 22 B3
Pyla-sur-Mer F 28 B1

Q

Quargnento I 27 C5
Quarré-les-Tombes F 18 B2
Quarteira P 54 B1
Quatre-Champs F 11 B4
Queige F 26 B3
Queipo E 55 B3
Queixans E 40 B2
Quel E 38 B1
Quelaines-St-Gault F 16 B1
Queljada P 42 A1
Quemada E 37 C3
Queralbs E 41 B3
Quérigut F 40 B3
Quero E 51 A4
Querqueville F 8 A2
Quesada E 58 B1
Questembert F 15 B3
Quettehou F 8 A2
Quevauvillers F 10 B2
Quevy B 7 B4
Quiaois P 42 B1
Quiberon F 14 B2
Quiberville F 9 A4
Quiévrain B 7 B3
Quillan F 40 B3
Quillebeuf F 9 A4
Quimper F 14 A1
Quimperlé F 14 B2
Quincampoix F 9 A5
Quincoces de Yuso E 37 B3
Quincy F 17 B4
Quinéville F 8 A2
Quingey F 19 B4
Quinson F 32 B2
Quinssaines F 24 A2
Quinta-Grande P 48 C2
Quintana de la Serena
E 50 B2
Quintana del Castillo E 35 B4
Quintana del Marco E 35 B5
Quintana del Puenta E 36 B2
Quintana-Martin Galindez
E 37 B3
Quintanaortuño E 37 B3
Quintanapalla E 37 B3
Quintanar de la Orden
E 51 A4
Quintanar de la Sierra E 37 C3
Quintanar del Rey E 52 B2
Quintanilla de la Mata E 37 C3
Quintanilla del Coco E 37 C3
Quintanilla de Onésimo
E 44 A3
Quintanilla de Somoza
E 35 B4
Quintas de Valdelucio E 36 B2
Quintela P 42 B2
Quintin F 14 A3
Quinto E 47 A3
Quiroga E 35 B3
Quismondo E 44 B3
Quissac F 31 B2

R

Raamsdonksveer NL 7 A4
Rábade E 34 A3
Rabanales E 43 A3
Rabastens F 29 C4
Rabastens-de-Bigorre F 39 A4
Racconigi I 27 C4
Rachecourt-sur-Marne
F 11 C5
Radolfzell D 21 B3
Raigada E 35 B3
Rairiz de Veiga E 34 B3
Raiva
Aveiro P 42 A1
Coimbra P 42 B1
Ramacastañas E 44 B2
Ramales de la Victoria
E 37 A3
Rambervillers F 12 C2
Rambouillet F 10 C1
Rambucourt F 12 C1
Ramerupt F 11 C4
Ramirás E 34 B2
Ramiswil CH 20 B2
Ramonville-St Agne F 29 C4
Ramstein-Meisenbach
D 13 B3
Rance B 11 A4
Randan F 25 A3
Randin E 34 C3
Rânes F 9 B3
Rankweil A 21 B4
Ranvalhal P 48 B1
Raon-l'Étape F 12 C2
Raposa P 48 B2
Rapperswil CH 21 B3
Rasal E 39 B3
Rascafria E 45 B4
Rasines E 37 A3
Rasquera E 47 A4
Rastatt D 13 C4
Rasueros E 44 A2
Raucourt-et-Flaba F 11 B4
Raulhac F 24 C2
Rauville-la-Bigot F 8 A2
Rauzan F 28 B2
Ravels B 7 A4
Ravensburg D 21 B4
Razes F 23 B5
Razo E 34 A2
Réalmont F 30 B1
Rebais F 10 C3
Rebordelo P 43 A2
Recas E 45 B4
Recey-sur-Ource F 19 B3
Recezinhos P 42 A1
Recogne B 12 B1
Recoules-Prévinquières
F 30 A1
Redange L 12 B1
Redon F 15 B3
Redondela E 34 B2
Redondo P 49 C3
Régil E 38 A1
Regniéville F 12 C1
Regny F 25 B4
Rego da Leirosa P 48 A2
Regueiro E 34 B2
Reguengo
Portalegre P 49 B3
Santarém P 48 B2
Reguengos de Monsaraz
P 49 C3
Reichelsheim D 13 B4
Reichshoffen F 13 C3
Reiden CH 20 B2
Reigada
E 35 A4
P 43 B3
Reillanne F 32 B1
Reillo E 52 B2
Reims F 11 B4
Reinach CH 20 B3
Reinheim D 13 B4
Reinosa E 36 A2
Relleu E 53 C3
Rémalard F 9 B4
Rembercourt-aux-Pots
F 11 C5
Remedios P 48 B1
Remich L 12 B2
Rémilly F 12 B2
Remiremont F 19 A5
Remolinos E 38 C2
Remoulins F 31 B3
Rémuzat F 31 A4
Renaison F 25 A3
Renazé F 15 B4
Renchen D 13 C4
Rencurel F 26 B2
Renedo E 44 A3
Renens CH 19 C5
Rennes F 15 A4
Rennes-les-Bains F 40 B3
Rentería E 38 A2
Requena E 53 B2
Réquista F 30 A1
Resende P 42 A2
Ressons-sur-Matz F 10 B2
Restábal E 57 B4
Retamal E 49 C4
Rethel F 11 B4
Retie B 7 A5
Retiers F 15 B4
Retortillo E 43 B3
Retortillo de Soria E 45 A4
Retournac F 25 B4
Retuerta del Bullaque E 51 A3
Reuilly F 17 B4
Reus E 41 C2
Reusel NL 7 A5
Revel F 40 A2
Revello I 27 C4
Revenga E 45 B3
Revest-du-Bion F 32 A1
Revigny-sur-Ornain F 11 C4
Revin F 11 B4
Reyero E 36 B1
Rezé F 15 B4
Rhaunen D 13 B3
Rheinau D 13 C3
Rheinfelden D 20 B2
Rhêmes-Notre-Dame I 27 B4
Riallé F 15 B4
Riaño E 36 B1
Rians F 32 B1
Rianxo E 34 B2
Riaza E 45 A4
Riba E 37 A3
Ribadavia E 34 B2
Ribadeo E 35 A3
Riba de Saelices E 46 B1
Ribadesella E 36 A1
Ribaflecha E 37 B4
Ribaforada E 38 C2
Riba-roja d'Ebre E 47 A4
Riba-Roja de Turia E 53 B3
Ribeauvillé F 20 A2
Ribécourt-Dreslincourt
F 10 B2
Ribeira da Pena P 42 A2
Ribeira de Piquín E 35 A3
Ribemont F 11 B3
Ribérac F 29 A3
Ribera de Cardós E 40 B2
Ribera del Fresno E 50 B1
Ribesalbes E 53 A3
Ribes de Freser E 41 B3
Ribiers F 32 A1
Richebourg F 19 A4
Richelieu F 16 B2
Richisau CH 21 B3
Richterswil CH 21 B3
Ricla E 46 A2
Ridderkerk NL 7 A4
Riddes CH 27 A4
Riec-sur-Bélon F 14 B2
Riedlingen D 21 A4
Riedstadt D 13 B4
Riego de la Vega E 35 B5
Riego del Camino E 43 A4
Riello E 35 B5
Rienne B 11 B4
Riénsena E 36 A2
Rieumes F 40 A2
Rieupeyroux F 30 A1
Rieux-Volvestre F 40 A2
Riez F 32 B2
Riggisberg CH 20 C2
Rignac F 30 A1
Rijen NL 7 A4
Rijkevorsel B 7 A4
Rillé F 16 B2
Rillo de Gallo E 46 B2
Rimogne F 11 B4
Rincón de la Victoria E 57 B3
Rincón de Soto E 38 B2
Rinlo E 35 A3
Rio E 34 B3
Riobo E 34 B2
Riodeva E 46 B2
Rio do Coures P 48 B2
Rio Douro P 42 A2
Riofrio E 44 B3
Rio Frio P 48 C2
Riofrio de Aliste E 43 A3
Rio frio de Riaza E 45 A4
Riogordo E 57 B3
Rioja E 58 C2
Riolobos E 49 B4
Riom F 24 B3
Rio Maior P 48 B2
Riom-ès-Montagnes F 24 B2
Rion-des-Landes F 28 C2
Rionegro del Puente E 35 B4
Riopar E 52 C1
Riós E 35 C3
Rioseco E 36 A1
Rioseco de Tapia E 35 B5
Rio Tinto P 42 A1
Riotord F 25 B4
Riotorto E 35 A3
Rioz F 19 B5
Ripoll E 41 B3
Riscle F 28 C2
Riva Ligure I 33 B3
Rivarolo Canavese I 27 B4
Rive-de-Gier F 25 B4
Rivedoux-Plage F 22 B2
Rives F 26 B2
Rivesaltes F 40 B3
Rivoli I 27 B4
Rixheim F 20 B2
Roa E 37 C3
Roanne F 25 A4
Robleda E 43 B3
Robledillo de Trujillo E 50 A2
Robledo
Albacete E 52 C1
Orense E 35 B4
Robledo de Chavela E 45 B3
Robledo del Buey E 50 A3
Robledo del Mazo E 50 A3
Robledollano E 50 A2
Robles de la Valcueva
E 36 B1
Robliza de Cojos E 43 B4
Robres E 39 C3
Robres del Castillo E 38 B1
Rocafort de Queralt E 41 C2
Rocamadour F 29 B4
Rochechouart F 23 C4
Rochefort
B 7 B5
F 22 C3
Rochefort-en-Terre F 15 B3
Rochefort-Montagne F 24 B2
Rochefort-sur-Nenon F 19 B4
Roche-lez-Beaupré F 19 B5
Rochemaure F 31 A3
Rocheservière F 22 B2
Rociana del Condado E 55 B3
Rockenhausen D 13 B3
Rocroi F 11 B4
Roda de Bara E 41 C2
Roda de Ter E 41 C3
Rodalben D 13 B3
Rodeiro E 34 B2
Ródenas E 46 B2
Rödermark D 13 B4
Rodez F 30 A1
Rodoñá E 41 C2
Roesbrugge B 6 B2
Roeschwoog F 13 C4
Roeselare B 6 B3
Roffiac F 24 B3
Rogliano F 62 A2
Rognes F 31 B4
Rogny-les-7-Ecluses F 17 B4
Rohan F 15 A3
Rohrbach-lès-Bitche F 12 B3
Roisel F 10 B3
Rojales E 59 A4
Rolampont F 19 B4
Rollán E 43 B4
Rolle CH 19 C5
Romagnano Sésia I 27 B5
Romagné F 8 B2
Romanèche-Thorins F 25 A4
Romanshorn CH 21 B4
Romans-sur-Isère F 26 B2
Rombas F 12 B2
Romeán E 35 B3
Romenay F 19 C4
Romeral E 51 A4
Romilly-sur-Seine F 11 C3
Romont CH 20 C1
Romorantin-Lanthenay
F 17 B3
Roncal E 38 B3
Ronce-les-Bains F 22 C2
Ronchamp F 20 B1
Ronco Canavese I 27 B4
Ronda E 56 B2
Ronse B 7 B3
Roosendaal NL 7 A4
Ropuerelos del Páramo
E 35 B5
Roquebilière F 33 A3
Roquebrun F 30 B2
Roquecourbe F 30 B1
Roquefort F 28 B2
Roquemaure F 31 A3
Roquesteron F 32 B3
Roquetas de Mar E 58 C2
Roquetes E 47 B4
Roquevaire F 32 B1
Rorschach CH 21 B4
Rosal de la Frontera E 55 B2
Rosans F 32 A1
Rosário P 54 B1
Roscoff F 14 A2
Rosel GB 8 A1
Rosell E 47 B4
Roselló E 47 A4
Rosenfeld D 13 C4
Roses E 41 B4
Rosheim F 13 C3
Rosières-en-Santerre F 10 B2
Rosmaninhal P 49 B3
Rosoy F 18 A2
Rosporden F 14 B2
Rosquete P 48 B2
Rossas
Aveiro P 42 B1
Braga P 42 A1
Rossiglione I 33 A4
Rossignol B 12 B1
Rostrenen F 14 A2
Rota E 55 C3
Rothéneuf F 8 B2
Rotova E 53 C3
Rottenburg D 13 C4
Rotterdam NL 7 A4
Rottweil D 21 A3
Roubaix F 6 B3
Roudouallec F 14 A2
Rouen F 9 A5
Rouffach F 20 B2
Rougé F 15 B4
Rougemont F 19 B5
Rougemont le-Château
F 20 B1
Rouillac F 23 C3
Rouillé F 23 B4
Roujan F 30 B2
Roulans F 19 B5
Roussac F 23 B5
Roussennac F 30 A1
Rousses F 30 A2
Roussillon F 25 B4
Rouvroy-sur-Audry F 11 B4
Rouy F 18 B2
Royan F 22 C2
Royat F 24 B3
Roybon F 26 B2
Roye F 10 B2
Royère-de-Vassivière F 24 B1
Royos E 58 B2
Rozadas E 35 A4
Rozalén del Monte E 45 C5
Rozay-en-Brie F 10 C2
Rozoy-sur-Serre F 11 B4
Ruanes E 50 A2
Rubi E 41 C3
Rubiá E 35 B4
Rubiacedo de Abajo E 37 B3
Rubielos Bajos E 52 B1
Rubielos de Mora E 47 B3
Rucandio E 37 B3
Ruddervorde B 6 A3
Rüdesheim D 13 B3
Rue F 6 B1
Rueda E 44 A3
Rueda de Jalón E 46 A2
Ruelle-sur-Touvre F 23 C4
Ruerrero E 37 B3
Ruffec F 23 B4
Rugles F 9 B4
Ruidera E 52 C1
Ruillé-sur-le-Loir F 16 B2
Ruiselede B 6 A3
Rulles B 12 B1
Rülzheim D 13 B4
Rumigny F 11 B4
Rumilly F 26 B2
Rumont F 11 C5
Runa P 48 B1
Ruoms F 31 A3
Rupt-sur-Moselle F 20 B1
Rus E 51 B4
Rüsselsheim D 13 B4
Rustrel F 31 B4
Rute E 57 A3
Rüti CH 21 B3
Ruynes-en-Margeride F 24 C3

S

Saales F 12 C3
Saanen CH 20 C2
Saarbrücken D 12 B2
Saarburg D 12 B2
Saarlouis D 12 B2
Saas-Fee CH 27 A4
Sabadell E 41 C3
Sabero E 36 B1
Sabiñánigo E 39 B3
Sabiote E 51 B4
Sables-d'Or-les-Pins F 15 A3
Sablé-sur-Sarthe F 16 B1
Sabóia P 54 B1
Sabres F 28 B2
Sabrosa P 42 A2
Sabugal P 43 B2
Sacecorbo E 46 B1
Saceda del Rio E 45 B5
Sacedón E 45 B5
Saceruela E 50 B3
Sacramenia E 45 A4
Sada E 34 A2
Sádaba E 38 B2
Sadernes E 41 B3
Saelices E 45 C5
Saelices de Mayorga E 36 B1
Saeul L 12 B1
Safara P 55 A2
S'Agaro E 41 C4
Sagone F 62 A1
Sagres P 54 C1
Sagunt E 53 B3
Sagy F 19 C4
Sahagún E 36 B1
Saignelégier CH 20 B1
Saignes F 24 B2
Saillagouse F 40 B3
Saillans F 26 C2
Sains Richaumont F 11 B3
St Affrique F 30 B1
St Agnan F 18 C2
St Agnant F 22 C3
St Agrève F 25 B4
St Aignan F 17 B3
St Aignan-sur-Roë F 15 B4
St Alban-sur-Limagnole
F 25 C3
St Amand-en-Puisaye F 18 B2
St Amand-les-Eaux F 7 B3
St Amand-Longpré F 17 B3
St Amand-Montrond F 17 C4
St Amans F 25 C3
St Amans-Soult F 30 B1
St Amant-Roche-Savine
F 25 B3
St Amarin F 20 B1
St Ambroix F 31 A3
St Amé F 20 A1
St Amour F 26 A2
St André-de-Corcy F 25 B4
St André-de-Cubzac F 28 B2
St André-de-l'Eure F 9 B5
St André-de-Roquepertuis
F 31 A3
St André-de-Sangonis
F 30 B2
St Andre-de-Valborgne
F 30 A2
St André-les-Alpes F 32 B2
St Angel F 24 B2
St Anthème F 25 B3
St Antoine F 62 A2
St Antoine-de-Ficalba F 29 B3
St Antönien CH 21 C4
St Antonin-Noble-Val F 29 B4
St Août F 17 C3
St Armant-Tallende F 24 B3
St Arnoult F 10 C1
St Astier F 29 A3
St Auban F 32 B2
St Aubin
CH 20 C1
F 19 B4
GB 8 A1
St Aubin-d'Aubigne F 15 A4
St Aubin-du-Cormier F 15 A4
St Aubin-sur-Aire F 12 C1
St Aubin-sur-Mer F 9 A3
St Aulaye F 28 A3
St Avit F 24 B2
St Avold F 12 B2
St Aygulf F 32 B2
St Bauzille-de-Putois F 30 B2
St Béat F 39 B4
St Beauzély F 30 A1
St Benim-d'Azy F 18 C2
St Benoît-du-Sault F 23 B5
St Benoit-en-Woëvre F 12 C1
St Berthevin F 16 A1
St Blaise-la-Roche F 12 C3
St Blin F 19 A4
St Bonnet F 26 C3
St Bonnet Briance F 23 C5
St Bonnet-de-Joux F 18 C3
St Bonnet-le-Château F 25 B4
St Bonnet-le-Froid F 25 B4
St Brévin-les-Pins F 15 B3
St Briac-sur-Mer F 15 A3
St Brice-en-Coglès F 8 B2
St Brieuc F 15 A3
St Bris-le-Vineux F 18 B2
St Broladre F 8 B2
St Calais F 16 B2
St Cannat F 31 B4
St Cast-le-Guildo F 15 A3
St Céré F 29 B4
St Cergue CH 26 A3
St Cergues F 26 A3
St Cernin F 24 B2
St Chamant F 24 B1
St Chamas F 31 B4
St Chamond F 25 B4
St Chély-d'Apcher F 24 C3
St Chély-d'Aubrac F 24 C2
St Chinian F 30 B1
St Christol F 31 A4

St Christol-lès-Alès F . . .31 A3
St Christoly-Médoc F . .22 C3
St Christophe-du-Ligneron
F 22 B2
St Christophe-en-Brionnais
F 25 A4
St Ciers-sur-Gironde F . .28 A2
St Clair-sur-Epte F 10 B1
St Clar F 29 C3
St Claud F 23 C4
St Claude F 26 A2
St Come-d'Olt F 30 A1
St Cosme-en-Vairais F . .9 B4
St Cyprien
 Dordogne F 29 B4
 Pyrenées-Orientales F . .40 B4
St Cyr-sur-Loire F 16 B2
St Cyr-sur-Mer F 32 B1
St Cyr-sur-Methon F . . .25 A4
St Denis F 10 C2
St Denis-d'Oléron F . . .22 B2
St Denis d'Orques F . . .16 A1
St Didier F 25 A4
St Didier-en-Velay F . . .25 B4
St Dié F 12 C2
St Dier-d'Auvergne F . .25 B3
St Dizier F 11 C4
St Dizier-Leyrenne F . .24 A1
Ste Adresse F 9 A4
Ste Anne F 9 B4
Ste Anne-d'Auray F . . .14 B3
Ste Croix CH 19 C5
Ste Croix-Volvestre F . .40 A2
Ste Engrâce F 38 A3
Ste Enimie F 30 A2
Ste Efflam F 14 A2
Ste Foy-de-Peyrolières
F 40 A2
Ste Foy-la-Grande F . . .28 B3
Ste Foy l'Argentiere F . .25 B4
Ste Gauburge-Ste Colombe
F 9 B4
Ste Gemme la Plaine F .22 B2
Ste Geneviève F 10 B2
St Égrève F 26 B2
Ste Hélène F 28 B2
Ste Hélène-sur-Isère F . .26 B3
Ste Hermine F 22 B2
Ste Jalle F 31 A4
Ste Livrade-sur-Lot F . .29 B3
St Eloy-les-Mines F . . .24 A2
Ste Marie-aux-Mines F . .20 A2
Ste Marie-du-Mont F . . .8 A2
Ste Maure-de-Touraine
F 16 B2
Ste Maxime F 32 B2
Ste Ménéhould F 11 B4
Ste Mère-Église F 8 A2
St Emiland F 18 C3
St Émilion F 28 B2
Sainteny F 8 A2
Ste Ode B. 12 A1
Saintes F 22 C3
Ste Savine F 11 C4
Ste Sévère-sur-Indre F .17 C4
Ste Sigolène F 25 B4
St Esteben F 38 A2
St Estèphe F 28 A2
Ste Suzanne F 16 A1
St Étienne F 25 B4
St Etienne-de-Baigorry
F 38 A2
St Étienne-de-Cuines F .26 B3
St Étienne-de-Fursac F .24 A1
St Etienne-de-Montluc
F 15 B4
St Etienne-de-St Geoirs
F 26 B2
St Étienne-de-Tinée F . .32 A2
St Étienne-du-Bois F . . .26 A2
St Étienne-du-Rouvray F .9 A5
St Etienne-les-Orgues F .32 A1
Ste Tulle F 32 B1
St Fargeau F 18 B2
St Félicien F 25 B4
St Félix-de-Sorgues F . .30 B1
St Félix-Lauragais F . . .40 A2
St Firmin F 26 C3
St Florent F 62 A2
St Florentin F 18 B2
St Florent-le-Vieil F . . .15 B4
St Florent-sur-Cher F . .17 C4
St Flour F 24 B3
St Flovier F 17 C3
St Fort-sur-le-Né F 23 C3
St Fulgent F 22 B2
St Galmier F 25 B4
St Gaudens F 39 A4
St Gaultier F 23 B5
St Gély-du-Fesc F 30 B2
St Genest-Malifaux F . .25 B4
St Gengoux-le-National
F 18 C3
St Geniez F 32 A2
St Geniez-d'Olt F 30 A1
St Genis-de-Saintonge
F 22 C3
St Genis-Pouilly F 26 A3
St Genix-sur-Guiers F . .26 B2
St Georges Buttavent F . .8 B3
St Georges-d'Aurac F . .25 B3
St Georges-de-Commiers
F 26 B2
St Georges-de-Didonne
F 22 C3
St Georges-de-Luzençon
F 30 A1
St Georges-de-Mons F . .24 B2
St Georges-de-Reneins
F 25 A4
St Georges d'Oléron F . .22 C2
St Georges-en-Couzan
F 25 B3
St Georges-lès-Baillargeaux
F 23 B4
St Georges-sur-Loire F . .16 B1
St Georges-sur-Meuse B . .7 B5
St Geours-de-Maremne
F 28 C1
St Gérand-de-Vaux F . .25 A3
St Gérand-le-Puy F 25 A3
St Germain F 19 B5
St Germain-Chassenay
F 18 C2
St Germain-de-Calberte
F 30 A2

St Germain-de-Confolens
F 23 B4
St Germain-de-Joux F . .26 A2
St Germain-des-Fossés
F 25 A3
St Germain-du-Bois F . .19 C4
St Germain-du-Plain F . .19 C3
St Germain-du Puy F . .17 B4
St Germain-en-Laye F . .10 C2
St Germain-Laval F 25 B4
St Germain-Lembron F . .24 B3
St Germain-les-Belles F .24 B1
St Germain-Lespinasse
F 25 A3
St Germain-l'Herm F . . .25 B3
St Gervais-d'Auvergne
F 24 A2
St Gervais-les-Bains F . .26 B3
St Gervais-sur-Mare F . .30 B2
St Gildas-de-Rhuys F . .14 B3
St Gildas-des-Bois F . . .15 B3
St Gilles
 Gard F 31 B3
 Ille-et-Vilaine F 15 A4
St Gilles-Croix-de-Vie F .22 B2
St Gingolph F 27 A3
St Girons
 Ariège F 40 B2
 Landes F 28 C1
St Girons-Plage F 28 C1
St Gobain F 11 B3
St Gorgon-Main F 19 B5
St Guénolé F 14 B1
St Helier GB. 8 A1
St Herblain F 15 B4
St Hilaire
 Allier F 18 C2
 Aude F 40 A3
St Hilaire-de-Riez F 22 B2
St Hilaire-des-Loges F . .22 B3
St Hilaire-de-Villefranche
F 22 C3
St Hilaire-du-Harcouët F . .8 B2
St Hilaire-du-Rosier F . .26 B2
St Hippolyte
 Aveyron F 24 C2
 Doubs F 20 B1
St Hippolyte-du-Fort F . .30 B2
St Honoré-les-Bains F . .18 C2
St Hubert B 12 A1
St Imier CH 20 B2
St Izaire F 30 B1
St Jacques-de-la-Lande
F 15 A4
St Jacut-de-la-Mer F . . .15 A3
St James F 8 B2
St Jaume d'Enveja E . . .47 B4
St Jean-Brévelay F 15 B3
St Jean-d'Angély F 22 C3
St Jean-de-Belleville F . .26 B3
St Jean-de-Bournay F . .26 B2
St Jean-de-Braye F 17 B3
St Jean-de-Côle F 23 C4
St Jean-de-Daye F 8 A2
St Jean de Losne F 19 B4
St Jean-de-Luz F 38 A2
St Jean-de-Maurienne F .26 B3
St Jean-de-Monts F 22 B1
St Jean-d'Illac F 28 B2
St Jean-du-Bruel F 30 A2
St Jean-du-Gard F 31 A2
St Jean-en-Royans F . . .26 B2
St Jean-la-Riviere F 33 B3
St Jean-Pied-de-Port F . .38 A2
St Jean-Poutge F 29 C3
St Jeoire F 26 A3
St Joachim F 15 B3
St Jorioz F 26 B3
St Joris Winge B 7 B4
St Jouin-de-Marnes F . .16 C1
St Juéry F 30 B1
St Julien F 26 A2
St Julien-Chapteuil F . .25 B4
St Julien-de-Vouvantes
F 15 B4
St Julien-du-Sault F . . .18 A2
St Julien-du-Verdon F . .32 B2
St Julien-en-Born F 28 B1
St Julien-en-Genevois F .26 A3
St Julien-l'Ars F 23 B4
St Julien la-Vêtre F 25 B3
St Julien-Mont-Denis F . .26 B3
St Julien-sur-Reyssouze
F 26 A2
St Junien F 23 C4
St Just F 31 A3
St Just-en-Chaussée F . .10 B2
St Just-en-Chevalet F . .25 B3
St Justin F 28 C2
St Just-St Rambert F . . .25 B4
St Lary-Soulan F 39 B4
St Laurent-d'Aigouze F .31 B3
St Laurent-de-Chamousset
F 25 B4
St Laurent-de-Condel F . .9 A3
St Laurent-de-la-Cabrerisse
F 40 A3
St Laurent-de-la-Salanque
F 40 B3
St Laurent-des-Autels F .15 B4
St Laurent-du-Pont F . . .26 B2
St Laurent-en-Caux F . . .9 A4
St Laurent-en-Grandvaux
F 19 C4
St Laurent-Médoc F . . .28 A2
St Laurent-sur-Gorre F . .23 C4
St Laurent-sur-Mer F . . .8 A3
St Laurent-sur-Sèvre F . .22 B3
St Leger B 12 B1
St Léger-sous-Beuvray
F 18 C2
St Léger-sur-Dheune F . .18 C3
St Léonard-de-Noblat F .24 B1
St Lô F 8 A2
St Lon-les-Mines F 28 C1
St Louis F 20 B2
St Loup F 25 A3
St Loup-de-la-Salle F . .19 C3
St Loup-sur-Semouse F .19 B5
St Lunaire F 15 A3
St Lupicin F 26 A2
St Lyphard F 15 B3
St Lys F 40 A2
St Macaire F 28 B2
St Maclou F 9 A4

St Maixent-l'École F . . .23 B3
St Malo F 8 B1
St Mamet-la-Salvetat F . .24 C2
St Mandrier-sur-Mer F . .32 B1
St Marcel
 Drôme F 25 C4
 Saône-et-Loire F 19 C3
St Marcellin F 26 B2
St Marcellin sur Loire F .25 B4
St Marcet F 39 A4
St Mards-en-Othe F 18 A2
St Mars-la-Jaille F 15 B4
St Martin-d'Ablois F . . .11 C3
St Martin-d'Auxigny F . .17 B4
St Martin-de-Belleville F .26 B3
St Martin-de-Bossenay
F 11 C3
St Martin-de-Crau F . . .31 B3
St Martin-de-Londres F .30 B2
St Martin-d'Entraunes F .32 A2
St Martin-de-Queyrières
F 26 C3
St Martin-de-Ré F 22 B2
St Martin des Besaces F . .8 A3
St Martin-d'Estreaux F . .25 A3
St Martin-de-Valamas F .25 C4
St Martin-d'Hères F 26 B2
St Martin-du-Frêne F . . .26 A2
St Martin-en-Bresse F . .19 C4
St Martin-en-Haut F . . .25 B4
St Martin-la-Méanne F . .24 B1
St Martin-Osmonville F . .10 B1
St Martin-sur-Ouanne F .18 B2
St Martin-Valmeroux F . .24 B2
St Martin-Vésubie F 33 A3
St Martory F 39 A4
St Mathieu F 23 C4
St Mathieu-de-Tréviers
F 31 B2
St Maurice CH 27 A3
St Maurice-Navacelles
F 30 B2
St Maurice-sur-Moselle
F 20 B1
St Maximin-la-Ste Baume
F 32 B1
St Méard-de-Gurçon F . .28 B3
St Médard-de-Guizières
F 28 A2
St Médard-en-Jalles F . .28 B2
St Méen-le-Grand F 15 A3
St Menges F 11 B4
St M'Hervé F 15 A4
St Michel
 Aisne F 11 B4
 Gers F 39 A4
St Michel-Chef-Chef F . .15 B3
St Michel-de-Castelnau
F 28 B2
St Michel-de-Maurienne
F 26 B3
St Michel-en-Grève F . . .14 A2
St Michel-enl'Herm F . . .22 B2
St Michel-Mont-Mercure
F 22 B3
St Mihiel F 12 C1
St Montant F 31 A3
St Moritz CH 21 C4
St Nazaire F 15 B3
St Nazaire-en-Royans F .26 B2
St Nazaire-le-Désert F . .31 A4
St Nectaire F 24 B2
St Nicolas-de-Port F . . .12 C2
St Nicolas-de-Redon F . .15 B3
St Nicolas-du-Pélem F . .14 A2
St Niklaas F 7 A4
St Omer F 6 B2
St Pair-sur-Mer F 8 B2
St Palais F 38 A2
St Palais-sur-Mer F 22 C2
St Pardoux-la-Rivière F . .23 C4
St Paul-Cap-de-Joux F . .29 C4
St Paul-de-Fenouillet F . .40 B3
St Paul-de-Varax F 26 A2
St Paulien F 25 B3
St Paul-le-Jeune F 31 A3
St Paul-lès-Dax F 28 C1
St Paul-Trois-Châteaux
F 31 A3
St Pé-de-Bigorre F 39 A3
St Pée-sur-Nivelle F . . .38 A2
St Péravy-la-Colombe F .17 B3
St Péray F 25 C4
St Père-en-Retz F 15 B3
St Peter Port GB. 8 A1
St Philbert-de-Grand-Lieu
F 22 A2
St Pierre F 30 B1
St Pierre-d'Albigny F . . .26 B3
St Pierre-d'Allevard F . . .26 B3
St Pierre-de-Chartreuse
F 26 B2
St Pierre-de-Chignac F . .29 A3
St Pierre-la-Fage F 30 B2
St Pierre-d'Entremont F . .26 B2
St Pierre-d'Oléron F 22 C2
St Pierre-Eglise F 8 A2
St Pierre-en-Port F 9 A4
St Pierre-le-Moûtier F . .18 C2
St Pierre Montlimart F . .15 B4
St Pierre-Quiberon F . . .14 B2
St Pierre-sur-Dives F . . .9 A3
St Pierreville F 25 C4
St Pieters-Leeuw B 7 B4
St Plancard F 39 A4
St Poix F 15 B4
St Pol-de-Léon F 14 A2
St Polgues F 25 B3
St Pol-sur-Ternoise F . . .6 B2
St Pons-de-Thomières
F 30 B1
St Porchaire F 22 C3
St Pourçain-sur-Sioule
F 24 A3
St Priest F 25 B4
St Privat F 24 B2
St Quay-Portrieux F 14 A3
St Quentin F 10 B3
St Quentin-la-Poterie F . .31 A3
St Quentin-les-Anges F . .16 B1
St Rambert-d'Albon F . .25 B4
St Rambert-en-Bugey F . .26 B2
St Raphaël F 32 B2
St Rémy-de-Provence F .31 B3
St Rémy-du-Val F 9 B4

St Remy-en-Bouzemont
F 11 C4
St Renan F 14 A1
St Révérien F 18 B2
St Riquier F 10 A1
St Rome-de-Cernon F . .30 A1
St Rome-de-Tarn F 30 A1
St Sadurni-d'Anoia E . . .41 C2
St Saëns F 9 A5
St Sampson GB. 8 A1
St Samson-la-Poterie F .10 B1
St Saturnin-de-Lenne F .30 A2
St Saturnin-lès-Apt F . . .31 B4
St Sauflieu F 10 B2
St Saulge F 18 B2
St Sauveur
 Finistère F 14 A2
 Haute-Saône F 19 B5
St Sauveur-de-Montagut
F 25 C4
St Sauveur-en-Puisaye
F 18 B2
St Sauveur-le-Rue F . . .25 B4
St Sauveur-Lendelin F . .8 A2
St Sauveur-le-Vicomte F . .8 A2
St Sauveur-sur-Tinée F .32 A3
St Savin
 Gironde F 28 A2
 Vienne F 23 B4
St Savinien F 22 C3
St Savournin F 31 B4
St Seine-l'Abbaye F 19 B3
St Sernin-sur-Rance F . .30 B1
St Sevan-sur-Mer F 8 B1
St Sever F 28 C2
St Sever-Calvados F 8 B2
St Sorlin-d'Arves F 26 B3
St Soupplets F 10 B2
St Sulpice F 29 C4
St Sulpice-Laurière F . . .24 A1
St Sulpice-les-Feuilles
F 23 B5
St Symphorien F 28 B2
St Symphoriende-Lay F .25 B4
St Symphorien d'Ozon
F 25 B4
St Symphoriensur-Coise
F 25 B4
St Thégonnec F 14 A2
St Thiébault F 19 A4
St Trivier-de-Courtes F . .26 A2
St Trivier sur-Moignans
F 25 A4
St Trojan-les-Bains F . . .22 C2
St Tropez F 32 B2
St Truiden B 7 B5
St Vaast-la-Hougue F . . .8 A2
St Valérien F 18 A2
St Valery-en-Caux F 9 A4
St Valéry-sur-Somme F . .6 B1
St Vallier
 Drôme F 25 B4
 Saône-et-Loire F 18 C3
St Vallier-de-Thiey F . . .32 B2
St Varent F 16 C1
St Vaury F 24 A1
St Venant F 6 B2
St Véran F 27 C3
St Vincent I 27 B4
St Vincent-de-Tyrosse
F 28 C1
St Vit F 19 B4
St Vivien-de-Médoc F . .22 C2
St Yan F 25 A4
St Ybars F 40 A2
St Yorre F 25 A3
St Yrieix-la-Perche F . . .23 C5
Saissac F 40 A3
Saja E 36 A2
Salamanca E 44 B2
Salar E 57 A3
Salardú E 39 B4
Salas E 35 A4
Salas de los Infantes E .37 B3
Salau F 40 B2
Salavaux CH 20 C2
Salbertrand I 27 B3
Salbris F 17 B4
Salce E 35 B4
Saldaña E 36 B2
Salem D 21 B4
Salernes F 32 B2
Salers F 24 B2
Sales E 35 B4
Salies-de-Béarn F 38 A3
Salies-du-Salat F 39 A4
Salignac-Eyvigues F . . .29 B4
Saligney-sur-Roudon F .18 C2
Salinas
 Alicante E 53 C3
 Huesca E 39 B4
Salinas de Medinaceli E .46 A1
Salinas de Pisuerga E . .36 B2
Salindres F 31 A3
Salins-les-Bains F 19 C4
Salir P 54 B1
Sallanches F 26 B3
Sallent E 41 C2
Sallent de Gállego E . . .39 B3
Salles F 28 B2
Salles-Curan F 30 A1
Salles-sur-l'Hers F 40 A2
Salmerón E 46 B1
Salmiech F 30 A1
Salmoral E 44 B2
Salobreña E 57 B4
Salon-de-Provence F . . .31 B4
Salornay-sur-Guye F . . .18 C3
Salou E 41 C2
Salses-le-Chateau F . . .40 B3
Salt E 41 C3
Salto P 42 A2
Salussola I 27 B5
Saluzzo I 27 C4
Salvacañete E 46 B2
Salvada P 54 B2
Salvagnac F 29 C4
Salvaleon E 49 C4
Salvaterra de Magos P . .48 B2
Salvaterra do Extremo
P 49 B3
Salvatierra
 Avila E 44 B2

Salvatierra continued
 Badajoz E 49 C4
Salvatierra de Santiago
E 50 A1
Salviac F 29 B4
Samadet F 28 C2
Samatan F 40 A1
Samedan CH 21 C4
Samer F 6 B1
Samnaun CH 21 C5
Samoëns F 26 A3
Samogneux F 12 B1
Samora Correia P 48 C2
Samos E 35 B3
Samper de Calanda E . .47 A3
Sampéyre I 33 A3
Sampigny F 12 C1
San Adrián E 38 B2
San Agustin E 58 C2
San Agustin de Guadalix
E 45 B4
San Amaro E 34 B2
San Andrés del Rabanedo
E 36 B1
San Antolin de Ibias E . .35 A4
Sanary-sur-Mer F 32 B1
San Asensio E 37 B4
San Bartoloméde las
 Abiertas E 44 C3
San Bartoloméde la Torre
E 55 B2
San Bartoloméde Pinares
E 44 B3
San Benito E 50 B3
San Benito de la Contienda
E 49 C3
San Calixto E 50 C2
San Carlo CH 27 A5
San Carlos del Valle E . .51 B4
San Cebrián de Castro
E 43 A4
Sancergues F 18 B1
Sancerre F 17 B4
Sancey-le-Long F 19 B5
Sanchiorian E 44 B3
Sanchonuño E 45 A3
San Cibrao das Viñas E .34 B3
San Ciprián E 35 A3
San Clemente E 52 B1
San Clodio E 35 B3
Sancoins F 18 C1
San Crisóbal de Entreviñas
E 36 B1
San Cristóbal de la
 Polantera E 35 B5
San Cristóbal de la Vega
E 44 A3
San Cristovo E 35 C3
Sancti-Petri E 56 B1
Sancti-Spiritus E 43 B3
San Damiano d'Asti I . . .27 C5
San Damiano Macra I . . .33 A3
Sandillon F 17 B4
Sando E 43 B3
San Emiliano E 35 B5
San Enrique E 56 B2
San Esteban E 35 A4
San Esteban de Gormaz
E 45 A4
San Esteban de la Sierra
E 43 B4
San Esteban de Litera
E 39 C4
San Esteban del Molar
E 36 C1
San Esteban del Valle E .44 B3
San Esteban de Valdueza
E 35 B4
San Felices E 37 B3
San Felices de los Gallégos
E 43 B3
San Fernando E 56 B1
San Fernando de Henares
E 45 B4
Sangatte F 6 B1
San Germano Vercellese
I 27 B5
Sangonera la Verde E . .59 B3
Sangüesa E 38 B2
Sanguinet F 28 B1
San Javier E 59 B4
San Jorge P 48 B2
San José E 58 C2
San Juan E 37 B3
San Juan de Alicante E .59 A4
San Juan de la Nava E . .44 B3
San Justo de la Vega E .35 B4
Sankt Anton am Arlberg
E 21 B5
Sankt Blasien D. 20 B3
Sankt Gallen CH 21 B4
Sankt Gallenkirch A 21 B4
Sankt Georgen D. 20 A3
Sankt Ingbert D 12 B3
Sankt Margrethen CH . . .21 B4
Sankt Niklaus CH 27 A4
Sankt Paul F 32 A2
Sankt Peter D 20 A3
Sankt Wendel D. 12 B3
San Leonardo de Yagüe
E 37 C3
San Lorenzo al Mare I . . .33 B3
San Lorenzo de Calatrava
E 51 B4
San Lorenzo de El Escorial
E 45 B3
San Lorenzo de la Parrilla
E 52 B1
San Lourenco P 54 A1
Sanlúcar de Barrameda
E 55 C3
Sanlúcar de Guadiana
E 54 B2
Sanlúcar la Mayor E . . .55 B3
San Marcial E 43 A4
San Martin de Castañeda
E 35 B4
San Martin de la Vega E .45 B4
San Martin de la Vega del
 Alberche E 44 B2
San Martin del Tesorillo
E 56 B2
San Martin de Luiña E . .35 A4
San Martin de Montalbán
E 51 A3
San Martin de Oscos E . .35 A4

San Martin de Pusa E . .44 C3
San Martin de Unx E . . .38 B2
San Martin de Valdeiglesias
E 44 B3
San Mateo de Gallego E .38 C3
San Michele Mondov i l . .33 A3
San Miguel de Aguayo
E 36 A2
San Miguel de Bernuy E .45 A4
San Miguel del Arroyo
E 44 A3
San Miguel de Salinas
E 59 B4
San Millán de la Cogolla
E 37 B4
San Muñoz E 43 B3
San Nicolás del Puerto
E 50 C2
San Pablo de los Montes
E 51 A3
San Pedro
 Albacete E 52 C1
 Oviedo E 35 A4
San Pedro de Alcántara
E 56 B3
San Pedro de Ceque E . .35 B4
San Pedro de Arroyo E . .44 B3
San Pedro de Latarce E .36 C1
San Pedro del Pinatar E .59 B4
San Pedro del Romeral
E 37 A3
San Pedro de Merida E . .50 B1
San Pedro de Valderaduey
E 36 B2
San Pedro Manrique E . .38 B1
San Rafael del Rio E . . .47 B4
San Remo I 33 B3
San Román de Cameros
E 37 B4
San Roman de Hernija
E 44 A2
San Román de la Cuba
E 36 B2
San Roman de los Montes
E 44 B3
San Romao P. 49 C3
San Roque E 56 B2
San Roque de Riomera
E 37 A3
San Sabastián de los
 Ballesteros E 56 A3
San Salvador de
 Cantamuda E 36 B2
San Sebastián de los Reyes
E 45 B4
San Silvestre de Guzmán
E 55 B2
Santa Agnès E 60 B1
Santa Amalia E 50 A1
Santa Ana
 Cáceres E 50 A2
 Jaén E 57 A4
Santa Ana de Pusa E . .44 C3
Santa Barbara E 47 B4
Santa Bárbara P 54 B1
Santa Barbara de Casa
E 55 B2
Santa Bárbara de Padrões
P 54 B2
Santacara E 38 B2
Santa Catarina P 54 B2
Santa Clara-a-Nova P . .54 B1
Santa Clara-a-Velha P . .54 B1
Santa Clara de Louredo
P 54 B2
Santa Coloma de Farners
E 41 C3
Santa Coloma de Gramenet
E 41 C3
Santa Coloma de Queralt
E 41 C2
Santa Colomba de Curueño
E 36 B1
Santa Colomba de Somoza
E 35 B4
Santa Comba E 34 A2
Santa Comba Dáo P . . .42 B1
Santa Comba de Rossas
P 43 A3
Santa Cristina de la
 Polvorosa E 35 B5
Santa Cruz
 E 34 A2
 P 48 B1
Santa Cruz de Alhama
E 57 A4
Santa Cruz de Campezo
E 37 B4
Santa Cruz de Grio E . . .46 A2
Santa Cruz de la Salceda
E 45 A4
Santa Cruz de la Sierra
E 50 A2
Santa Cruz de la Zarza
E 45 C4
Santa Cruz del Retamar
E 45 B3
Santa Cruz del Valle E . .44 B2
Santa Cruz de Moya E . .53 B2
Santa Cruz de Mudela E .51 B4
Santa Cruz de Paniagua
E 43 B3
Santa Elena E 51 B4
Santa Elena de Jamuz
E 35 B5
Santaella E 56 A3
Santa Eufemia E 50 B3
Santa Eulália P 49 C3
Santa Eulalia de Oscos
E 35 A3
Santa Eulàlia des Riu E .60 C1
Santa Fe E 57 A4
Sant Agust ide Lluçanès
E 41 B3
Santa Iria P 54 B2
Santa Leocadia P 42 A1
Santa Lucia-de-Porto-
 Vecchio P 62 B2
Santa Luzia P 54 B1
Santa Magdalena de Polpis
E 47 B4

Santa Margalida E. 61 B3
Santa Margarida P. 48 B2
Santa Margarida do Sado
P 54 A1
Santa Margaridao de
Montbui E. 41 C2
Santa Maria E. 38 B3
Santa Maria da Feira P. .42 B1
Santa Maria de Cayón
E. 37 A3
Santa Maria de Corco E .41 B3
Santa Maria de Huerta
E. 46 A1
Santa Maria de la Alameda
E. 45 B3
Santa Maria de las Hoyas
E. 37 C3
Santa Maria del Cami E .61 B2
Santa Maria del Campo
E. 37 B3
Santa Maria del Campo Rus
E. 52 B1
Santa Maria del Páramo
E. 36 B1
Santa Maria de Mercadillo
E. 37 C3
Santa Maria de Nieva E. .58 B3
Santa Maria de Trassierra
E. 50 C3
Santa María la Real de
Nieva E. 44 A3
Santa Maria Maggiore I. .27 A5
Santa Maria Ribarredonda
E. 37 B3
Santa Marina del Rey E .35 B5
Santa Marta
Albacete E. 52 B1
Badajoz E 49 C4
Santa Marta de Magasca
E. 50 A1
Santa Marta de Penaguião
P 42 A2
Santa Marta de Tormes
E. 44 B2
Santana
Évora P 48 C2
Setúbal P. 48 C1
Santana da Serra P. 54 B2
Sant'Ana de Cambas P. .54 B2
Santana do Mato P 48 C2
Santander E. 37 A3
Sant Antoni de Calonge
E. 41 C4
Sant Antoni de Portmany
E. 60 C1
Santanyi E 61 B3
Santa Olalla
Huelva E 55 B3
Toledo E 44 B3
Santa Pau E. 41 B3
Santa Pola E. 59 A4
Santa Ponça E. 60 B2
Santarém P 48 B2
Santa Severa F. 62 A2
Santas Martas E 36 B1
Santa Susana E. 48 C2
Santa Suzana P. 49 C3
Santa Uxía E. 34 B2
Sant Boi de Llobregat E .41 C3
Sant Carles de la Ràpita
E. 47 B4
Sant Carlos E. 60 B1
Sant Celoni E. 41 C3
Sant Climent E. 61 B4
Santed E. 46 A2
Santelices E 37 A3
San Telmo E 55 B3
Santervas de la Vega E. .36 B2
Sant Feliu E. 41 C3
Sant Feliu de Codines
E. 41 C3
Sant Feliu de Guíxols E .41 C4
Sant Feliu Sasserra E. . .41 C3
Sant Ferran E 60 C1
Sant Francesc de
Formentera E. 60 C1
Sant Francesc de ses
Salines E. 60 C1
Santhià I. 27 B5
Sant Hilari Sacalm E. . . .41 C3
Sant Hipòlit de Voltregà
E. 41 B3
Santiago de Alcántara
E. 49 B3
Santiago de Calatrava E .57 A3
Santiago de Compostela
E. 34 B2
Santiago de la Espade
E. 58 A2
Santiago de la Puebla E .44 B2
Santiago de la Ribera E .59 B4
Santiago del Campo E . .49 B4
Santiago de Litem P. . . .48 B2
Santiago do Cacém P. . .54 B1
Santiago do Escoural P .48 C2
Santiago Maior P. 48 C2
Santibáñez de Béjar E. .44 B2
Santibáñez de la Peña
E. 36 B2
Santibáñez de Murias
E. 36 A1
Santibáñez de Vidriales
E. 35 B4
Santibáñez el Alto E. . . .43 B3
Santibáñez el Bajo E. . .43 B3
Santillana E 36 A2
Santiponce E. 56 A1
San Tirso de Abres E . . .35 A3
Santisteban del Puerto
E. 51 B4
Santiuste de San Juan
Bautiste E. 44 A3
Santiz E. 43 A4
Sant Jaume dels Domenys
E. 41 C2
Sant Joan Baptista E . . .60 B1
Sant Joan de les Abadesses
E. 41 B3
Sant Jordi E. 47 B4
Sant Josep de sa Talaia
E. 60 C1
Sant Juliáde Loria AND .40 B2

Sant Llorençde Morunys
E. 41 B2
Sant Llorençdes Carctassar
E. 61 B3
Sant Llorenç Savall E. . .41 C3
Sant Luis E 61 B4
Sant Mart ide Llemaná
E. 41 B3
Sant Martí de Maldá E. .41 C2
Sant Martí Sarroca E. . .41 C2
Sant Mateu E. 47 B4
Sant Miquel E. 60 B1
Santo Aleixo P. 55 A2
Santo Amado P 55 A2
Santo Amaro P 49 C3
Santo André E 54 A1
Santo Domingo E 49 C3
Santo Domingo de la
Calzada E. 37 B4
Santo Domingo de Silos
E. 37 C3
Santo Estêvão
Faro P 54 B2
Santarém P 48 C2
Santomera E 59 A3
Santoña E. 37 A3
Santo-Pietro-di Tenda F .62 A2
Santo Tirso P 42 A1
Santotis E 36 A2
Santo Tomé E 58 A1
Santovenia
Burgos E 37 B3
Zamora E. 36 C1
Sant Pau de Seguries E .41 B3
Santpedor E 41 C2
Sant Pere de Riudebitles
E. 41 C2
Sant Pere Pescador E. .41 B4
Sant Pere Sallavinera E .41 C2
Sant Quirze de Besora
E. 41 B3
Sant Rafel E. 60 C1
Sant Ramon E 41 C2
Santutzi E 37 A4
Sant Vincençede Castellet
E. 41 C2
San Vicente de Alcántara
E. 49 B3
San Vicente de Arana E .38 B1
San Vicente de la Barquera
E. 36 A2
San Vicente de la Sonsierra
E. 37 B4
San Vicente de Toranzo
E. 37 A3
San Vietro E. 43 A3
San Vincente del Raspeig
E. 59 A4
Sanxenxo E 34 B2
São Aleixo P 49 C3
São Barnabé P 54 B1
São Bartoloméda Serra
P 54 A1
São Bartolomeu de
Messines P. 54 B1
São Bento P. 34 C2
São Brás P. 54 B2
São Brás de Alportel P .54 B2
São Braz do Reguedoura
P 48 C2
São Cristóvão P. 48 C2
São Domingos P. 54 B1
São Geraldo P. 48 C2
São Jacinto P 42 B1
São João da Madeira P. .42 B1
São João da Pesqueira
P 42 A2
São João da Ribeira P . .48 B2
São João da Serra P . . .42 B1
São João da Venda P . .54 B2
São João dos Caldeireiros
P 54 B2
São Julião P 49 B3
São Leonardo P 49 C3
São Luis P 54 B1
São Manços P 49 C3
São Marcos da Ataboeira
P 54 B2
São Marcos da Serra P .54 B1
São Marcos de Campo
P 49 C3
São Martinho da Cortiça
P 42 B1
São Martinho das
Amoreiras P. 54 B1
São Martinho do Porto
P 48 B1
São Matias
Beja P 54 A2
Évora P. 48 C2
São Miguel d'Acha P. . .49 A3
São Miguel de Machede
P 49 C3
São Pedro da Torre P . .34 C2
São Pedro de Cadeira
P 48 B1
São Pedro de Muel P. . .48 B1
São Pedro de Solis P . .54 B2
São Pedro do Sul P. . . .42 B1
Saorge P 33 B3
São Romão P 54 B1
São Sebastião dos Carros
P 54 B2
São Teotónio P 54 B1
São Torcato P 42 A1
Sapataria P. 48 C1
Sapiãos P. 42 A2
Sa Pobla E. 61 B3
Saramon F. 29 C3
Sa Rapita E 61 B3
Sarcelles F. 10 B2
Sardoal P. 48 B2
Sardón de Duero E. 44 A3
Sare F. 38 A2
S'Arenal E. 60 B2
Sargans CH 21 B4
Sari-d'Orcino F. 62 A1
Sarilhos Grandes P. 48 C2
Sariñena E 39 C3
Sarlat-la-Canéda F. 29 B4
Sarliac-sur-l'Isle F. 29 A3
Sarnadas P. 49 B3
Sarnen CH. 20 C3
Sarpoil F. 25 B3
Sarracín E 37 B3
Sarral E. 41 C2

Sarralbe F 12 B3
Sarrancolin F. 39 B4
Sarras F. 25 B4
Sarre I 27 B4
Sarreaus E. 34 B3
Sarrebourg F. 12 C3
Sarreguemines F. 12 B3
Sarre-Union F 12 C3
Sarria E 35 B3
Sarriàde Ter E 41 B3
Sarrión E 47 B3
Sarroca de Lleida E 47 A4
Sarron F. 28 C2
Sartène F 62 B1
Sartilly F 8 B2
Sarzeau F. 15 B3
Sarzedas P. 49 B3
Sasamón E 36 B2
Sa Savina E. 60 C1
Sassello I. 33 A4
Sástago E 47 A3
Sas van Gent NL. 7 A3
Satão P. 42 B2
Satillieu F 25 B4
Satteins A. 21 B4
Saucats F. 28 B2
Saucelle E 43 A3
Saugues F. 25 C3
Saujon F. 22 C3
Saulces Monclin F 11 B4
Saulgau D 21 A4
Saulieu F 18 B3
Saulnot F. 20 B1
Sault F 31 A4
Sault-Brénaz F 26 B2
Sault-de-Navailles F. . . .28 C2
Saulx F. 19 B5
Saulxures-sur-Moselotte
F. 20 B1
Saulzais-le-Potier F. 17 C4
Saumos F 28 B1
Saumur F 16 B1
Saurat F. 40 B2
Sausset-les-Pins F 31 B4
Sauteyrargues F 31 B2
Sauvagnat F 24 B2
Sauve F. 31 B2
Sauveterre-de-Béarn F. .38 A3
Sauveterre-de-Guyenne
F. 28 B2
Sauviat-sur-Vige F. 24 B1
Sauxillanges F 25 B3
Sauzet
Drôme F. 25 C4
Lot F. 29 B4
Sauzé-Vaussais F. 23 B4
Sauzon F 14 B2
Savenay F. 15 B4
Saverdun F 40 A2
Saverne F. 13 C3
Savières F. 11 C3
Savigliano I 27 C4
Savignac-les-Eglises F. .29 A3
Savigny-sur-Braye F. . . .16 B2
Saviñán E 46 A2
Savines-le-lac F 32 A2
Savognin CH 21 C4
Savona I. 33 A4
Savournon F. 32 A1
Sax E. 53 C3
Sayalonga E 57 B3
Sayatón E 45 B5
Scaër F. 14 A2
Scey-sur-Saône et St Albin
F. 19 B4
Schaffhausen CH 21 B3
Schangnau CH. 20 C2
Schapbach D. 13 C4
Scheidegg D 21 B4
Schiedam NL. 7 A4
Schiers CH 21 C4
Schillingen D. 12 B2
Schiltach D 13 C4
Schiltigheim F. 13 C3
Schirmeck F 12 C3
Schliengen D. 20 B2
Schluchsee D 20 B3
Schmelz D 12 B2
Schomberg D 21 A3
Schönau D. 20 B2
Schoondijke NL. 7 A3
Schoonhoven NL 7 A4
Schopfheim D 20 B2
Schramberg D 20 A3
Schröcken A 21 B5
Schruns A 21 B4
Schüpfheim CH. 20 C3
Schwaigern D 13 B5
Schwanden CH 21 C4
Schwarzenburg CH. 20 C2
Schweich D 12 B2
Schweighausen D. 20 A2
Schwenningen D. 21 A3
Schwetzingen D 13 B4
Schwyz CH 21 B3
Scionzier F. 26 A3
Scopello I. 27 B5
Scuol CH 21 C5
Sebazac-Concourès F. . .30 A1
Seborga I 33 B3
Séchault F. 11 B4
Seclin F. 6 B3
Secondigny F. 22 B3
Seda P. 49 B3
Sedan F 11 B4
Sedano E. 37 B3
Sedella E 57 B3
Séderon F 31 A4
Seebach D 13 C3
Seeheim-Jugenheim D. .13 B4
Seelbach D 13 C3
Sées F. 9 B4
Segonzac F 23 C3
Segorbe E. 53 B3
Segovia E 45 B3
Segré F 15 B5
Segura
E. 38 B1
P 49 B3
Segura de León E 55 A3
Segura de los Baños E. .46 B3
Ségur-les-Villas F 24 B2
Segurrilla E 44 B3
Seia P. 42 B2
Seiches-sur-le-Loir F . . .16 B1
Seignelay F 18 B2

Seijo E 34 C2
Seilhac F. 24 B1
Seilles B. 7 B5
Seissan F 39 A4
Seixal P. 48 C1
Sélestat F. 20 A2
Selgua E 39 C4
Selles-St Denis F. 17 B3
Selles-sur-Cher F 17 B3
Sellières F 19 C4
Selongey F 19 B4
Selonnet F 32 A2
Seltz F. 13 C4
Selva E. 61 B2
Semide
F 11 B4
P 42 B1
Semur-en-Auxois F. 18 B3
Sena E 39 C3
Sena de Luna E 35 B5
Senarpont F. 10 B1
Sénas F 31 B4
Sencelles E. 61 B2
Sendim P. 43 A3
Seneffe B 7 B4
Senés E. 58 B2
Senez F 32 B2
Sengouagnet F 39 B4
Senlis F 10 B2
Sennecey-le-Grand F . . .19 C3
Sennwald CH. 21 B4
Senonches F. 9 B5
Senones F. 12 C2
Sens F. 18 A2
Sens-de-Bretagne F. . . .15 A4
Senterada E. 39 B4
Seoane E. 35 B3
Seon CH. 20 B3
Sépeaux F 18 B2
Sépey CH. 27 A4
Seppois F. 20 B2
Septeuil F 10 C1
Sepúlveda E 45 A4
Sequeros E. 43 B3
Seraincourt F 11 B4
Sérent F 15 B3
Sérifontaine F. 10 B1
Sérignan F. 30 B2
Sermaises F 10 C2
Sermaize-les-Bains F . . .11 C4
Sernache de Bonjardim
P 48 B2
Sernancelhe P. 42 B2
Serón E 58 B2
Serón de Najima E. 46 A1
Serooskerke NL. 7 A3
Seròs E 47 A4
Serpa P 54 B2
Serrada E. 44 A3
Serra de Outes E. 34 B2
Serradilla E 49 B4
Serradilla del Arroyo E. .43 B3
Serradilla del Llano E. . .43 B3
Serranillos E 44 B3
Serravalle I 27 B5
Serrejón E 44 C2
Serres F 32 A1
Serrières F. 25 B4
Serrières-de-Briord F . . .26 B2
Sertã P. 48 B2
Sertig Dörfli CH. 21 C4
Servance F. 20 B1
Serverette F 25 C3
Servian F. 30 B2
Serviers F 31 A3
Serzedelo P. 42 A1
Serzedilla E 45 B4
Sesimbra P 48 C1
Sesma E. 38 B1
Ses Salines E 61 B3
Sestao E 37 A4
Sestriere I 27 C3
Setcases E 40 B3
Sète F 30 B2
Setenil E 56 B2
Séttimo Torinese I. 27 B4
Settimo Vittone I. 27 B4
Setúbal P. 48 C2
Seúrre F 19 C4
Sévérac-le-Château F. . .30 A2
Sever do Vouga P 42 B1
Sévigny F. 11 B4
Seville = Sevilla E. 56 A2
Sevilla la Nueva E. 45 B3
Seville = Sevilla E. 56 A2
Sevilleja de la Jara E. . .50 A3
Sevrier F. 26 B3
Seyches F 29 B3
Seyne F. 32 A2
Seynes F. 31 A3
Seyssel F. 26 B2
Sézanne F 11 C3
Sezulfe P. 43 A2
's-Gravendeel NL. 7 A4
's-Gravenzande NL. 7 A4
's-Hertogenbosch NL . . .7 A5
Siauges-St Romain F . . .25 B3
Sierck-les-Bains F. 12 B2
Sierentz F. 20 B2
Sierra de Fuentes E 49 B4
Sierra de Luna E 38 B3
Sierra de Yeguas E. 56 A3
Sierre CH. 27 A4
Sietamo E 39 B3
Sigean F. 30 B1
Sigmaringen D. 21 A4
Signa I. 29 C1
Signes F 32 B1
Signy-l'Abbaye F 11 B4
Signy-le-Petit F 11 B4
Sigogne F 23 C3
Sigüenza E. 45 A5
Sigüés E. 38 B2
Siles E. 58 A2
Silgueiros P. 42 B2
Silla E. 53 B3
Silleda E. 34 B2
Sillé-le-Guillaume F. 16 A1
Sils E 41 C3
Silvaplana CH 21 C4
Silvares P. 42 B2
Silves P 54 B1
Simandre F. 19 C4
Simard F 19 C4
Simat de Valldigna E . . .53 B3

Simmerberg D. 21 B4
Simmern D. 13 B3
Simplon CH. 27 A5
Sinarcas E. 53 B2
Sindelfingen D 13 C5
Sines P. 54 B1
Singen D 21 B3
Sinlabajos E 44 A3
Sins CH. 20 B3
Sinsheim D. 13 B4
Sint Annaland NL. 7 A4
Sint Oedenrode NL 7 A5
Sintra P. 48 C1
Sinzheim D. 13 C4
Sion CH. 27 A4
Siorac-en-Périgord F . . .29 B3
Siruela E. 50 B2
Sisante E 52 B1
Sissach CH. 20 B2
Sissonne F 11 B3
Sistelo P 34 C2
Sisteron F 32 A1
Sitges E. 41 C2
Sixt-Fer-á-Cheval F. 27 A3
Sizun F 14 A1
Sluis NL 6 A3
Sober E 34 B3
Sobernheim D 13 B3
Sobrado
Coruña E 34 A2
Lugo E 35 B3
Sobral da Adica P 55 A2
Sobral de Monte Agraço
P 48 C1
Sobreira Formosa P. . . .48 B3
Socovos E 58 A3
Socuéllamos E 52 B1
Sodupe E. 37 A3
Soengas P 42 A1
Sohren D. 13 B3
Soignies B 7 B4
Soissons F 10 B3
Solana de los Barros E. .49 C4
Solana del Pino E 51 B3
Solares E. 37 A3
Soleils F 32 B2
Solera E. 57 A4
Solesmes F 7 B3
Solgne F 12 C2
Solignac F 23 C5
Solivella E 41 C2
Sollana E 53 B3
Sóller E 60 B2
Solliès-Pont F 32 B2
Solomiac F 29 C3
Solórzano E 37 A3
Solothurn CH 20 B2
Solre-le-Château F 7 B4
Solsona E 41 C2
Somain F 6 B3
Sombernon F 18 B3
Sombreffe B 7 B4
Sommariva del Bosco I .27 C4
Sommeilles F 11 C4
Sommepy-Tahure F 11 B4
Sommesous F 11 C4
Somme-Tourbe F 11 B4
Sommières F. 31 B3
Sommières-du-Clain F . .23 B4
Somo E 37 A3
Somontin E 58 B2
Somosiero E 45 A4
Sompuis F 11 C4
Son Bou E 61 B4
Sonceboz CH 20 B2
Soncillo E 37 B3
Soneja E 53 B3
Songeons F 10 B1
Sonseca E 51 A4
Son Servera E 61 B3
Sonthofen D 21 B5
Sopelana E 37 A4
Sorbas E 58 B2
Sore F 28 B2
Sörenberg CH 20 C3
Soreze F 40 A3
Sorges F 23 C4
Sorgues F 31 A3
Soria E 37 C4
Soriheula del Guadalimar
E. 58 A1
Sornac F 24 B2
Sort E 40 B2
Sos F 28 B3
Sos del Rey Católico E. .38 B2
Sospel F. 33 B3
Sotillo de Adrada E. 44 B3
Sotillo de la Ribera E . . .37 C3
Sotobañado y Priorato
E. 36 B2
Soto de la Marina E. 37 A3
Soto del Barco E 35 A4
Soto de los Infantes E . .35 A4
Soto de Real E. 45 B4
Soto de Ribera E. 35 A5
Sotoserrano E 43 B3
Soto y Amío E. 35 B5
Sotresgudo E. 36 B2
Sotrondio E. 36 A1
Sotta F. 62 B2
Sotuelamos E. 52 B1
Souain F 11 B4
Soual F 40 A3
Soucy F 18 A2
Soudron F. 11 C4
Souesmes F 17 B4
Soufflenheim F 13 C3
Souillac F. 29 B4
Souilly F. 11 B5
Soulac-sur-Mer F 22 C2
Soulaines-Dhuys F 11 C4
Soulatgé F 40 B3
Soultz-Haut-Rhin F 20 B2
Soultz-sous-Forêts F . . .13 C3
Soumoulou F 39 A3
Souppes-sur-Loing F. . . .17 A4
Souprosse F 28 C2
Sourdeval F 8 B2
Soure P 48 A2
Sournia F 40 B3
Souro Pires P 43 B2
Sours F 10 C1
Sousceyrac F 24 C2
Sousel P. 49 C3

Soustons F 28 C1
Souteló de Montes E . . .34 B2
Souto P 42 B2
Soutochao E 35 C3
Souto da Carpalhosa P .48 B2
Souvigny F 18 C2
Souzay-Champigny F . . .16 B1
Soyaux F 23 C4
Spaichingen D. 21 A3
Speicher D. 12 B2
Speyer D 13 B4
Spézet F. 14 A2
Spiez CH 20 C2
Spigno Monferrato I 33 A4
Spijkenisse NL 7 A4
Spincourt F 12 B1
Splügen CH 21 C4
Spotorno I. 33 A4
Stabroek B. 7 A4
Staden B 6 B3
Stäfa CH 21 B3
Stainville F. 11 C5
Stalden CH 27 A4
Stans CH. 20 C3
Staufen D. 20 B2
Stavenisse NL 7 A4
Stechelberg CH. 20 C2
Steckborn CH 21 B3
Steeg A 21 B5
Steenbergen NL 7 A4
Steenvoorde F. 6 B2
Steffisburg CH 20 C2
Steinach D. 20 A3
Stein an Rhein CH. 21 B3
Steinen D 20 B2
Steinheim D 21 A5
Stekene B 7 A4
Stellendam NL. 7 A4
Stenay F 11 B5
Stes Maries-de-la-Mer F 31 B3
Stockach D 21 B4
Stöckalp CH 20 C3
Strasbourg F 13 C3
Stresa I 27 B5
Strijen NL. 7 A4
Stromberg D 13 B3
Stroppiana I 27 B5
Stuben A 21 B5
Suances E 36 A2
Sucina E 59 B4
Sueca E 53 B3
Sugères F 25 B3
Sugny B 11 B4
Suippes F 11 B4
Sulgen CH 21 B4
Sully-sur-Loire F 17 B4
Sülz D. 13 C4
Sulzbach
Bayern D 13 B5
Saarland D. 12 B3
Sumiswald CH. 20 B2
Sunbilla E 38 A2
Super Sauze F 32 A2
Surgères F. 22 B3
Súria E 41 C2
Surin F 23 B4
Sursee CH 20 B3
Sury-le-Comtal F 25 B4
Susa I 27 B4
Susch CH 21 C5
Suze-la-Rousse F 31 A3

T

Tabanera la Luenga E. . .45 A3
Tabaqueros E 52 B2
Tábara E 43 A4
Tabenera de Cerrato E. .36 B2
Tabernas E. 58 B2
Taboada E 34 B3
Taboadela E 34 B3
Tábua P 42 B1
Tabuaco P 42 A2
Tabuenca E 46 A2
Tabuyo del Monte E. . . .35 B4
Tafalla E. 38 B2
Taganheira P. 54 B1
Tággia I 33 B3
Tagnon F 11 B4
Tahal E. 58 B2
Tailfingen D. 21 A4
Taillis F. 15 A4
Tain-l'Hermitage F. 25 B4
Taipadas P. 48 C2
Tal E. 34 B2
Talant F 19 B3
Talarrubias E 50 A2
Talaván E 49 B4
Talavera de la Reina E . .44 C3
Talavera la Real E 49 C4
Talayuela E 44 C2
Talayuelas E 53 B2
Talhadas P. 42 B1
Táliga E 49 C3
Talizat F 24 B3
Tallard F. 32 A2
Talloires F 26 B3
Talmay F 19 B4
Talmont-St Hilaire F 22 B2
Talmont-sur-Gironde F. .22 C3
Tamajón E. 45 B4
Tamame E 43 A4
Tamames E 43 B3
Tamarit de Mar E. 41 C2
Tamarite de Litera E . . .39 C4
Tamariu E. 41 C4
Tamarón E 35 A4
Tamurejo E 50 B3
Tanabueyes E 37 B3
Tancarville F 9 A4
Tanis F. 26 A3
Tannay
Ardennes F 11 B4
Nièvre F 18 B2
Tanus F 30 A1
Tapia de Casariego E . .35 A4
Tapio E. 40 A2
Taradell E. 41 C3
Taramundi E. 35 A3
Tarancón E 45 B4
Tarare F 25 B4
Tarascon F. 31 B3
Tarascon-sur-Ariège F . .40 B2
Tarazona E 38 C2

Tarazona de la Mancha
E 52 B2
Tarbena E. 53 C3
Tarbes F. 39 A4
Tardajos E. 37 B3
Tardelcuende E. 45 A5
Tardets-Sorholus F. 38 A3
Tardienta E 39 C3
Targon F. 28 B2
Tarifa E. 56 B2
Tariquejas E. 55 B2
Tarnos F. 28 C1
Tarragona E. 41 C2
Tàrrega E. 41 C2
Tartas F 28 C2
Täsch CH 27 A4
Taulé F 14 A2
Taulignan F 31 A3
Tauste E. 38 C2
Tauves F 24 B2
Tavaux F 19 B4
Tavernes de la Valldigna
E 53 B3
Taverny F 10 B2
Tavescan E 40 B2
Tavira P 54 B2
Tazones E 36 A1
Teba E 56 B3
Teillay F 15 B4
Teillet F 30 B1
Teixeiro E 34 A2
Tejada de Tiétar E 44 B2
Tejado E 46 A1
Tejares E 44 B2
Tembleque E 51 A4
Temiño E 37 B3
Temse B 7 A4
Tenay F 26 B2
Tence F 25 B4
Tende F 33 A3
Tenneville B. 12 A1
Teo E 34 B2
Tera E 37 C4
Terena P. 49 C3
Teresa de Cofrentes E . .53 B2
Tergnier F 10 B3
Termas de Monfortinho
P 49 A4
Terme di Valdieri I 33 A3
Termens E 39 C4
Termes F 24 C3
Terneuzen NL 7 A3
Terras do Bouro P. 42 A1
Terrassa E 41 C3
Terrasson-la-Villedieu F .29 A4
Terrazos E 37 B3
Terriente E 46 B2
Terrugem P 49 C3
Teruel E 46 B2
Tervuren B 7 B4
Terzaga E 46 B2
Tessy-sur-Vire F 8 B2
Teterchen F 12 B2
Tettnang D 21 B4
Teulada E 53 C4
Thalfang D 12 B2
Thalkirch CH 21 C4
Thalwil CH 21 B3
Thann F 20 B2
Thaon-les-Vosges F 19 A5
Tharsis E 55 B2
Thayngen CH 21 B3
Thénezay F 16 C1
Thenon F 29 A4
Therouanne F 6 B2
Thézar-les-Corbières F . .40 A3
Thèze F 39 A3
Thiberville F 9 A4
Thibie F 11 C4
Thiéblemont-Farémont
F 11 C4
Thierrens CH. 20 C1
Thiers F 25 B3
Thiezac F 24 B2
Thionville F 12 B2
Thiron-Gardais F. 9 B4
Thivars F 10 C1
Thiviers F. 23 C4
Thizy F 25 A4
Tholen NL 7 A4
Tholey D 12 B3
Thônes F 26 B3
Thonnance-les-Joinville
F 11 C5
Thonon-les-Bains F 26 A3
Thorame-Basse F 32 A2
Thorame-Haute F 32 A2
Thorens-Glières F 26 A3
Thorigny-sur-Oreuse F. . .11 C3
Thouarcé F 16 B1
Thouars F 16 C1
Thueyts F 25 C4
Thuin B 7 B4
Thuir F 40 B3
Thun CH. 20 C2
Thuret F 24 B3
Thurey F 19 C4
Thüringen A. 21 B4
Thurins F 25 B4
Thury-Harcourt F 9 B3
Thusis CH 21 C4
Tibi E 53 C3
Tiedra E 44 A2
Tiefencastel CH. 21 C4
Tiel NL 7 A5
Tielmes E 45 B4
Tielt B. 6 A3
Tienen B 7 B4
Tiengen D 20 B3
Tiercé F 16 B1
Tierga E 46 A2
Tiermas E 38 B2
Tierrantona E. 39 B4
Tignes F 27 B3
Tigy F. 17 B4
Tíjola E. 58 B2
Tilburg NL 7 A5
Til Châtel F 19 B4
Tilh F 28 C2
Tillac F 39 A4
Tille F 10 B2
Tilloy Bellay F. 11 B4
Tilly F 23 B5
Tilly-sur-Seulles F. 8 A3

Tinajas E 46 B1
Tinalhas P 49 B3
Tinchebray F 8 B3
Tincques F. 6 B2
Tineo E. 35 A4
Tinténiac F 15 A4
Tintigny B 12 B1
Tiriez E 52 C1
Tirig E. 47 B4
Tirteafuera E 51 B3
Titaguas E. 53 B2
Titisee-Neustadt D 20 B3
Tivisa E 47 A4
Tobarra E. 52 C2
Tocane-St Apre F 29 A3
Tocha P 42 B1
Tocina E 56 A2
Tocón E 57 A4
Todtmoos D 20 B3
Todtnau D 20 B2
Toén E 34 B3
Toledo E. 45 C3
Tolosa
E 38 A1
P 49 B3
Tolox E. 56 B3
Tolva E 39 B4
Tomar P 48 B2
Tombeboeuf F 29 B3
Tomellosa E. 45 B5
Tomelloso E 51 A4
Tomiño E 34 C2
Tona E 41 C3
Tondela P 42 B1
Tongeren B 7 B5
Tonnay-Boutonne F 22 C3
Tonnay-Charente F 22 C3
Tonneins F 29 B3
Tonnerre F 18 B2
Topares E. 58 B2
Topas E 44 A2
Toques E 34 B3
Torà E 41 C2
Toral de los Guzmanes
E 36 B1
Toral de los Vados E. . . .35 B4
Torcy-le-Petit F 9 A5
Tordehumos E. 36 C1
Tordera E. 41 C3
Tordesillas E 44 A2
Tordesilos E. 46 B2
Torelló E. 41 B3
Toreno E 35 B4
Torfou F 22 A2
Torgueda P 42 A2
Torhout B 6 A3
Torigni-sur-Vire F 8 A3
Torija E. 45 B4
Toril E 46 B2
Torino = Turin I 27 B4
Torla E 39 B3
Tornada P 48 B1
Tornavacas E 44 B2
Tornos E 46 B2
Toro E 44 A2
Torquemada E 36 B2
Torralba de Burgo E 45 A5
Torralba de Calatrava E . .51 A4
Torrão P 48 C2
Torreblacos E 37 C4
Torreblanca E 47 B4
Torreblascopedro E 51 B4
Torrecaballeros E 45 A3
Torrecampo E 50 B3
Torre Cardela E 57 A4
Torrecilla E 46 B1
Torrecilla de la Jara E . . .50 A3
Torrecilla de la Orden E . .44 A2
Torrecilla del Pinar E 45 A3
Torrecilla en Cameros
E 37 B4
Torrecillas de la Tiesa E .50 A2
Torre das Vargens P. 48 B3
Torre de Coelheiros P. . . .48 C3
Torre de Dom Chama P . .43 A2
Torre de Juan Abad E . . .51 B4
Torre de la Higuera E . . .55 B3
Torre del Bierzo E 35 B4
Torre del Burgo E 45 B4
Torre del Campo E 57 A4
Torre del Mar E 57 B3
Torredembarra E. 41 C2
Torre de Miguel Sesmero
E 49 C4
Torre de Moncorvo P. . . .43 A2
Torre de Santa Maria E . .50 A1
Torredonjimeno E. 57 A4
Torre do Terranho P 42 B2
Torregrossa E 41 C1
Torreira P 42 B1
Torrejoncillo E. 49 B4
Torrejón de Ardoz E 45 B4
Torrejón de la Calzada
E 45 B4
Torrejón del Rey E 45 B4
Torrejon el Rubio E. 50 A1
Torrelaguna E 45 B4
Torrelapaja E 46 A2
Torre la Ribera E 39 B4
Torrelavega E 36 A2
Torrelobatón E 44 A2
Torrelodones E 45 B4
Torre los Negros E 46 B2
Torremanzanas E 53 C3
Torremayor E 49 C4
Torremocha E 50 A1
Torremolinos E 57 B3
Torrenostra E 47 B4
Torrent E 53 B3
Torrente de Cinca E 47 A4
Torrenueva
Ciudad Real E 51 B4
Granada E 57 B4
Torreorgaz E 49 B4
Torre-Pacheco E 59 B4
Torre Péllice I 27 C4
Torreperogil E 51 B4
Torres E 57 A4
Torres-Cabrera E. 57 A3
Torresandino E 37 C3
Torres de la Alameda E . .45 B4
Torres Novas P 48 B2
Torres Vedras P. 48 B1
Torrevieja E 59 B4
Torrijos E. 45 C3

Torroal P 48 C2
Torroella de Montgrí E. . .41 B4
Torrox E 57 B4
Tórtoles E 44 B2
Tórtoles de Esgueva E . . .36 C2
Tortosa E. 47 B4
Tortosendo P. 42 B2
Tortuero E 45 B4
Torviscón E. 57 B4
Tossa de Mar E 41 C3
Tosse F 28 C1
Totana E 59 B3
Tôtes F. 9 A5
Touça P 43 A2
Toucy F 18 B2
Toul F 12 C1
Toulon F. 32 B1
Toulon-sur-Allier F 18 C2
Toulon-sur-Arroux F 18 C3
Toulouse F 29 C4
Tourcoing F 6 B3
Tour de la Parata F 62 B1
Tourlaville F 8 A2
Tournai B 6 B3
Tournan-en-Brie F. 10 C2
Tournay F 39 A4
Tournon-d'Agenais F 29 B3
Tournon-St Martin F 23 B4
Tournon-sur-Rhône F . . .25 B4
Tournus F 19 C3
Touro
E 34 B2
P 42 B2
Tourouvre F 9 B4
Tourriers F. 23 C4
Tours F 16 B2
Tourteron F 11 B4
Tourves F 32 B1
Toury F 17 A3
Touvedo P 42 A1
Touvois F 22 B2
Trabada E 35 A3
Trabadelo E 35 B4
Trabanca E 43 A3
Trabazos E. 43 A3
Traben-Trarbach D 12 B3
Trafaria P 48 C1
Tragacete E 46 B2
Traiguera E 47 B4
Trainel F 11 C3
Tramacastilla de Tena E .39 B3
Tramagal P. 48 B2
Tramelan CH 20 B2
Trampot F 12 C1
Trana I 27 B4
Trancoso P 42 B2
Trans-en-Provence F 32 B2
Trappes F. 10 C2
Trasierra E. 50 B1
Trasmiras E. 34 B3
Traspinedo E 44 A3
Travo F 62 B2
Treban F 24 A3
Trébeurden F 14 A2
Trebujena E. 55 C3
Treffort F 26 A2
Trégastel-Plage F 14 A2
Tréguier F 14 A2
Trégunc F 14 B2
Treignac F 24 B1
Treignat F 24 A2
Treignes B 11 A4
Trélazé F 16 B1
Trélissac F 29 A3
Trélon F 11 A4
Trélou-sur-Marne F 11 B3
Tremblay-le-Vicomte F. . .9 B5
Tremés P 48 B2
Tremp E 39 B4
Trensacq F. 28 B2
Trept F 26 B2
Trespaderne E 37 B3
Trets F 32 B1
Trevelez E 57 B4
Treviana E 37 B3
Trévoux F. 25 B4
Trézelles F 25 A3
Triaize F. 22 B2
Triacastela E 35 B3
Triaucourt-en-Argonne
F 11 C5
Triberg D 20 A3
Trier D 12 B2
Trie-sur-Baïse F 39 A4
Trignac F 15 B3
Triguères F 55 B3
Trigueros del Valle E 36 C2
Trillo E 46 B1
Trilport F 10 C2
Trindade
Beja P 54 B2
Bragança P 43 A2
Trino I 27 B5
Trinta P 42 B2
Triora I 33 B3
Triste E. 38 B3
Trivero I 27 B5
Troarn F 9 A3
Trofa E 42 A1
Troia I. 48 C2
Troisvierges L 12 A2
Tronget F 24 A3
Tronzano-Vercellese I . . .27 B5
Trôo F 16 B2
Trosly-Breuil F 10 B3
Trossingen D. 21 A3
Trouville-sur-Mer F 9 A4
Troyes F 18 A3
Trubia E 35 A5
Truchas E 35 B4
Trujillanos E 50 B1
Trujillo E 50 A2
Trun
CH 21 C3
F 9 B4
Tschagguns A 21 B4
Tua P 42 A2
Tubilla del Lago E 37 C3
Tübingen D 13 C5
Tubize B 7 B4
Tuchan F 40 B3
Tudela E. 38 B2
Tudela de Duero E. 44 A3
Tuejar E 53 B2
Tuffé F 16 A2

Tui E. 34 B2
Tulette F 31 A3
Tulle F 24 B1
Tullins F. 26 B2
Tunes P 54 B1
Turbenthal CH 21 B3
Turcia E 35 B5
Turcifal P 48 B1
Turckheim F. 20 A2
Turégano E. 45 A4
Turin = Torino I 27 B4
Turis E. 53 B3
Turleque E 51 A4
Turnhout B. 7 A4
Turón E 58 C1
Turquel P. 48 B1
Turries F. 32 A2
Turtmann CH 27 A4
Tuttlingen D. 21 B3

U

Úbeda E. 51 B4
Überlingen D. 21 B4
Ubidea E 37 A4
Ubrique E. 56 B2
Ucero E 37 C3
Uchaud F 31 B3
Uclés E 45 C5
Uetendorf CH 20 C2
Ugarana E. 37 A4
Ugíjar E 58 C1
Ugine F 26 B3
Ujué E 38 B2
Uleila del Campo E. 58 B2
Ulldecona E. 47 B4
Ulldemolins E 41 C1
Ulme P. 48 B2
Uncastillo E. 38 B2
Unhais da Serra P. 42 B2
Unquera E 36 A2
Unterägeri CH 21 B3
Unteriberg CH 21 B3
Unterschächen CH 21 C3
Ur F 40 B2
Urçay F 17 C4
Urda E 51 A4
Urdax E 38 A2
Urdilde E 34 B2
Urdos F 39 B3
Urnäsch CH 21 B4
Urracal E. 58 B2
Urries E 38 B2
Urroz E. 38 B2
Ury F 10 C2
Usagre E. 50 B1
Useldange L 12 B1
Ussé F 16 B2
Usséglio I 27 B4
Ussel
Cantal F 24 B2
Corrèze F. 24 B2
Usson-du-Poitou F 23 B4
Usson-en-Forez F 25 B3
Usson-les-Bains F 40 B3
Ustaritz F 38 A2
Uster CH 21 B3
Utebo E. 46 A3
Utiel E 53 B2
Utrera E 56 A2
Utrillas E 47 B3
Uttenweiler D. 21 A4
Uza F 28 B1
Uzein F. 39 A3
Uzel F 14 A3
Uzerche F 24 B1
Uzès F 31 A3
Uznach CH 21 B3

V

Vaas F 16 B2
Vabre F. 30 B1
Vacqueyras F 31 A3
Vadillo de la Sierra E. . . .44 B2
Vadillos E 46 B1
Vado Ligure I 33 A4
Vaduz FL 21 B4
Vagney F 20 A1
Vagos P 42 B1
Vaiges F 16 A1
Vaihingen D. 13 C4
Vaillant F 19 B4
Vailly-sur-Aisne F 11 B3
Vailly-sur-Sauldre F 17 B4
Vaison-la-Romaine F 31 A4
Vaite F 19 B4
Valada P. 48 B2
Valadares E 42 A1
Valado P. 48 B1
Valberg F 32 A2
Valbom P 42 A1
Valbonnais F 26 C2
Valbuena de Duero E. . . .36 C2
Valdahon F 19 B5
Valdaracete E. 45 B4
Valdealgorfa E. 47 B3
Valdecaballeros E. 50 A2
Valdecabras E. 46 B1
Valdeconcha E. 45 B5
Valdeflores E 55 B3
Valdefresno E. 36 B1
Valdeganga E 52 B2
Valdelacasa E. 44 B2
Valdelacasa de Tajo E . . .50 A2
Valdelarco E 55 B3
Valdelosa E. 43 A4
Valdeltormo E. 47 B4
Valdemanco de Esteras
E 50 B3
Valdemorillo E. 45 B3
Valdemoro E. 45 B4
Valdemoro Sierra E 46 B2
Valdenoceda E. 37 B3
Valdeobispo E. 44 B1
Valdeolivas E. 46 B1
Valdepeñas E 51 B4
Valdepeñas de Jaén E . . .57 A4
Valdepiélago E 36 B1
Valdepolo E. 36 B1
Valderas E 36 B1
Valderrobres E. 47 B4

Valderrueda E 36 B2
Val de San Lorenzo E. . . .35 B4
Val de Santo Domingo
E 44 B3
Val d'Esquières F 32 B2
Valdestillas E. 44 A3
Valdetorres E. 50 B1
Valdetorres de Jarama
E 45 B4
Valdeverdeja E 44 C2
Valdevimbre E. 36 B1
Valdieri I. 33 A3
Valdilecha E. 45 B4
Val-d'Isère F 27 B4
Valdocondes E 37 C3
Valdoviño E 34 A2
Vale de Açor
Beja P 54 B2
Portalegre P. 48 B3
Vale de Agua P 54 B1
Vale de Cambra P 42 B1
Vale de Lobo P 54 B1
Vale de Prazeres P 42 B2
Vale de Reis P 48 C2
Vale de Rosa P 54 B2
Vale de Santarém P. 48 B2
Vale de Vargo P 54 B2
Vale do Peso P 49 B3
Valega P. 42 B1
Valeiro P. 48 C2
Valença P. 34 B2
Valença F. 17 B3
Valence
Charente F 23 C4
Drôme F. 25 C4
Valence d'Agen F 29 B3
Valence d'Albigeois F . . .30 A1
Valence-sur-Baïse F 29 C3
Valencia
E 53 B3
Valencia de Alcántara
E 49 B3
Valencia de Don Juan E .36 B1
Valencia de las Torres
E 50 B1
Valencia del Ventoso E. . .55 A3
Valencia de Mombuey E .55 A2
Valenciennes F 7 B3
Valensole F 32 B1
Valentigney F 20 B1
Valentine F 39 A4
Valenzuela E 57 A3
Valenzuela de Calatrava
E 51 B4
Valera de Abajo E 52 B1
Valeria E. 52 B1
Valflaunes F 31 B2
Valgorge F 31 A3
Valgrisenche I 27 B4
Valhelhas P 42 B2
Valkenswaard NL 7 A5
Vallada E 53 C3
Vallado E 35 A4
Valladolid E 44 A3
Vall d'Alba E 47 B3
Valldemossa E 60 B2
Valle de Abdalajís E 57 B3
Valle de Cabuérniga E . . .36 A2
Valle de la Serena E 50 B2
Valle de Matamoros E . . .49 C4
Valle de Santa Ana E . . .49 C4
Vallelado E. 44 A3
Valle Mosso I 27 B5
Valleraugue F 30 A2
Vallerois-le-Bois F 19 B5
Vallet F. 15 B4
Vallfogona de Riucorb
E 41 C2
Valloire F 26 B3
Vallon-Pont-d'Arc F 31 A3
Vallorbe CH 19 C5
Vallouise F 26 C3
Valls E. 41 C2
Valmadrid E. 47 A3
Valmojado E 45 B3
Valmont F 9 A4
Valognes F 8 A2
Valonga P. 42 B1
Valongo P. 42 A1
Válor E 58 C1
Valoria la Buena E. 36 C2
Valpaços P 42 A2
Valpelline I 27 B4
Valras-Plage F 30 B2
Valréas F 31 A3
Vals CH 21 C4
Valsavarenche I 27 B4
Valsequillo E 50 B2
Vals-les-Bains F 25 C4
Valsonne F. 25 B4
Val-Suzon F 19 B3
Valtablado del Río E 46 B1
Val Thorens F 26 B3
Valtierra E 38 B2
Valtournenche I 27 B4
Valverde
E 49 C4
Valverde de Burguillos
E 49 C4
Valverde de Júcar E 52 B1
Valverde de la Vera E . . .44 B2
Valverde de la Virgen E. .36 B1
Valverde del Camino E. . .55 B3
Valverde del Fresno E . . .43 B3
Valverde de Llerena E. . .50 B2
Valverde de Mérida E. . . .50 B1
Vanault-les-Dames F. . . .11 C4
Vandenesse F 18 C2
Vandenesse-en-Auxois
F 19 B4
Vannes F 15 B3
Vaour F 29 B4
Vaqueiros P. 54 B2
Varacieux F. 26 B2
Varades F 15 B4
Varages F. 32 B2
Varallo I 27 B5
Varazze I 33 A4
Varengeville-sur-Mer F . .9 A4
Varennes-en-Argonne F. .11 B5
Varennes-le-Grand F 19 C3
Varennes-St Sauveur F . .19 C4
Varennes-sur-Allier F . . .25 A3
Varennes-sur-Amance
F 19 B4
Vargas
E 37 A3
P 48 B2

Varilhes F. 40 A2
Váriz P 43 A3
Varreddes F 10 C2
Vars F. 26 C3
Varzjelas P. 42 B1
Varzo I 27 A5
Varzy F. 18 B2
Vassieux-en-Vercors F . .26 C2
Vassy F 8 B3
Vatan F 17 B3
Vatry F 11 C4
Vättis CH 21 C4
Vauchamps F 11 C3
Vauchassis F 18 A2
Vaucouleurs F. 12 C1
Vaudoy-en-Brie F 10 C3
Vaulruz CH. 20 C1
Vaulx Vraucourt F 10 A2
Vaumas F. 18 C2
Vausseroux F 23 B3
Vauvenargues F. 32 B1
Vauvert F 31 B3
Vauvillers F 19 B5
Vaux-sur-Sure B 12 B1
Vayrac F 29 B4
Vecinos E. 43 B4
Vedra E 34 B2
Vega
Asturias E 36 A1
Asturias E 36 A1
Vega de Espinareda E . . .35 B4
Vega de Infanzones E. . . .36 B1
Vegadeo E. 35 A3
Vega de Pas E 37 A3
Vega de Valcarce E. 35 B4
Vega de Valdetronco E. . .44 A2
Vegas de Coria E. 43 B3
Vegas del Condado E . . .36 B1
Veguillas E. 45 B4
Vejer de la Frontera E. . . .56 B2
Velada E 44 B3
Velayos E 44 B3
Velefique E 58 B2
Velez Blanco E 58 B2
Vélez de Benaudalla E . . .57 B4
Vélez-Málaga E 57 B3
Vélez Rubio E 58 B2
Velilla del Río Carrió E . . .36 B2
Velilla de San Antonio
E 45 B4
Velles F 17 C3
Vellisca E. 45 B5
Velliza E. 44 A3
Venaco F 62 A2
Venarey-les-Laumes F . . .18 B3
Venaría I 27 B4
Venasca I 33 A3
Vence F 32 B3
Venda Nova
Coimbra P. 48 A2
Leiria P 48 B2
Vendas Novas P 48 C2
Vendays-Montalivet F. . . .22 C2
Vendeuil F. 11 B3
Vendeuvre-sur-Barse F . .18 A3
Vendoeuvres F. 23 B5
Vendôme F 17 B3
Venelles F. 31 B4
Venialbo E 44 A2
Vénissieux F 25 B4
Vennezey F. 12 C2
Venta de Baños E 36 C2
Venta del Moro E. 52 B2
Venta de los Santos E. . .51 B4
Venta las Ranas E 36 A1
Ventanueva E 35 A4
Ventas de Huelma E 57 A4
Ventas de Zafarraya E . . .57 B3
Ventavon F 32 A1
Ventimiglia I 33 B3
Ventosa de la Sierra E . . .37 C4
Ventosilla E 37 C4
Venzolasca F. 62 A2
Vera E. 58 B3
Vera Cruz P 54 A2
Vera de Bidasoa E. 38 A2
Vera de Moncayo E. 38 C2
Verbánia I 27 B5
Verberie F 10 B2
Verbier CH 27 A4
Vercelli I 27 B5
Vercel-Villedieu-le-Camp
F 19 B5
Vercheny F. 26 C2
Verclause F 31 A4
Verdille F. 23 C3
Verdú E 41 C2
Verdun F 12 B1
Verdun-sur-Garonne F . . .29 C4
Verdun-sur-le-Doubs F . .19 C4
Verfeil F 29 C4
Vergel E 53 C4
Verges E 41 B4
Vergt F 29 A3
Verín E 35 C3
Veringenstadt D 21 A4
Vermand F 10 B3
Vermelha P 48 B1
Vermenton F 18 B2
Vernante I 33 A3
Vernantes F. 16 B2
Vernayaz CH 27 A4
Vern-d'Anjou F 16 B1
Vernet F. 40 A2
Vernet-les-Bains F 40 B3
Verneuil F. 11 B3
Verneuil-sur-Avre F. 9 B4
Vernier CH. 26 A3
Vernon F 9 B5
Vernoux-en-Vivarais F . . .25 C4
Verrès I 27 B4
Verrey-sous-Salmaise F .18 B3
Verrières F 23 C4
Versailles F 10 C2
Versam CH. 21 C4
Versoix CH. 26 A3
Verteillac F. 23 C4
Vertou F 15 B4
Vertus F. 11 C3
Vervins F 11 B3
Verzuolo I 33 A3
Verzy F. 11 B4
Vescovato F 62 A2

Vésime I 27 C5
Vesoul F 19 B5
Vétroz CH 27 A4
Veules-les-Roses F 9 A4
Veulettes-sur-Mer F 9 A4
Veurne B 6 A2
Vevey CH 20 C1
Vex CH 27 A4
Veynes F 32 A1
Veyre-Monton F 24 B3
Veyrier F 26 B3
Vézelay F 18 B2
Vézelise F 12 C2
Vézenobres F 31 A3
Vezins F 16 B1
Vézins-de-Lévézou F 30 A1
Vezzani F 62 A2
Via Gloria P 54 B2
Viana F 37 B4
Viana do Alentejo P 48 C2
Viana do Bolo E 35 B3
Viana do Castelo P 42 A1
Vianden L 12 B2
Viator E 58 C2
Vibraye F 16 A2
Vic F 41 C3
Vícar E 58 C2
Vicdessos F 40 B2
Vic-en-Bigorre F 39 A4
Vic-Fézensac F 29 C3
Vichy F 25 A3
Vic-le-Comte F 24 B3
Vico F 62 A1
Vic-sur-Aisne F 10 B3
Vic-sur-Cère F 24 C2
Vidago P 42 A2
Vidauban F 32 B2
Vide P 42 B2
Vidigueira P 54 A2
Vieille-Brioude F 25 B3
Vieira P 48 B2
Vieira do Minho P 42 A1
Vieiros P 49 C3
Vielha E 39 B4
Vielle-Aure F 39 B4
Viellespesse F 24 B3
Viellevigne F 22 B2
Vielmur-sur-Agout F 30 B1
Viels Maison F 11 C3
Vienne F 25 B4
Viernheim D 13 B4
Vierville-sur-Mer F 8 A3
Vierzon F 17 B4
Vieteren B 6 B2
Vieux-Boucau-les-Bains F 28 C1
Vif F 26 B2
Vigeois F 24 B1
Vignale I 27 B5
Vigneulles-lès-Hattonchâtel F 12 C1
Vignevieille F 40 B3
Vignory F 19 A4
Vignoux-sur Barangeon F 17 B4
Vigo E 34 B2
Vigone I 27 C4
Vihiers F 16 B1
Vila Boim P 49 C3
Vila Chã de Ourique P 48 B2
Viladamat E 41 B4
Vila de Cruces E 34 B2
Vila de Rei P 48 B2
Vila do Bispo P 54 B1
Vila do Conde P 42 A1
Viladrau E 41 C3
Vila Flor P 43 A2
Vila Franca das Navas P 43 B2
Vilafranca del Maestrat E 47 B3
Vilafranca del Penedès E 41 C2
Vila Franca de Xira P 48 C1
Vila Fresca E 48 C1
Vilagarcía de Arousa E 34 B2
Vilajuïga E 41 B4
Vilamarín E 34 B3
Vilamartín de Valdeorras E 35 B3
Vila Nogueira P 48 C1
Vila Nova da Baronia P 48 C2
Vilanova de Castelló E 53 B3
Vila Nova de Cerveira E 34 C2
Vila Nova de Famalicão P 42 A1
Vila Nova de Foz Côa P 43 A2
Vila Nova de Gaia P 42 A1
Vila Nova de Milfontes P 54 B1
Vila Nova de Paiva P 42 B2
Vila Nova de São Bento P 55 B2
Vilanova de Sau E 41 C3
Vilanova i la Geltrú E 41 C2
Vilapedre E 34 A3
Vila Pouca de Aguiar P 42 A2
Vila Praia de Ancora P 42 A1
Vilarandelo P 42 A2
Vilar de Santos E 34 B3
Vilardevós E 35 C3
Vila Real P 42 A2
Vila-real dos Infantes E 53 B3
Vila Real de Santo António P 54 B2
Vilar Formoso P 43 B3
Vila-Rodona E 41 C2
Vila Ruiva P 54 A2
Vilasantar E 34 A2
Vilaseca E 41 C2
Vila Seca P 42 B1
Vilassar de Mar E 41 C3
Vila Velha de Ródão P 49 B3
Vila Verde
  Braga P 42 A1
  Lisboa P 48 B1
Vila Verde de Filcalho P 55 B2
Vila Viçosa P 49 C3
Vilches E 51 B4
Villabáñez E 44 A3
Villablanca E 55 B2

Villablino E 35 B4
Villabona E 38 A1
Villabragima E 36 C1
Villabuena del Puente E 44 A2
Villacadima E 45 A4
Villacañas E 51 A4
Villacarriedo E 37 A3
Villacarrillo E 58 A1
Villacastín E 44 B3
Villaconejos E 45 B4
Villaconejos de Trabaque E 46 B1
Villa Cova de Lixa P 42 A1
Villada E 36 B2
Villadangos del Páramo E 35 B5
Villadecanes E 35 B4
Villa del Prado E 44 B3
Villa del Rio E 51 C3
Villadepera E 43 A3
Villa de Peralonso E 43 A3
Villadiego E 37 B3
Villadompardo E 57 A3
Villadóssola I 27 A5
Villaeles de Valdavia E 36 B2
Villaescusa de Haro E 52 B1
Villafáfila E 36 C1
Villafeliche E 46 A2
Villaflores E 44 A2
Villafrades de Campos E 36 B2
Villafranca
  Avila E 44 B2
  Navarra E 38 B2
Villafranca de Córdoba E 51 C3
Villafranca del Bierzo E 35 B4
Villafranca de los Barros E 49 C4
Villafranca de los Caballeros E 51 A4
Villafranca-Montes de Oca E 37 B3
Villafranco del Campo E 46 B2
Villafranco del Guadalquivir E 55 B3
Villafrechós E 36 C1
Villafruela E 37 C3
Villagarcia de las Torres E 50 B1
Villagonzalo E 50 B1
Villagotón E 35 B4
Villagrains F 28 B2
Villaharta E 50 B3
Villahermosa E 52 C1
Villaherreros E 36 B2
Villahoz E 37 B3
Villaines-la-Juhel F 9 B3
Villajoyosa E 53 C3
Villalba E 34 A3
Villalba de Calatrava E 51 B4
Villalba de Guardo E 36 B2
Villalba del Alcor E 55 B3
Villalba de la Sierra E 46 B1
Villalba de los Alcores E 36 C2
Villalba de los Barros E 49 C4
Villalba del Rey E 45 B5
Villalcampo E 43 A3
Villalcázar de Sirga E 36 B2
Villalengua E 46 A2
Villalgordo del Júcar E 52 B1
Villalgordo del Marquesado E 52 B1
Villalmóndar E 37 B3
Villalón de Campos E 36 B1
Villalonga E 53 C3
Villalonso E 44 A2
Villalpando E 36 C1
Villaluenga E 45 B4
Villalumbroso E 36 B2
Villálvaro E 37 C3
Villamalea E 52 B2
Villamanán E 36 B1
Villamanín E 36 B1
Villamanrique E 51 B5
Villamanrique de la Condesa E 55 B3
Villamanta E 45 B3
Villamantilla E 45 B3
Villamartín E 56 B2
Villamartín de Campos E 36 B2
Villamartín de Don Sancho E 36 B1
Villamayor E 36 A1
Villamayor de Calatrava E 51 B3
Villamayor de Campos E 36 C1
Villamayor de Santiago E 51 A5
Villamblard F 29 A3
Villamejil E 35 B4
Villameras E 50 A2
Villaminaya E 51 A4
Villamor de los Escuderos E 44 A2
Villamoronta E 36 B2
Villamuelas E 45 C4
Villamuriel de Cerrato E 36 C2
Villandraut F 28 B2
Villanova d'Asti I 27 C4
Villanova Mondovì I 33 A3
Villante E 37 B3
Villanubla E 36 C2
Villanueva de Alcardete E 51 A4
Villanueva de Alcorón E 46 B1
Villanueva de Algaidas E 57 A3
Villanueva de Argaña E 37 B3
Villanueva de Bogas E 51 A4
Villanueva de Córdoba E 50 B3
Villanueva de Gállego E 38 C3
Villanueva del Aceral E 44 A3
Villanueva de la Concepcion E 57 B3
Villanueva de la Fuente E 52 C1
Villanueva de la Jara E 52 B2

Villanueva de la Reina E 51 B4
Villanueva del Arzobispo E 58 A2
Villanueva de la Serena E 50 B2
Villanueva de la Sierra E 43 B3
Villanueva de las Manzanas E 36 B1
Villanueva de las Peras E 35 C5
Villanueva de las Torres E 58 B1
Villanueva de la Vera E 44 B2
Villanueva del Campo E 36 C1
Villanueva del Duque E 50 B3
Villanueva del Fresno E 49 C3
Villanueva del Huerva E 46 A2
Villanueva de los Castillejos E 55 B2
Villanueva de los Infantes E 51 B5
Villanueva del Rey E 50 B2
Villanueva del Rio E 56 A2
Villanueva del Rio y Minas E 56 A2
Villanueva del Rosario E 57 B3
Villanueva del Trabuco E 57 A3
Villanueva de Mesia E 57 A4
Villanueva de Nia E 36 B2
Villanueva de Oscos E 35 A4
Villanueva de San Carlos E 51 B4
Villanueva de San Juan E 56 A2
Villanueva de Tapia E 57 A3
Villanueva de Valdegovia E 37 B3
Villaquejida E 36 B1
Villaquilambre E 36 B1
Villaquirán de los Infantes E 36 B2
Villaralto E 50 B3
Villarcayo E 37 B3
Villard-de-Lans F 26 B2
Villar de Barrio E 34 B3
Villar de Cañas E 52 B1
Villar de Chinchilla E 52 C2
Villar de Ciervo E 43 B3
Villardeciervos E 35 C4
Villar de Domingo Garcia E 46 B1
Villardefrades E 36 C1
Villar del Arzobispo E 53 B3
Villar del Buey E 43 A3
Villar del Cobo E 46 B2
Villar del Humo E 52 B2
Villar de los Navarros E 46 A2
Villar del Pedroso E 50 A2
Villar del Rey E 49 B4
Villar del Rio E 37 B4
Villar del Saz de Navalón E 46 B1
Villar de Rena E 50 A2
Villarejo E 45 A4
Villarejo de Fuentes E 52 B1
Villarejo de Orbigo E 35 B5
Villarejo de Salvanes E 45 B4
Villarejo-Periesteban E 52 B1
Villares del Saz E 52 B1
Villarotto I 27 B4
Villargordo del Cabriel E 52 B2
Villarino E 43 A3
Villarino de Conso E 35 B3
Villarluengo E 47 B3
Villarobe E 37 B3
Villar Perosa I 27 C4
Villarramiel E 36 B2
Villarrasa E 55 B3
Villarreal de San Carlos E 44 C1
Villarrín de Campos E 36 C1
Villarrobledo E 52 B1
Villarroya de la Sierra E 46 A2
Villarroya de los Pinares E 47 B3
Villarrubia de los Ojos E 51 A4
Villarrubia de Santiago E 45 C4
Villarrubio E 45 C5
Villars-les-Dombes F 25 A5
Villarta E 52 B2
Villarta de los Montes E 50 A3
Villarta de San Juan E 51 A4
Villasana de Mena E 37 A3
Villasandino E 36 B2
Villasante E 37 A3
Villasarracino E 36 B2
Villasayas E 45 A5
Villasdardo E 43 A3
Villaseca de Henares E 45 B5
Villaseca de Laciana E 35 B4
Villaseca de la Sagra E 45 C4
Villaseco de los Gamitos E 43 A3
Villaseco de los Reyes E 43 A3
Villasequilla de Yepes E 45 C4
Villastar E 46 B2
Villastellone I 27 C4
Villatobas E 45 C4
Villatorp E 44 B2
Villatoya E 52 B2
Villavaliente E 52 B2
Villavelayo E 37 B4
Villaver de de Guadalimar E 52 C1
Villaverde del Rio E 56 A2
Villaviciosa E 36 A1
Villaviciosa de Córdoba E 50 B3
Villaviciosa de Odón E 45 B4
Villavieja de Yeltes E 43 B3
Villayón E 35 A4
Villé F 13 C3
Villebois-Lavalette F 10 C2
Villecerf F 10 C2
Villecomtal F 30 A1

Villedieu-les-Poêles F 8 B2
Villedieu-sur-Indre F 17 C3
Ville-di-Pietrabugno F 62 A2
Villedômain F 17 B3
Villefagnan F 23 B4
Villefontaine F 26 B2
Villefort F 31 A2
Villefranche-d'Albigeois F 30 B1
Villefranche-d'Allier F 24 A2
Villefranche-de-Lauragais F 40 A2
Villefranche-de-Lonchat F 28 B3
Villefranche-de-Panat F 30 A1
Villefranche-de-Rouergue F 30 A1
Villefranche-du-Périgord F 29 B4
Villefranche-sur-Cher F 17 B3
Villefranche-sur-Mer F 33 B3
Villefranche-sur-Saône F 25 A4
Villegenon F 17 B4
Villel E 46 B2
Villemaur-sur-Vanne F 18 A2
Villemontais F 25 B3
Villemur-sur-Tarn F 29 C4
Villena E 53 C3
Villenauxe-la-Grande F 11 C3
Villenave-d'Ornon F 28 B2
Villeneuve
  CH 27 A3
  F 29 B5
Villeneuve-d'Ascq F 6 B3
Villeneuve-de-Berg F 31 A3
Villeneuve-de-Marsan F 28 C2
Villeneuve-de-Rivière F 39 A4
Villeneuve-la-Guyard F 10 C3
Villeneuve-l'Archevêque F 18 A2
Villeneuve-le-Comte F 10 C2
Villeneuve-lès-Avignon F 31 B3
Villeneuve-les-Corbières F 40 B3
Villeneuve-St Georges F 10 C2
Villeneuve-sur-Allier F 18 C2
Villeneuve-sur-Lot F 29 B3
Villeneuve-sur-Yonne F 18 A2
Villeréal F 29 B3
Villerias E 36 C2
Villeromain F 17 B3
Villers-Bocage
  Calvados F 8 A3
  Somme F 10 B2
Villers-Bretonneux F 10 B2
Villers-Carbonnel F 10 B2
Villers-Cotterêts F 10 B2
Villersexel F 19 B5
Villers-Farlay F 19 C4
Villers-le-Gambon B 7 B4
Villers-le-Lac F 20 B1
Villers-sur-Mer F 9 A3
Villerupt F 12 B1
Villerville F 9 A4
Villeseneux F 11 C4
Ville-sous-la-Ferté F 19 A3
Ville-sur-Illon F 19 A5
Ville-sur-Tourbe F 11 B4
Villetrun F 17 B3
Villeurbanne F 25 B4
Villeveyrac F 30 B2
Villevocance F 25 B4
Villiers-St Benoît F 18 B2
Villiers-St Georges F 11 C3
Villingen D 20 A3
Villoldo E 36 B2
Villon F 18 B3
Villoria E 44 B2
Vilvestre E 43 A3
Vilvoorde B 7 B4
Vimeiro P 48 B1
Vimianzo E 34 A1
Vimieiro P 48 C3
Vimioso P 43 A3
Vimoutiers F 9 B4
Vimy F 6 B2
Vinadio I 33 A3
Vinaixa E 41 C1
Vinarós E 47 B4
Vinay F 26 B2
Vinca F 40 B3
Vinets F 11 C4
Vineuil F 17 B3
Vingrau F 40 B3
Vinhais P 43 A3
Viniegra de Arriba E 37 B4
Vinon F 17 B4
Vinon-sur-Verdon F 32 B1
Viñuela E 57 B3
Viñuela de Sayago E 43 A4
Viñuelas E 45 B4
Vinuesa E 37 C4
Viola I 33 A3
Violay F 25 B4
Vire F 8 B3
Vireux F 11 A4
Virgen de la Cabeza E 51 B3
Virieu F 26 B2
Virieu-le-Grand F 26 B2
Virton B 12 B1
Viry F 26 A3
Viseu P 42 B2
Visiedo E 46 B2
Viso del Marqués E 51 B4
Visone I 27 C5
Visp CH 27 A4
Vistabella del Maestrat E 47 B3
Vitigudino E 43 A3
Vitoria-Gasteiz E 37 B4
Vitré F 15 A4
Vitrey-sur-Mance F 19 B4
Vitry-en-Artois F 6 B2
Vitry-le-François F 11 C4
Vitry-sur-Seine F 10 C2
Vitteaux F 18 B3
Vittel F 19 A4
Viù I 27 B4
Vivario F 62 A2
Vivel del Rio Martin E 46 B2
Viver E 53 B3

Viverols F 25 B3
Viveros E 52 C1
Viviers F 31 A3
Vivonne F 23 B4
Vivy F 16 B1
Vizille F 26 B2
Vizzavona F 62 A2
Vlissingen NL 7 A3
Vogogna I 27 A5
Vogüé F 31 A3
Vöhrenbach D 20 A3
Void-Vacon F 12 C1
Voiron F 26 B2
Voise F 10 C1
Voisey F 19 B4
Voiteur F 19 C4
Völklingen D 12 B2
Vollore-Montagne F 25 B3
Voltri I 33 A4
Volvic F 24 B3
Volx F 32 B1
Voreppe F 26 B2
Vorey F 25 B3
Voué F 11 C4
Vouillé F 23 B4
Voulx F 10 C2
Voussac F 24 A3
Vouvray F 16 B2
Vouvry CH 27 A3
Vouzela P 42 B1
Vouziers F 11 B4
Voves F 17 A3
Vrigne-aux-Bois F 11 B4
Vron F 6 B1
Vught NL 7 A5
Vuillafans F 19 B5
Vy-lès Lure F 19 B5

W

Waalwijk NL 7 A5
Waarschoot B 7 A3
Wädenswil CH 21 B3
Wadern D 12 B2
Waghäusel D 13 B4
Wald CH 21 B3
Waldböckelheim D 13 B3
Waldkirch D 20 A2
Wald-Michelbach D 13 B4
Waldmohr D 13 B3
Waldshut D 20 B3
Waldstatt CH 21 B4
Waldwisse F 12 B2
Walenstadt CH 21 B4
Walincourt F 10 A3
Wallers F 6 B3
Walshoutem B 7 B5
Waltenhofen D 21 B5
Wamba E 36 C2
Wangen im Allgäu D 21 B4
Wängi CH 21 B3
Waregem B 7 B3
Waremme B 7 B5
Warth A 21 B5
Wasselonne F 13 C3
Wassen CH 21 C3
Wasserauen CH 21 B4
Wassy F 11 C4
Waterloo B 7 B4
Watten F 6 B2
Wattwil CH 21 B4
Wavignies F 10 B2
Wavre B 7 B4
Weggis CH 20 B3
Wehr D 20 B2
Weierbach D 13 B3
Weil am Rhein D 20 B2
Weil der Stadt D 13 C4
Weinfelden CH 21 B4
Weingarten
  Baden-Württemberg D 13 B4
  Baden-Württemberg D 21 B4
Weinheim D 13 B4
Weissstannen CH 21 C4
Weitnau D 21 B5
Wellin B 11 A5
Weischenrohr CH 20 D2
Wengen CH 20 C2
Werkendam NL 7 A4
Westerlo B 7 A4
Westkapelle
  B 6 A3
  NL 7 A3
Wetteren B 7 A3
Wetzikon CH 21 B3
Weyersheim F 13 C3
Wiesbaden D 13 A4
Wiesen CH 21 C4
Wiesloch D 13 B4
Wiggen CH 20 C2
Wil CH 21 B4
Wildbad D 13 C4
Wildberg D 13 C4
Wildegg CH 20 B3
Wilhelmsdorf D 21 B4
Willebroek B 7 A4
Willgottheim F 13 C3
Willisau CH 20 B3
Wiltz L 12 B1
Wimereux F 6 B1
Wimmenau F 13 C3
Wimmis CH 20 C2
Wingene B 6 A3
Winnweiler D 13 B3
Winterthur CH 21 B3
Wintzenheim F 20 A2
Wissant F 6 B1
Wissembourg F 13 B3
Witry-les-Reims F 11 B4
Wittelsheim F 20 B2
Wittenheim F 20 B2
Wittlich D 12 B2
Woerth F 13 C3
Wohlen CH 20 B3
Woippy F 12 B2
Wolfach D 13 C4
Wolfegg D 21 B4
Wolfstein D 13 B3
Wolfurt A 21 B4
Wolhusen CH 20 B3
Worb CH 20 C2

Wormhout F 6 B2
Worms D 13 B4
Wörrstadt D 13 B4
Wörth
  Bayern D 13 B5
  Rheinland-Pfalz D 13 B4
Woumen B 6 A2
Wuustwezel B 7 A4

X

Xàtiva E 53 C3
Xeraco E 53 B3
Xert E 47 B4
Xerta E 47 B4
Xertigny F 19 A5
Xinzo de Limia E 34 B3
Xixón = Gijón E 36 A1
Xove E 34 A3
Xubia E 34 A2
Xunqueira de Ambia E 34 B3
Xunqueira de Espadañedo E 34 B3

Y

Ydes F 24 B2
Yebra de Basa E 39 B3
Yecla E 53 C2
Yecla de Yeltes E 43 B3
Yenne F 26 B2
Yepes E 45 C4
Yerseke NL 7 A4
Yerville F 9 A4
Yeste E 58 A2
Ygos-St Saturnin F 28 C2
Ygrande F 18 C1
Ymonville F 17 A3
Yport F 9 A4
Ypres = Ieper B 6 B2
Yssingeaux F 25 B4
Yuncos E 45 B4
Yunquera E 56 B3
Yunquera de Henares E 45 B4
Yverdon-les-Bains CH 20 C1
Yvetot F 9 A4
Yvignac F 15 A3
Yvoir B 7 B4
Yvonand CH 20 C1
Yzeure F 18 C2

Z

Zaamslag NL 7 A3
Zafarraya E 57 B3
Zafra E 49 C4
Zagrilla E 57 A3
Zahara E 56 B2
Zahara de los Atunes E 56 B2
Zahinos E 49 C4
Zaidín E 47 A4
Zalamea de la Serena E 50 B2
Zalamea la Real E 55 B3
Zaldibar E 37 A4
Zalla E 37 A3
Zaltbommel NL 7 A5
Zambra E 57 A3
Zambugueira do Mar P 54 B1
Zamora E 43 A4
Zandhoven B 7 A4
Zaorejas E 46 B1
Zaragoza E 47 A3
Zarautz E 38 A1
Zarcilla de Ramos E 58 B3
Zarren B 6 A2
Zarza Capilla E 50 B2
Zarza de Alange E 50 B1
Zarza de Granadilla E 43 B3
Zarza de Tajo E 45 B4
Zarzadilla de Totana E 58 B3
Zarza la Mayor E 49 B4
Zarzuela del Monte E 44 B3
Zarzuela del Pinar E 45 A3
Zas E 34 A2
Zeberio E 37 A4
Zebreira P 49 B3
Zeebrugge B 6 A3
Zele B 7 A4
Zell
  CH 20 B2
  Baden-Württemberg D 13 C4
  Baden-Württemberg D 20 B4
  Rheinland-Pfalz D 12 A3
Zelzate B 7 A3
Zemst B 7 B4
Zerf D 12 B2
Zermatt CH 27 A4
Zernez CH 21 C5
Zestoa E 38 A1
Zevenbergen NL 7 A4
Zicavo F 62 B2
Zierikzee NL 7 A3
Zinal CH 27 A4
Zofingen CH 20 B2
Zomergem B 7 A3
Zoñán E 35 A3
Zonhoven B 7 B5
Zonza F 62 B2
Zorita E 50 A2
Zottegem B 7 B3
Zubieta E 38 A2
Zubiri E 38 B2
Zucaina E 47 B3
Zuera E 38 C3
Zufre E 55 B3
Zug CH 21 B3
Zuheros E 57 A3
Zújar E 58 B2
Zumaia E 38 A1
Zumárraga E 37 A4
Zundert NL 7 A4
Zurgena E 58 B2
Zürich CH 21 B3
Zurzach CH 20 B3
Zweibrücken D 13 B3
Zweisimmen CH 20 C2
Zwiefalten D 21 A4